Conserving Culture

A Publication of the American Folklore Society

New Series

General Editor, Patrick B. Mullen

Conserving Culture

A New Discourse on Heritage

Edited by Mary Hufford

Published for the American Folklife Center
at the Library of Congress by the
UNIVERSITY OF ILLINOIS PRESS Urbana and Chicago

Manufactured in the United States of America
1 2 3 4 5 C P 5 4 3 2 1

This book is printed on acid-free paper.

Library of Congress Cataloging-in-Publication Data
Conserving culture : a new discourse on heritage / edited by Mary Hufford.
p. cm.
Includes bibliographical references and index.
ISBN 0-252-02060-X (cloth: acid-free paper). — ISBN 0-252-06354-6 (paper : acid-free paper)
1. Ethnology—Research. 2. Folklore—Research. I. Hufford, Mary, 1952–
GN345.C656 1994
305.8'0072—dc20 93-23922
CIP

Contents

Acknowledgments

This volume of essays grew out of a conference entitled "Cultural Conservation: Reconfiguring the Cultural Mission," held at the Library of Congress in May of 1990. Those attending the conference included professionals from the fields of folklore, anthropology, archaeology, environmental studies, historic preservation, landscape architecture and design, and urban and regional planning. The present volume owes a great debt not only to the essayists but also to all who participated in the conference, shaping its debates and clarifying its issues. Especially deserving of thanks are the ten members of the conference "team," who helped steer the conference through its planning stages and led the conference's lively roundtable discussions: Elaine Eff, Burt Feintuch, Benita Howell, Eugene Hunn, Chester Liebs, Ormond Loomis, Setha Low, Patricia Parker, Gary Stanton, and Shalom Staub. Credit also belongs to Ann Dancy, whose sense of order and humor caused the myriad parts of the conference to cohere. For insightful comments that helped transform a collection of papers into a volume of essays I am also grateful to Burt Feintuch, Eugene Hunn, Chester Liebs, John Sinton, and Jamil Zainaldin. A number of colleagues at the American Folklife Center warrant special thanks. The manuscript benefited from incisive readings by James Hardin, the center's writer/editor. Hillary Glatt readied the manuscript for publication with patience and good humor. Thea Caemmerer, Doris Craig, Magdalena Gilinsky, and Lisa Oshins generously assisted with mailings and other logistics when deadlines loomed. The final round of appreciation goes to Alan Jabbour, whose guidance, imagination, and vision continue to inspire a steadily growing movement.

Introduction: Rethinking the Cultural Mission

Mary Hufford

To speak of rethinking the federal government's cultural mission is to provoke questions about the nature and scope of that cultural mission as it is currently constituted. Indeed, some might wonder whether *mission* is the proper term for the broad, loosely knit array of policies and instrumentalities constituting the government's present position on heritage. The concept of cultural conservation appeared in the early 1980s as a means of gathering together and focusing government initiatives pertaining to cultural heritage. In the decade since the term made its debut, scholars and activists have wrestled with the perplexing implications of cultural conservation as concept and practice. The conference held in May of 1990 provided a forum for critically rethinking the national system of heritage protection. In the course of that conference there was talk of shifting the government's preservation paradigm—away from a top-down, prescriptive approach to heritage planning toward an approach more open and responsive to grass-roots cultural concerns.

The current configuration for national heritage protection and cultural affairs took shape in the 1960s and 1970s, when prescriptions for what Lyndon Johnson called "the total relationship between man and the world around him" were written into law.[1] Within a single decade Congress enacted a number of measures designed to encourage cultural and environmental diversity, including the National Foundation for the Arts and Humanities Act (1965), the National Historic Preservation Act (1966), the National Environmental Policy Act (1969), and the American Folklife Preservation Act (1976). The legislation added to the federal system such agencies and instrumentalities as the National Endowments for the Arts and Humanities, the Advisory Council on Historic Preservation, the National Register of Historic Places, the President's Council on Environmental Quality, and the American Folklife Center, and it lent support to growing networks at the state and local levels.[2] By the early 1980s a whole new infrastructure of private organizations and public agencies, committed to programs in the arts and humanities, conservation of land and wildlife, preservation of the built environment, and representation and maintenance of living cultural diversity, had spread throughout the country.

Mirroring divisions of the world maintained in our academies and other cultural and scientific institutions, the legislative measures of the 1960s and 1970s designated three arenas of action: (1) nature (natural species and ecosystems); (2) the built environment (historic and prehistoric artifacts, buildings, sites, and districts); and (3) folklife/culture (living artistic expressions and traditional communities and processes). Each arena had its professionals, legislative mandates, public and private supporters, and assorted goals and visions.

Federal heritage policies, when considered in their entirety, seemed to provide for all the ingredients of heritage. Yet several underlying assumptions about the interrelations of those ingredients actually hindered comprehensive, coordinated planning. It was not long before professionals working in all three arenas grew frustrated over the dissonance between the map of heritage implied in agency policies and guidelines and the actual territories in which they were working. There were two main problems. The first was the tendency of heritage to resist its assigned categories. The language of the laws upheld distinctions between "nature" and "culture" and further divided cultural heritage into "tangible" and "intangible" aspects. Yet natural land forms and wildlife species could serve as touchstones to community life and values as readily as structures of the built environment could. (Indeed, complexes of "natural" species and habitats were proving to be partly shaped by traditional knowledge and skills.) History was as likely to reside in a craft dependent on natural resources as it was in an example of eighteenth-century architecture. Distinguishing between tangible and intangible resources obscured the complex interdependencies of culture and environment, made manifest in toponymy, narrative, ritual, and other stylized behaviors.[3] Though professionals with an interest in combining auspices and expertise occasionally integrated their research, other obstacles posed by the bureaucracy and its enabling legislation were not so easily overcome.

The second problem arose when those representing the "national" interest tried to impose external standards on local communities and sites spanning a broad cultural spectrum. Recognizing the cross-cultural nature of their decision making, some professionals pointed out not only that federal policies define resources too narrowly but also that determining the "significance" and "integrity" of resources is a highly subjective undertaking. Separating heritage into "tangible" and "intangible" elements left to planners the task of assigning significance to environmental features. Such features could thus come to represent cultural values belonging to professional planners more than to others with a stake in the same environment. The heavy reliance of folklife projects on arts organizations for funding led to an emphasis on traditions that were detachable and aesthetically pleasing, some of which had to be aestheticized to justify funding. The tendency of heritage planning to authenticate past cultures and environments effectively reduced the power of present-day communities to manage the environments on which their dynamic cultures depend. Clearly, despite their underlying intentions, heritage policies can be used to diminish cultural pluralism as well as to support it.

Amending the National Historic Preservation Act in 1980, the Ninty-sixth Congress requested a report from the Department of the Interior and the American Folklife Center on the status of "intangible cultural resources." The resulting policy study, published in 1983, recommended that the term *cultural conservation* be adopted as a "concept for organizing the profusion of public and private efforts that deal with traditional community cultural life."[4] Not only did the term offer an overarching framework for the protection of cultural heritage, it encapsulated some radical policy implications.[5] In effect it proposed moving from a fragmented approach to heritage protection dominated by elite and professional constituencies to an integrated approach based on grass-roots cultural concerns and guided by ethnographic perspectives.

Advantages of the term soon became apparent to cultural specialists in a variety of fields. As an alternative to *preservation, conservation* registers the dynamism of cultural resources, implying that, like natural phenomena, cultural phenomena inevitably change. *Cultural conservation* further suggests that resource identification be guided as much as possible by those whose cultures are affected.[6] Moreover, its breadth and focus on action make cultural conservation the province of no single discipline, offering an ideal rubric for interdisciplinary initiatives.

Since the report's release, the concept has attracted adherents from multiple sectors. *Cultural conservation* has appeared as the title for tracks at professional meetings, the topic for conferences and seminars at state and regional levels, and the focus of field research and festivals alike. Collaborating on particular projects, governmental agencies have explored the potential for incorporating folklife research in planning for historic preservation and environmental protection.[7] With the assistance of newly created agencies and updated guidelines,[8] professionals have tried to apply the powerful language available in the National Historic Preservation Act, the National Environmental Policy Act, and the American Folklife Preservation Act to specific cases.[9]

The term *cultural conservation*, then, applies to advocacy in all three heritage arenas, advocacy that is ethnographic rather than ethnocentric. Cultural conservation professionals include folklorists, anthropologists, archaeologists, historic preservationists, environmental planners, and scientists engaged in cultural conservation activities. The term *conservationist* unites professionals in the applied sciences and humanities as advocates who bring their views of culture and ecology to bear on threatened facets of the world. As several essayists make clear, these views and approaches are not "objective" but are grounded in subjective assumptions about how nature and society fit together. Naturalists, some of them guided by an ecological model of a less populous, preindustrial world, may apply their research in defense of natural diversity. By the same token cultural conservationists may apply their research in the service of groups not served by the dominant culture, in order to shape and sustain a culturally pluralistic society.

A central task of cultural conservation is to discover the full range of resources people use to construct and sustain their cultures. Knowledge of this sort might be applied in supporting local groups as they manage environmental change and in planning for the full range of governmentally sponsored services that affect the education, health, and general welfare of a culturally diverse population.

The practice of cultural conservation relies on ethnography, "a disciplined attempt to discover and describe the symbolic resources with which members of a society conceptualize and interpret their experience."[10] When undertaken for the sake of heritage protection, ethnography comprises the investigation of how local groups constitute their own heritage, map it onto their surroundings, and make use of it in their daily lives. Such information can lead to the discovery of how the federal government might support such efforts, often through creative combinations of cultural theory, legislative tools, and institutional resources. Viewing environment and culture as an indivisible whole, and viewing environmental planning as cultural practice, the ethnographic perspective can redress the fragmented state of cultural affairs and the homogeneous images of culture produced through centralized planning.

There are many ways of imbuing a physical entity with significance, of making it a "resource." Indeed, over the past century the U.S. government itself has attached diametrically opposed frames of reference to the same resources. Where wolves, coyotes, and eagles were once systematically exterminated as cruel predators, they are now carefully managed as inhabitants of ecosystems and purveyed in some instances as featured attractions at such wilderness events as "howling sessions."[11] In the early decades of this century the archaeological treasures of the Southwest demonstrated for some the superiority of Europeans who conquered the wilderness over aboriginal peoples who failed to survive it. The same sites now encourage visitors to reflect on the destruction by Europeans of native lifeways far more harmoniously attuned to nature than our own (a romanticized view fraught with its own hazards).[12] In this period of heavy immigration and industrialization folksong collectors sought the relics of a pure Anglo-Saxon civilization in the southern mountains, and ethnologists recorded the vanishing remnants of Native American cultures. While such efforts enhanced the collections of the Bureau of American Ethnology and the Library of Congress, in some instances they furthered xenophobic and racist aims.[13] Now in the service of various public agencies professional ethnographers document and present traditions in transformation to encourage cultural diversity.[14]

The dramatic differences between concepts of resources held by the government early in the century and concepts held today relate to a central theme of this collection: heritage is not a given in the world; rather, we, together with our "constituents," share in the act of making it. What Barbara Kirshenblatt-Gimblett writes of folklorists may be said of conservation professionals: they "do not discover, they constitute; and the relation of what they constitute to the 'real' is not one of verification. In this sense, folklorists, and anthropologists [read: conservation professionals], may be said to 'invent' culture." This act of invention, implicated in the act of description, is a creative, culturally generative act, and paradoxically it renders the ethnographer a collaborator in the making of heritage.[15] Culture is indeed "politically constituted."[16]

In recent decades cultural conservation professionals have struggled to make the established heritage protection system work, not just for the elite, enclaved, and more outspoken sectors of the population but also for communities that lack distinctive cultural profiles in the public mind or whose public images have been shaped by mistaken and stereotypical notions. Examples considered in this volume include postindustrial communities in Massachusetts (DeNatale) and Pennsylvania (Abrams), the Navajo nation in Arizona (Downer et al.), trappers in the Ozark mountains (Brady), ethnic social clubs in New York City (Zeitlin), family farmers (Rikoon, Heffernan, and Heffernan), basketmakers in the Carolina lowcountry (Rosengarten), and those making places for their communities in poor urban neighborhoods (Low).

What is at issue is the process for determining the significance of contested resources. Assigning significance to any resource is a matter of describing the context within which the resource makes sense. Ethnographers involved in heritage planning have thus expanded and applied the notion of the vernacular system. This distinction between the native or vernacular view, on the one hand, and the scholarly, official, or elite view, on the other, derives from the anthropological distinction between emic and etic ways of dividing up and classifying the world. Essayists here elaborate this theoretical distinction into "traditional" and "Western academic" versions of history (Downer et al.), "vernacular" and "official" heritage displays (Abrams), "memory" and "counter-memory" (Mondale), "vernacular" and "federal" notions of place (DeNatale), and "lineage husbandry" and "managerial ecology" (Marks). Viewed within elite or scientific systems, myth, legend, and belief may appear quaint, arcane, or anachronistic. Viewed as aspects of vernacular systems, these modes of expression can become crucial resources for planning.

By the late 1980s conservation professionals had become more fully aware of the promise and limitations of various conceptual and legislative tools. Yet within discrete disciplines and agencies no existing forum enabled the kind of in-depth exploration of emerging issues necessary to move the field ahead. Sensing the time was ripe for such an event, the American Folklife Center convened a conference. Approximately a hundred and fifty conservation professionals assembled to examine more critically the emerging practice of cultural conservation, together with its theoretical and legislative implications, and to begin consolidating themselves as a network. For four days participants presented papers, shared information and debated issues in roundtable discussions, and drafted resolutions and recommendations for focusing conservation efforts over the next decade.[17]

The essays in this volume suggest that over the past decade cultural conservation has grown from a proposal to coordinate heritage efforts into a distinct paradigm for conservation, grounded in the ethnographic perspective. This paradigm combines an integrated view of heritage with an emphasis on local involvement in heritage planning. Developing one of the conference's prominent themes, the essays explore and explicate the role of that perspective in the heritage planning process.

Taking as points of departure the government's principal categories of heritage, this collection of essays is organized into three major sections: "Conserving History," "Protecting Biocultural Diversity," and "Encouraging Folklife." While these sections reflect the current divisions of heritage labor in the government, the essays demonstrate that history, nature, and living culture (in this case, folklife) have been much too narrowly defined and that each category opens a window onto one large domain: cultural heritage. The section headings are concepts for reconfiguring the present bureaucratic and disciplinary boundaries.

The notion of conserving history shifts attention beyond sites and structures to the dynamic nature of the past itself and its multiform manifestations and uses. The tendency of conventional conservation approaches to naturalize historic resources, while dehistoricizing natural resources, places both in a timeless, prelapsarian setting (Abrahams). Essayists explore the implications of vernacular systems of history-making for preservation planning. Vernacular histories, whether stored in myths, artifacts, festivals, or landscapes, are vital resources for the ongoing construction and maintenance of places and the social identities dependent on them. As such, vernacular histories contain important lessons and models for heritage planners, professional place-makers, and others seeking to support what James Abrams calls "free public expressions of plurality."

Similarly, the term *biocultural diversity* suggests that, along with natural resources, local knowledge of and systems for managing them are fitting objects of conservation. Essayists here describe some of the environmental and cultural costs of promoting nature and culture separately for tourism, a growing source of support for conservation efforts worldwide. Again, essayists examine ways in which traditional systems of knowledge can form a basis for managing culture and environment as a whole. In her account of those who rallied around the sweetgrass basketmakers' search for sweetgrass, Dale Rosengarten suggests a model for the case-by-case construction of interdisciplinary and interagency collaboration entailed in cultural conservation.

Essays in "Encouraging Folklife" describe and examine such tools as professionally produced festivals, cultural impact assessments, zoning ordinances, technical assistance to grass-roots movements, and heritage parks as strategies for defending traditional ways of life. Essayists examine some of our ways of establishing contexts within which such discrete cultural expressions as German cookies, Mayan glyphs, family farms, and ethnic social clubs become meaningful—not only to planners but also to the general public, whose support is indispensable. The Heritage Parks Program, described by Shalom Staub, appears to herald a new form on the horizon. Taking shape in the early 1990s in a number of states, heritage centers, corridors, and parks merit close critical attention and input from specialists across the conservation spectrum.

In a milieu devoted to multiculturalism, the documentation and promotion of cultural distinctiveness has gained political favor. Yet our own history teaches us that uncritical celebrations of cultural distinctiveness can serve to obscure underlying structures responsible for shared conditions of poverty and disenfranchisement.[18] Such celebrations, as John Comaroff has warned, merely "allow us to be voyeurs, to look in and not be vexed by the differences."[19] Concerned with the differences and cutting through the surface distinctions, Archie Green closes the volume with a rousing call to coalition and action. Taken as a whole, the essays cast into bold relief some of the perilous and promising terrain in which cultural conservationists of the 1990s and beyond are beginning to make their way.

NOTES

1. Lyndon Baines Johnson, "Message on Preserving Natural Beauty," delivered to Congress in 1966.

2. For a "Review of Significant Legislation, Activities, and Events Relating to Cultural Conservation in the United States," see Ormond Loomis, coordinator, *Cultural Conservation: The Protection of Cultural Heritage in the United States,* Publications of the American Folklife Center, no. 10 (Washington, D.C.: American Folklife Center, Library of Congress, 1983), 87–108.

3. A number of scholars have articulated linkages among folklorists, archaeologists, naturalists, and historic preservationists as well as between the academic and applied spheres of research. Thomas F. King, Patricia Parker Hickman, and Gary Berg, *Anthropology in Historic Preservation: Caring for Culture's Clutter* (New York: Academic Press, 1977), 10, argue for including prehistoric and historic resources under the umbrella of historic resources: "Using a single term for all the objects of historic preservation's interest . . . helps discourage the unwarranted but pervasive assumptions that archaeologists are concerned only with prehistory, that structures are the sole province of the architect, and that once written records are available about a people only historians need study their leavings." See also Henry Glassie, "Archaeology and Folklore: Common Anxieties, Common Hopes," in *Historic Archaeology and the Importance of Material Things,* Special Publications Series 2, ed. Leland Ferguson (Lansing, Mich.: Society for Historical Archaeology, 1977), 23–35. For a discussion of the aestheticization of folklore to obtain support through funding for the arts, see Barbara Kirshenblatt-Gimblett, "Mistaken Dichotomies," *Journal of American Folklore* 101 (1988): 143. For a discussion of the interface of research on folklife and natural history for environmental planning, see Mary Hufford, "Stalking the Native View: The Protection of Folklife in Natural Habitats," in *The Conservation of Culture,* ed. Burt Feintuch (Lexington: University Press of Kentucky, 1988), 217–29.

4. Loomis, *Cultural Conservation,* iv.

5. See John Peterson, "Cultural Conservation: Policy and Discipline Implications in a Term," in *Cultural Heritage Conservation in the American South,* Southern Antropological Society Proceedings, no. 23, ed. Benita J. Howell (Athens: University of Georgia Press, 1990), 5–19.

6. In other words, whereas the preservation effort is not unlike putting up pickles, the conservationist's goal is to ensure the proper conditions for the continued growth of cucumbers. Alan Jabbour, cited in Peterson, "Cultural Conservation," and elaborated in Benita Howell, "Public and Private Partnerships: Case Studies in Cultural Conservation from Kentucky and Tennessee" (Presentation at the Preservation in Profile Conference, sponsored by the Ken-

tucky Heritage Council, Covington, Kentucky, September 25–28, 1991). However, one of the reasons people grow cucumbers is to make pickles out of them, according to their own recipes. The cultural conservationist's task is not to make pickles out of cucumbers others have grown but to identify the many ways people have of growing cucumbers and pickling them themselves and to identify ways in which the government can support those efforts.

7. These initiatives sprang up at various levels of government and in various quarters in the private sector. For results of American Folklife Center field projects that explored ways to combine ethnography with environmental science and historic preservation in planning, see Mary Hufford, *One Space, Many Places: Folklife and Land Use in New Jersey's Pinelands National Reserve* (Washington, D.C.: American Folklife Center, Library of Congress, 1986); Thomas Carter and Carl Fleischhauer, *The Grouse Creek Cultural Survey: Integrating Folklife and Historic Preservation Research* (Washington, D.C.: American Folklife Center, Library of Congress, 1988); and David Taylor, *Documenting Maritime Folklife* (Washington, D.C.: American Folklife Center, Library of Congress, 1992). The Smithsonian Institution's Office of Folklife Programs spotlighted cultural conservation for five years at its annual Festival of American Folklife (1985–89). See Marjorie Hunt and Peter Seitel, "Cultural Conservation," in *1985 Festival of American Folklife*, ed. Thomas Vennum, Jr. (Washington, D.C.: Smithsonian Institution, 1985), 38–39. A number of conferences have been held at state and regional levels. Sponsors include the Pennsylvania Governor's Heritage Affairs Commission (1987), the Kentucky Heritage Council (1991), and the Southern Arts Federation (1991). Professional organizations featuring panels and tracks devoted to the topic of cultural conservation include the American Anthropological Association (1983), the Conference of Public Sector Folklorists at the University of Kentucky (1985), the Southern Anthropological Association (1988), and the American Association for State and Local History (1990). Several of these conferences resulted in published collections of essays. See Burt Feintuch, ed., *The Conservation of Culture: Folklorists and the Public Sector* (Lexington: University Press of Kentucky, 1988); and Howell, *Cultural Heritage Conservation in the American South*. For related publications of the Department of the Interior, see Patricia L. Parker, *Keepers of the Treasures: Protecting Historic Properties and Cultural Traditions on Indian Lands* (Washington, D.C.: National Park Service, Department of the Interior, 1990); and Patricia L. Parker and Thomas F. King, *Guidelines for Evaluating and Documenting Traditional Cultural Properties*, National Register Bulletin, no. 38 (Washington, D.C.: National Park Service, Department of the Interior, 1990).

8. The newly formed American Folklife Center was drawn into various preservation initiatives with the National Park Service, the National Trust for Historic Preservation, and various state historic preservation efforts. The Advisory Council on Historic Preservation, in accordance with the Historic Preservation Act, provided oversight for what has come to be known as the Section 106 review process, or "section 106." (See note 9 for the language.)

Parker and King's *Guidelines* provides the most succinct and unambiguous guidelines for evaluating and documenting traditional cultural properties available to date.

9. The language of all three acts provides a broad basis for cultural conservation. The National Environmental Policy Act requires both social and environmental impact assessments to "create and maintain conditions under which man and nature can exist in harmony, and fulfill the social, economic, and other requirements of present and future generations of Americans" (section 101, part a), as well as to "preserve important historic, cultural, and natural aspects of our national heritage, and maintain, wherever possible, an environment which supports diversity and variety of individual choice" (section 101, part b[4]).

Section 106 of the Historic Preservation Act states that any federally assisted undertaking shall "take into account the effect of the undertaking on any district, site, building, structure, or object that is included in or eligible for inclusion in the National Register," and it requires that the head of any such undertaking give the Advisory Council on Historic Preservation an opportunity to comment on the plan.

Section 2 of the American Folklife Preservation Act states that "the encouragement and support of American folklife, while primarily a matter for private and local initiative, is also an appropriate matter of concern to the Federal Government."

10. Keith H. Basso and Henry A. Selby, *Meaning in Anthropology* (Albuquerque: University of New Mexico Press, 1976), 3. Parker and King define *ethnography* as "the descriptive and analytic study of the culture of particular groups or communities. An ethnographer seeks to understand a community through interviews with its members and often through living in and observing it (a practice referred to as 'participant observation')." Citing the National Park Service's internal cultural resource management guidelines, Parker and King define *culture* as "a system of behaviors, values, ideologies, and social arrangements. These features, in addition to tools and expressive elements such as graphic arts, help humans interpret their universe as well as deal with features of their environments, natural and social." Parker and King, *Guidelines,* 4, 22.

11. Thomas R. Dunlap, *Saving America's Wildlife* (Princeton, N.J.: Princeton University Press, 1988), 108, alludes to the howling sessions at Algonquin Park in Ontario, where "bands of tourists howl like wolves in the hope of answers from the wild (the sessions remain popular because wolves will respond even to poor imitations of howling)."

12. Describing the rationales used to gain popular support for the preservation of antiquities, Hal Rothman, *Preserving Different Pasts: The American National Monuments* (Urbana: University of Illinois Press, 1989), 53, observes that "the demise of prehistoric culture gave Americans confidence in their destiny. In the aftermath of the Spanish-American War, xenophobic Americans regarded their subjugation of the wilderness as evidence of the superiority of English-speaking people." Kathleen Fine, "The Politics of Interpretation at Mesa Verde National Park," *Anthropological Quarterly* 61 (1988):

177–86, provides a description of the more romanticized present-day presentations of American Indians at Mesa Verde. This movement from destruction of resources for the sake of progress to enshrinement of them typifies a pattern that Allen Batteau, *The Invention of Appalachia* (Tucson: University of Arizona Press, 1990), identifies as "sacrifice and sacralization," which he relates to the development of Appalachian images over the past century.

13. See David Whisnant, *All that Is Native and Fine: The Politics of Culture in an American Region* (Chapel Hill: University of North Carolina Press, 1983), especially the chapter on the White Top Folk Festival.

14. For instance, the American Folklife Center's Federal Cylinder Project has transferred wax cylinder recordings of Native American ceremonies and performances onto cassette tapes, which they have presented to Native American groups. Some Native Americans have responded by incorporating recorded materials into contemporary ceremonies many decades after the traditions were supposed to have vanished.

15. Kirshenblatt-Gimblett, "Mistaken Dichotomies," 143. Mary Douglas, *Rules and Meanings: The Anthropology of Everyday Knowledge* (Middlesex, England: Penguin, 1973), points out that concealing the man-made origins of social structures is a way of claiming authority. Other works disclosing, as it were, "the man behind the curtain," include Eric Hobsbawm and Terence Ranger, *The Invention of Tradition* (Cambridge: Cambridge University Press, 1983); and Batteau, *The Invention of Appalachia.*

16. Allen Batteau, "Appalachia and the Concept of Culture: A Theory of Shared Misunderstanding," *Appalachian Journal* 7 (1979): 9–31.

17. See "Roundtable Recommendations and Resolutions," *Folklife Center News* 12, nos. 3 and 4 (1990): 14–19.

18. Batteau, "Appalachia and the Concept of Culture," 31.

19. Comaroff espouses instead a "critical multiculturalism," wherein the project is to "de-center ourselves by asking what it is that the confrontation with other cultural contexts reveals of our taken-for-granted, our commonsensical axioms about the nature of our own world." Excerpt of speech published in *University of Chicago Magazine,* April 1992, 15.

Part 1

Conserving History

1

Conserving a Problematic Past

Clarence Mondale

When we conserve a past, we make history. We make history because we must, to understand ourselves and our present circumstances. Because the past we conserve is necessarily problematic, we need to be self-critical and self-reflective in coming to collective decisions about what to remember and what to forget. Selecting particular pasts to conserve is necessarily a matter of continuous negotiations among all interested parties. Our pasts have consequences: if we celebrate a meretricious past, we cheapen ourselves.

What we make of the past is itself a historical product, as David Lowenthal has argued at length. Until 1850, say, the Western world looked to the past for inspiration and emulation, imagining it to be continuous with the present. The onset of the historic preservation movement (often dated from the Centennial Exhibition of 1876) coincided with an unprecedented rate of social and technological change. Because by then we were no longer able to see the past and the present connectedly, Lowenthal argues, Western, particularly American, culture became obsessed with the preservation of miscellaneous things.[1] Increasingly, pastness became its own excuse for being.

Thomas Jefferson is just one of many influential Americans who have argued that "the dead have no rights." Ours has often been represented as a "tradition of the new." The great outcome of the frontier experience, Frederick Jackson Turner proclaimed, was escape from "the bondage of the past." Of course Turner was himself a historian, and Jefferson was wonderfully alive to classical tradition, so it cannot be argued that they were insensitive to the uses of the past. But Jefferson, Turner, and legions of other influential Americans clearly warn us against clinging to a useless past.[2]

It is sobering to live in Washington, D.C., as I do, and contemplate the monuments here. Most of the brass and granite dedicated to such monuments was put in place during the 1875–1925 period. Washington abounds in such monuments; Los Angeles, to speak in urban types, does not. What this distinction in urban types suggests is that a kind of monumentality was in style at a given period and that it is now out of style. An older, "classical" emphasis on heroic individuals and grand events has been superseded (since 1925, say) by attempts to re-create past environments in which ordinary people do everyday things.[3]

Two thoughts suggest themselves. Why don't we provide for periodic and systematic reviews of the current meanings of our intentionally conserved pasts? Let the criteria be generous, even indulgent, but let the point be made that the pasts we conserve are expected to have an understood present relevance. And, shouldn't more be made of the time-boundedness of monuments—as, for example, the time-boundedness of the "classical" kind of monument and the imperial vision of a capital city, of which it was a part?

Any past is in some degree invented or contrived, and any such contrivance is likely to have a political agenda. For example, recent scholarship makes it clear that the American colonial revival movement derived from the efforts of old-stock Americans, appalled by the onset of industrial capitalism, to find refuge in a precapitalist past.[4] That such efforts at the invention of a past much purer than life were successful is attested to by the colonial revival facades and furnishings of countless American homes (the more expensive, the more solemn the effort to achieve "authenticity"), as well as by the street and subdivision names in any number of suburban "villages." In general the colonial revival movement corresponds to the urbanization of our society and could be described as a suburbanization of the past. How a suburbanized past functions is described by John Dorst in *The Written Suburb,* a study of an affluent Delaware River suburban enclave. A local history society with its annual fair contributes its part to the "look" of the area and is helped along by a local arts museum with national connections. The "look" of the area is that of a high-priced historyland, a preserve set aside from (while absolutely dependent on) nearby highways and cities.[5] Less prestigious suburbs emulate the suburb Dorst describes.

It is a version of history that more than pays its way, as is suggested by a letter I received a while back. Inserted in the envelope of that letter was a card upon which was printed as its entire content, in the manner of an invitation to a special event, "Come see the seasons change in a place that's stayed the same for over 200 years." What is being touted to individuals of retirement age, like me, is a real estate development with all of the amenities, particularly "the charm of historic Williamsburg as a backdrop."[6] The emptiness of the language is positively breathtaking. Without doubt, the language is composed in strict reference to advanced market research about what sells homes.

Edward Relph describes the modern urban landscape as combining the sleekness of the architecture in business districts ("cityscape") with an archaic cuteness in residential areas ("townscape"). In the townscape there is a new taste for what Relph calls "quaintspace," where new buildings and neighborhoods are engineered to look old and thereby cost more. The quaintness refers to no particular past but rather to a patina or illusion of pastness, which is flaunted as a kind of neighborhood logo.[7]

We are all familiar with that kind of overprocessed past. Olivia Cadaval has described an unprocessed past, or, rather, the process of inventing, even creating, a new past. Her subject is the annual parade and festival of Latinos in Washington, D. C. Washingtonians speak of Latinos to denote an incredible miscellaneousness of peoples and cultures. Contributing to that miscellaneousness is the recency of any shared past among that population. The festival and parade give the Latinos an annual opportunity to redefine what they mean to themselves, what face they will choose to present to the onlooking public, and, not least of all, who is in charge of deciding such matters. Cadaval traces the event from its inception to date, and in doing so she is able to make out an emergent sense of peoplehood among the "Latinos" and an attendant sense of what matters about the past they share.[8]

I would hazard the guess that the intentionally preserved past (under the sponsorship of private and public agencies) is much more likely to conserve history as an amenity and an objet d'art, as quaintspace, than as an elemental, almost desperate struggle for shared meaning, as among the Washington Latinos. So far as that is the case, it is another issue deserving self-reflection on the part of professional conservers.

I spoke of how the past is the product of continuous negotiations among all interested parties. Those negotiations must take into account the distinction between history beyond our experience and history that we know first or second hand.

We no doubt want to keep that Civil War soldier's memorial in the town square even though the war and the names on that memorial are forgotten. It can be argued that it is there and should stay there, partly, as a history lesson (though with Union soldier monuments in the North and Confederate soldier monuments in the South, the lesson itself is ambiguous). Simply because of its indistinct references for anyone in the present generation, the memorial suggests an immemoriality, a "once upon a time," that comfortably frames the present moment.[9] Further, the monument has become a landmark in the everyday landscape of the downtown area, whatever its intended meaning. Finally, there is no compelling reason to remove it. This array of reasons, however, is different from those applying to memorials to the remembered past.

The Vietnam Veterans Memorial is, for many of us, part of the remembered past. The names of the dead recorded there are for many the names of the near and dear. The monument clearly taps a deep well of feeling, of grief, on the part of those now alive who survived that war. Just as much to the point, it took some time to agree to have a memorial. During the war and in its immediate aftermath, feelings about it were impossibly protean. The process was not unlike that employed by the Washington Latinos in arriving at a form for their festival. In time, committees were assembled to decide there should be a memorial to the war and then to decide what it should be. What had been a shapeless past was finally given form, albeit a continuingly contested form.[10]

In due time, of course, that war will be lost to living memory. Then issues of preservation of this currently popular memorial will have to be addressed with the impersonal logic applying to the Civil War soldier in the town square. The issue for self-reflection here is how to acknowledge distinctions between memorials to history as experienced and those commemorating a more distant and impersonal past.

The past may just recede, becoming lost to memory, but it may also take on an unpredictable life of its own. In the 1920s it was decided that the proper memorial to Abraham Lincoln was an Olympian figure in a Greek temple, a curious apotheosis for a man celebrated for his homely origins. The designers of that memorial could not have guessed that their Greek temple would serve as the mythically appropriate stage and theater for the massive 1963 March on Washington and for Martin Luther King's pronouncement that segregation was dead.[11]

Students of such matters speak of "counter-memory" to denote the curious twists and turns of collective memories not provided in official versions of the past. A stunning example of how counter-memory works is provided by Wu Hang's analysis of the uses of China's Tiananmen Square under the Communist regime. Mao Zedong wanted a public square large enough to hold the entire population of China, to celebrate the new order. To that end, the imperial complex of gates and buildings was almost completely destroyed. A gate that had been part of the earlier complex was now to overlook the new square. The center of empire was thus transmuted into the center of the people's republic. A Monument to the People's Heroes faced the square, commemorating the history of the revolution. With no precedent and altogether spontaneously, massive demonstrations in 1976 fixed on the monument as a memorial to Zhou Enlai and as a symbol of resistance to the post-Mao regime (Wu suggests that perhaps they did so because the classic form of the monument resembled a gravestone). The 1989 protesters had the 1976 precedent in mind when they again made the monument a symbol of resistance (this time in conjunction with a memorializing of Hu Yaobang). We all know how this recent protest culminated in the erection of a facsimile of the Statue of Liberty directly in front of the mammoth official portrait of Mao overlooking the square. The regime destroyed that statue, and in precisely the spot where the statue had stood it erected what can only be called a counter-monument, celebrating faithfulness to the standing order. Memory and counter-memory thus contend for what is understood to be the mythically central place in Chinese geography and history.[12]

Issues for self-reflection abound in such examples. We have to insist that the past be useful, but in doing so we must be circumspect. The meaningful monument takes on a life of its own, interweaving official meanings with the unpredictable and sometimes powerful play of counter-memories. Official and vernacular versions of history instruct one another, with a subtlety we have not yet begun to comprehend.[13] Those of us concerned with historic sites also need to understand why the site of a monument takes on a meaning almost independent of the monument itself (as with the centrality of Tiananmen, whatever the regime, or the present-day centrality of Washington's monumental mall).[14]

Memory functions independently of monuments and intentions. We are all familiar with the American habit of setting aside historic homes and sites in almost perfect indifference to the surrounding environments. A tiny island of "history" in a sea of unrelated events can be used as a metaphor for the proportions and relations between the intentionally conserved past and the unintended pasts implicit in everyday events and landscapes. Lowenthal quotes from Proust: "As Habit weakens everything, what best reminds us of a person is precisely what we had forgotten."[15] This principle applies to the subject at hand. We have only recently come to appreciate the central importance to individual and group identity of the habitual round, the taken-for-granted world ("precisely what we had forgotten").[16]

Most of what we most value is forgotten most of the time. Our thoroughly urbanized, commodified "everywhere community"[17] is often thought of as dead to tradition, and yet in the second or third week of every December amazing numbers of us "remember" that it is time to get a Christmas tree. The ritual defies simple description; its meanings to its many participants are at once indefinite and multiple. The act involves cultural conservation rather than historic preservation. The individual tree does not matter much. What does matter is the annual reenactment of an important ritual that must be called back to memory through a series of acts, one of the first of which is getting into the car to look for a tree.

J. B. Jackson is a pioneer in the study of ordinary or vernacular or "forgotten" landscapes. The study of such landscapes requires a sensitivity to the welter of everyday activities on the part of all social classes at all times. Jackson finds meanings where others have not looked: in the trailer park, the commercial strip, or the paths followed by strangers to a city once they leave its bus or train depots and search for some place to spend the night.[18] You might say that with his help we "remember" the meaning of such quintessentially familiar everyday landscapes. The contrast, of course, is with the "islands" of self-consciously preserved landscapes commemorating famous people or the taste of the well-to-do.

Finally, in coming to terms with our problematic past, we need to understand the rhythms of memory for given individuals, the everyday uses of memory, and the changes in its use over a lifetime. There are different kinds of memory. Some have little to do with conserving the past: a short-term memory gets us by from minute to minute but has no lasting consequence; an instrumental memory is entirely dedicated to the transaction of business (to remembering an appointment, for example). Other kinds of memory are basic to what we make of the past. Memory as enacted in habitual behavior, our unself-conscious second nature, is the grounding for the more self-conscious acts of recall and reverie.[19] Self-consciousness about the past is likely to be the product of idle moments. Yi-Fu Tuan contrasts time as perceived when we are walking toward a particular destination with the kind of "timelessness" that takes over when we march to music. Reminiscence or reverie, like marching to music, is likely to be unconcerned about destinations.[20]

The past means different things at different stages in life. For youngsters, the past is what happened to other people. Adolescents are likely to rebel against an immediate past and perhaps idealize a past beyond their memories.[21] Middle-aged people tend to put the past off to one side. The elderly—and there are more of us all the time—tend to sift through memories, increasingly as they age, often as a means of connecting a blurring present with increasingly vivid memories of a remote past.[22]

The past we institutionally conserve should minister to life in the round. Memory is for the sake of life, not the other way around. Pastness for its own sake breeds mindlessness of a kind we all recognize: facades with no particular connection to what lies behind them; reconstructions that have a manifestly factitious relation to the past; irrelevant and ossified, not to mention politically vicious, forms of monumentality; indulgence in the merely nostalgic aspects of memory, often tied to sophisticated notions of what can be marketed on the strength of that nostalgia; and, generally, a disjuncture between what is formally conserved and what truly matters.

NOTES

1. David Lowenthal, *The Past Is a Foreign Country* (Cambridge: Cambridge University Press, 1985), esp. 385–406. Joseph S. Wood, "Providing Substance: His-

toric Preservation as Cultural Environmentalism," *North American Culture* 4 (1988): 22–37, making a similar point, uses a remark attributed to Mamie Eisenhower as an epigraph: "Things are more like they used to be now than they have ever been before."

2. The phrase comes from a letter from Thomas Jefferson to John W. Eppes, June 24, 1813, in Thomas Jefferson, *The Writings of Thomas Jefferson,* vol. 12 (Washington, D.C.: Thomas Jefferson Memorial Association, 1907), 260–61, as quoted in Lowenthal, *The Past Is a Foreign Country,* 108; Frederick Jackson Turner, "The Significance of the Frontier in American History," in *The Frontier in American History* (New York: Henry Holt, 1921), 1–38, esp. 210.

3. On the change in monumental style, see J. B. Jackson, "The Necessity for Ruins," in *The Necessity for Ruins* (Amherst: University of Massachusetts Press, 1980), 89–102, esp. 98. A related source on a similar topic is Eric Hobsbawm, "Mass-Producing Traditions: Europe, 1879–1914," in *The Invention of Tradition,* ed. Eric Hobsbawm and Terence Ranger (Cambridge: Cambridge University Press, 1983), 263–307. Pierre Nora, "Between Memory and History: *Les Lieux de Memoire,*" *Representations* 26 (Spring 1989): 10–11, with nineteenth-century France as his topic, speaks of a now obsolescent notion of a memory-nation, in which history is identified with an imputedly sacred nation-state; the "classic" monumentality bespeaks such a memory-nation.

4. See, for example, Alan Axelrod, ed., *The Colonial Revival in America* (New York: W. W. Norton, 1985). Shalom Staub, "Folklore and Authenticity: A Myopic Marriage in Public-Sector Programs," in *The Conservation of Culture: Folklorists and the Public Sector,* ed. Bert Feintuch (Lexington: University Press of Kentucky, 1988), 166–79, astutely analyzes the class biases implicit in a folkloristic notion of authenticity, which takes its meaning from its contrast to the everyday life of the folklorist. In such terms an authentic folk artist can have nothing to do with the presumably inauthentic commercial and popular society in which the folklorist makes his or her living. There is an analogy between such notions of authenticity and the "otherness" of a precapitalist past.

5. John Dorst, *The Written Suburb: An American Site, an Ethnographic Dilemma* (Philadelphia: University of Pennsylvania Press, 1989).

6. The materials were received in a letter of March 1990 (no more particular date specified) from Ford's Colony at Williamsburg (a "very special address").

7. Edward Relph, *The Modern Urban Landscape* (Baltimore: Johns Hopkins University Press, 1987), chaps. 11, 12.

8. Olivia Cadaval, "The Hispano-American Festival and the Latino Community: Creating an Identity in the Nation's Capital" (Ph.D. diss., George Washington University, 1989).

9. On this whole subject, see Yi-Fu Tuan, *Space and Place* (Minneapolis: University of Minnesota Press, 1977), esp. chap. 9. Lowenthal, *The Past Is a Foreign Country,* 359, emphasizes the differences between the remote and the "near and middle past." Daniel J. Boorstin, *The Image* (New York: Atheneum, 1987 [1961]), 64, talks about how "to become a great hero is actually to become lifeless; to become a face on a coin or a postage stamp." Or, one could add, to become a statue or memorial.

10. The complicated process is described in James M. Mayo, *War Memorials as Political Process* (New York: Praeger, 1988), 198–208. On issues of the contested form of the memorial, see Marita Sturken, "The Wall, the Screen and the Image: The Vietnam Veterans Memorial," *Representations* 35 (Summer 1991): 118–42. That issue of the periodical is devoted to "Monumental Histories." Susan Soderberg, "'Lest We Forget': Confederate Monuments and Cemeteries in Maryland" (M.A. thesis, George Washington University, 1992), tells the fascinating story of how the people of a border state, with deeply divided loyalties, gradually come to commemorate the lost Confederate cause under a Union flag.

11. Jeanne Houck, "Generations Remember: The Lincoln Memorial as a Contested Site for Memory of the Civil War, 1900–1945" (Paper delivered at the American Studies Association Convention, Baltimore, Md., 1991), describes the evolution of the memorial. She makes clear that Frederick Douglass, for example, wanted something very different from the memorial finally built. On the civic sculpture ideal involved in the memorial, see Michele H. Bogart, *Public Sculpture and the Civic Ideal in New York City, 1890–1930* (Chicago: University of Chicago Press, 1989). The establishment of Resurrection City at the foot of the memorial in 1968 was an attempt to capitalize on the success of the 1963 march.

12. Wu Hung, "Tiananmen Square: A Political History of Monuments," *Representations* 35 (Summer 1991): 84–117. Another excellent example of counter-memories at work is described by James E. Young, "The Biography of a Memorial Icon: Nathan Rapoport's Warsaw Ghetto Monument," *Representations* 26 (Spring 1989): 69–106, which is part of an special issue devoted to "Memory and Counter-Memory," edited by Natalie Zemon Davis and Randolph Starn. The concept of counter-memory derives from Michel Foucault, *Language, Counter-Memory, Practice,* ed. Donald F. Bouchard (Ithaca, N.Y.: Cornell University Press, 1977), esp. 139–64.

13. John Bodnar, "Power and Memory in Oral History: Workers and Managers at Studebaker," *Journal of American History* 75 (1989): 1201–21, uses oral histories to describe the ways in which vernacular versions of history and official (corporate) versions of history instruct one another. Bodnar's essay is part of a special issue devoted to "Memory and American History." David Thelen's introduction to that issue (1117–29) is thoughtful and wide-ranging in its discussion of the social construction of memory.

14. Nora, "Between Memory and History," 22, remarks, "Memory attaches itself to sites, whereas history attaches itself to events." Davis and Starn, in the introduction to the issue in which the Nora article appears (2–4), remind us that the ancient discipline of mnemonics emphasized places, both figurative and material.

15. Marcel Proust, *Remembrance of Things Past,* vol. 1, trans. C. K. Scott-Moncrieff and Terence Kilmartin (New York: Penguin, 1983), 692, as quoted in Lowenthal, *The Past Is a Foreign Country,* 205.

16. See, for example, Tuan, *Space and Place,* esp. chaps. 2, 4.

17. The phrase is from Daniel J. Boorstin, *The Americans: The Democratic Community* (New York: Vintage Books, 1974), 1. Boorstin characterizes the contemporary American community as a largely placeless entity.

18. The examples are taken from J. B. Jackson, *Landscapes,* ed. Ervin H. Zube

(Amherst: University of Massachusetts Press, 1970). Jackson is probably the best known of the students of ordinary landscape, but their numbers are legion. An excellent assemblage of essays on aspects of the ordinary landscape as related to architecture is Dell Upton and John Michael Vlach, eds., *Common Places: Readings in American Vernacular Architecture* (Athens: University of Georgia Press, 1986). The recent popularity of the subject is likely to obscure the fact that common landscape has been a central concern of geographers for as long as that discipline has been around.

19. Lowenthal, *The Past Is a Foreign Country,* 193–210.

20. On music in relation to "purposeful action," see Tuan, *Space and Place,* 128.

21. Two books by Kenneth Keniston are old but good discussions of how adolescents feel about the past: *The Uncommitted: Alienated Youth in American Society* (New York: Dell Publishing, 1965); and *Young Radicals: Notes on Committed Youth* (New York: Harcourt, Brace and World, 1968).

22. See Clarence Mondale, "Under Reduced Circumstances: Space and Place for the Aging," *Journal of American Studies* 22 (1988), 347–70.

2

Lost Frames of Reference: Sightings of History and Memory in Pennsylvania's Documentary Landscape

James F. Abrams

> . . . what is the strange power that the miners have over the imaginations of these people?
>
> —George Leighton, "Shenandoah, Pennsylvania"

> . . . the worse the "industrial" experience, the more authentic the resulting attraction.
>
> —John Urry, "Culture Change and Contemporary Holiday-Making"

> . . . simulation is the master, and nostalgia, the phantasmal, parodic rehabilitation of all lost frames of reference, is our just desserts.
>
> —Jean Baudrillard, *Simulations*

Call it fin-de-siècle malaise, the localized anguish of global economic restructuring, or a folklorist's struggle with representational crisis, but from where I sit in western Pennsylvania the social and cultural terrain of everyday life appears progressively more disjointed and ruptured. Deindustrialization and unemployment, out-migration of the region's children, as well as the declining significance of big-union politics have left working communities gasping for air. Yet when rehearsing this litany of social, economic, political, and cultural disjunctions, I find myself all too easily setting the stage for the entrance of cultural repair workers (such as myself), who, through a general recasting of the public sphere in the name of "heritage," are to salve the wounds inflicted on the region by capital flight, wire-brush the rustbelt for tourist promotion, and reunite the frayed and unraveling strands of our contemporary cultural experience.

The liberal- and progressive-sounding language of social crisis vis-à-vis economic restructuring, underwritten by the decisions and priorities of transnational capital, appears to have created a new discursive formation less inclined to critique the economic policies of capital than to justify and legitimate the ameliorating cultural activities of the state. As a folklorist working amid the cultural technologies of the state, I have become sensitized to, and rather wary of, institutionally based discourses of social crisis and its mirror concept "heritage." In this essay I argue that if we are to practice cultural conservation as critically oriented public educators within the emergent discursive echo chambers currently under construction by various levels of government, we must listen carefully for popular accents of gender, class, and ethnicity, which circulate and proliferate in response and resistance to the representational priorities of the state. I also subject the term *heritage* to particular scrutiny and examine its uses in various bureaucratic settings and working communities to address the cultural politics embedded in the practice of heritage preservation. More specifically, I focus on the struggle for collective memory currently being waged by Pennsylvania coal town residents and state historical agencies in highly textualized social spaces that I term "documentary landscapes."

Let me begin this essay by stating its central theme: on a general and analytical level the concept of heritage strikes me as an ideologically charged textualizing practice intended, with varying degrees of self-consciousness, to mediate and reimpose order on the destabilizing forces of culture change. Heritage discourse is formulated during and after periods of significant social transformation, and it functions as an act of cultural redefinition and repair. Migration, economic dislocation, and a sense of generational discontinuity are a few stimuli that provoke intense feelings of loss, absence, and yearning, conditions that heritage projects attempt to assuage by recovering memories and traditions presumed emblematic of a group's desired cultural continuity. As the anthropologist Richard Handler has noted in several publications, these emblems are then bracketed from the flow of everyday experience, and they become discursive or physical sites within which the struggle for cultural self-definition takes place.[1] The invention of heritage discourse thus acts as a barometer for social and cultural transformation rather than for stability. The more vehement the marshalling of one's cultural "resources" in the name of heritage, the more urgent the need for vigilant maintenance and protection of one's cultural identity seems to be.[2] Just beneath the surface of much heritage discourse seethes social rage, for the relative quietude of heritage communication joins dialectically with the anger of the outraged. Heritage discourse and social rage are but two sides of the same coin. Personal experience with the torments of identity related to religion, ethnicity, class, color, and gender, or the fear associated with potential victimization, is never far from the social fantasies of heritage discourse or from the desire to recoup coherence.[3]

"We" have *a past* that is "ours" and that makes "us" different. "We" recognize "our" differences *by virtue* of traditions that "we" agree to enact and sustain and that nourish "us." The possessive pronouns of heritage discourse constitute a malleable social space, and they migrate along a continuum of ownership claims so that nearly any set of generally desired cultural traits or images can be possessed by a household, an ethnic group, or the state. Of course, when various governmental agencies assert identity claims regarding "our Native American heritage" or "America's industrial heritage," members of the nation-state share a sense of affiliation and proprietorship very different from that of a western Apache-speaking person who advocates language revitalization for members of her community or a labor union official who recounts a strike story on a picket line. The migration of identity claims between lived and represented experience and consequent struggles for the meaning of places have, at best, sparked some fruitful cross-class discussion about the cluster of relations linking institutional policy to popular mechanisms of cultural reproduction and, at worst, caused the effacement of popular memory through a defensive professionalization of the past.

The self-conscious and tendentious use of the past in the reconstruction of cultural identity has recently attracted much scholarly attention, from reflexive and critically oriented ethnographic accounts to practice-based manuals describing the methods of heritage programming and preservation. The rapidly expanding literature on heritage projects can be divided roughly between the policy and methodological concerns of practitioners in public folklore and history, on the one hand, and the epistemological/political critiques of state-sponsored heritage activities developed in ethnographic case studies by anthropologists, sociologists, and scholars in cultural studies, on the other hand.[4] In the latter category, commentators point to numerous problematics in the social construction of heritage projects, including interventions that result in "cultural objectification"—the process of reifying previously taken-for-granted behaviors as cultural property and turning them into a medium for exchange; "heritage as diversion" or as "protective illusion"—the substitution of heritage displays for direct political action against the forces deemed responsible for economic and political marginalization; and "the suppression of unruly histories"—an effort to regulate the moral and expressive resources of community and to engineer compliance with a set of preferred memories and images through the mechanisms of cultural programming and supervision deployed by the state.[5]

Taken together, this incisive literature constitutes a trenchant critique of cultural conservation as a politically innocent activity. Yet precisely because many of these studies have focused on the issue of institutional hegemony, heritage initiatives at the community or grass-roots level remain generally unexplored. Much research also fails to account for the structured but variable ways that people recontextualize and rework messages presented by powerful institutions. An exclusive focus on institutions as agencies of hegemony obscures the fact that cultural sites, like heritage projects, are never made once and for all but are indeterminate and subject to continual reinvention.[6] Deindustrialization, cultural tourism, and the media of nostalgia have generated a new international industrial heritage movement that unites workers of the world—as images. But surely these images and themes are consumed, resisted, and reinvented differently in, for example, southwestern Pennsylvania and South Wales.

Of relevance to the argument advanced so far is the distinction posited by the sociologist Craig Calhoun between the "imagined communities" of indirect social relationships, which are institutionally and electronically mediated and involved with the elicitation of cultural *categories,* and the face-to-face interpersonal relations that link members of *groups* in complex patterns of association and belonging. Within mediascapes characterized by indirect social relationships, images and enactments of tradition are primarily involved with the construction of relatively fixed ascriptive categories (such as "folk," "heritage," or "worker"). Sociability in face-to-face relations, on the other hand, can be described as performative and improvisational, albeit generally within the bonds of interpersonal relations characteristic of everyday social experience.[7] The formation and coherence of everyday occupational identity in places like Pennsylvania seem increasingly intermixed with such media presentations as those documentary forms encountered in heritage environments.[8]

Intensely textualized heritage environments in various theme pockets of the deindustrialized, overdeveloped world constitute new "documentary landscapes." Redesigned as historical settings for the tourist trade, industrial documentary landscapes encompass entire regions that have been marooned by capital. They are spaces of deliberate remembering (and forgetting) in which protected industrial artifacts, such as abandoned coal tipples and workers' housing, lend distinctive place-identities to otherwise displaced social environments. Time freezes and "monumentalizes" to a period of unquestioned industrial strength.[9] Space becomes playful. Scripts, plans, timetables, inventories, evaluations of significance, ethnographic documentation, and the full armory of the state's cultural technologies concentrate on framing space as text.

Following Kenneth Burke's ideas about role congruence in textual environments, we can view the documentary landscape as a densely communicative "stage set" that motivates action and behavior in a manner consistent with the containing "scene."[10] The set influences the perception and reception of actors in a scene, and once established it situates action as the work of either reproduction or resistance. Later I describe cases of role conflict vis-à-vis the ordering motives of the documentary landscape, but here I want to suggest one nuts-and-bolts implication: a setting evoking the essential historical nature of labor does not convey the pressing relevance of labor to current economic or cultural realities. If textualized and thematized space is frozen into images of the past, people within the frame become actors, objects of memory, spectators to their own history, or categories.

The literary and social critic Raymond Williams described the making of a documentary landscape in South Wales during a talk on Welsh culture broadcast by BBC radio in 1975. He asked listeners to follow him on a jaunt through the Welsh Folk Museum at St. Fagans, and after describing the museum as a "lovely place," he wondered aloud, "What happens to a people when it calls itself, even temporarily, a folk?" Williams saw in the reerected farmhouses and cottages, weaving mill, and tannery an attempt to locate the "real" culture of Wales in the period just prior to the industrial revolution and just beyond the horizon of everyday life. The folk, in Williams's reading of the museum, embodied a distant pastoral otherness completely divorced from the work-a-day world of the coal mines, steel mills, and factories of industrial South Wales, wherein the majority of the Welsh population actually worked. He went on rather sardonically to suggest that if depopulation and unemployment continued apace, then before long "a nostalgic colliery cage would rise beyond the tannery. An out-of-date ironworks would share a stream with the weaving. A depressed and ravaged country, passing quickly through the status of a marginal region, would find its cultural reincarnation in the lovingly preserved material relics of an open air museum."[11]

Only a few years later, the forward march of deindustrialization in South Wales did indeed prompt a massive effort to resurrect, display, and memorialize the heritage of industrial workers in a series of attractions throughout the region. With the collapse of the industrial economy, workers had come to occupy an iconic position in the Welsh documentary landscape similar to that formerly occupied exclusively by agricultural laborers. Industrial workers too had become the "folk."

The rapid social and political marginalization of industrial workers in Britain and North America has given rise to two distinctive retrospective visions. On the one hand, the cultural brokerage of industrial decline involves fixing images of workers securely in the past, where they can be colonized, commodified, and consumed as signs of an already defeated social class. In this mode, textures of contemporary poverty, unemployment, and urban decay blur into the carefully preserved styles and look of an earlier period "when times were really tough."[12] As signs of an earlier, past period, industrial artifacts in the documentary landscape elude association with contemporary industrial workers and communities. Members of working-class communities, who are mainly elderly because the young have migrated elsewhere, also take on a grainy verisimilitude of a preferred industrial "golden age."

On the other hand, many institutionally based, critical perspectives on the past hardly find it discomfiting to raise the specters of class and gender oppression, as long as specters of oppression can be ultimately transformed into spectacles of consumption. In this mode of perception, the patina of grime and rust metaphorically covering many industrial artifacts points accusingly at the exploitative excesses of industrialists and the moral legitimacy of their opulent life-styles. With perfect postmodern excess, however, the heritage industry can have it both ways, for, as the sociologist John Urry observes, "the worse the 'industrial' experience, the more authentic the resulting attraction."[13] In sum, the phantom exploitation of working people on view in industrial documentary landscapes rarely links the concrete historical decisions of capital to the stern political and economic realities currently besetting rustbelt communities in Great Britain, Pennsylvania, and elsewhere.

The historical cultures associated with the coal industry in Pennsylvania are receiving unprecedented attention and concern. Elements of the physical landscape, such as coal breakers and tipples, "patch" houses, and sites of labor-capital conflict, evoke memories of hard work, community, and resistance to exploitation to some, while for others they represent a past much better forgotten. Local labor monuments and memorials dedicated to miners anchor memories to particular sites, transforming physical space into landmarks of emotion and moral suasion. Small-scale museum-bars and vernacular museums examine institutional representations for omissions and silences related to exploitation and discrimination. Former miners leading coal mine tours speak for dead comrades. Department stores, businesses, and banks stamp the communal past with their own exceptional currency. Parades memorializing the coal industry reflect ways in which memory is reorganized in the imagery of contemporary concerns. Clearly, in the coal regions of Pennsylvania the past cracks into two heritage movements, each enshrining autonomous spheres of the social world. Vernacular landscapes encountered in the semi-open spaces of home garages, local bars, and community parks delimit social zones of belonging to name, claim, and personalize memory for a known community. Institutional representations of industrial history disperse images and narratives to an unknowable public. The vernacular continuously and actively scans the institutional for regulated silences, voicing allegiance to lived collective experience through the embodied memory of a "witness."

Both varieties of heritage display mediate the process of industrial decline and transformation. Neither is more "authentic" than the other since each represents ratios of power and emotion consistent with its relation to contemporary modes of information technology. As indicated earlier, the face-to-face, oral communication found in vernacular heritage space links a display to its referent—the miner, his family, and community—usually through the body of a former miner now acting as the guide to his collection.[14] The vernacular collection seems nearly always to include a "value center," an item or assemblage of particular emotional resonance, around which individuals narrate their own or their community's life story. Within most institutional documentary landscapes communication takes place primarily through images, not embodied speaking. The flow of images, scripts, and simulations creates its own self-referential context within which the figure of the living embodied miner disappears. As the journalist George Leighton noted in his 1937 *Harper's* article on Pennsylvania coal towns, the sudden reappearance of the referent can be cause for alarm:

> There is, at Pottsville, the countyseat [of Schuylkill County], a hotel, called the *Necho Allen* after the man who is supposed to have discovered anthracite. This hotel has a Coal Mine Taproom. One section of the wall represents the mouth of a gangway with a car piled with coal emerging into the taproom. Part of the wall is mine timbered and all about are scattered mining tools, carbide lamps, and other paraphernalia. The side walls of the booths are fitted with handsome photographic murals which show the begrimed miner at work. And at the tables—the linen is very heavy and the silver glitters—sit the elect of Pottsville, making the cocktail hour something more than an excuse for a drink. . . .
>
> . . . There is a gray-haired woman, a little touched up, with a young man and both are pretty drunk. When the woman waves her hands at the murals her bracelets jangle. She says that the young man won't see anything like this anywhere, and that is quite true. She says the mines are simply fascinating. And they are. There are no murals of the general offices of the Philadelphia and Reading Coal and Iron Company nor the Chairman of the Board shown dictating a letter. No, there are only miners, only Maxeys and McShanes and Kalvaruskis and Brazzeses make up this odd gallery of heroes. Heroes? How uneasy, how uncomfortable these people would be if a crowd of such heroes should suddenly enter the taproom and sit down. Why, then, the murals on the walls, what is the strange power that the miners have over the imaginations of these people? Someone ought to explain this mystery, this furtive vicarious blood transfusion. But

no explanation is offered on the cocktail list; there is only some publicity writer's blurb about Necho Allen.[15]

Leighton's understated yet acerbic description reads like an excerpt from fieldnotes recorded while sitting alone at a table, observing, and estranged. The taproom furnishes his fieldsite. Other than his own political sensibilities, he recognizes in this documentary milieu two especially radiant exclusions: any imagery pertaining to the coal industry's dominant culture, and the embodied presence of workers. Absentee owners of the anthracite region remain absent from the representational field of the taproom lest their portrayed privilege juxtapose harshly with "the begrimed miner." On the other hand, Leighton playfully suggests names for the workers, but he makes this move only to establish the fact that their ethnicity constitutes part of the display. In the taproom, as in most cross-class documentary landscapes, workers are ethnically and occupationally marked yet anonymous—an imagined "collective other."[16] As dust-enshrouded images and categories without specific names or biographies, these miners represent fetishized market roles rather than selves.[17] Leighton never revealed whether the begrimed (black-faced) images of order and subordination ever materialized as embodied subjects in the taproom of the Necho Allen. But the play between the dominant class's embodied presence and the absence of its image, on the one hand, and working-class embodied absence and its imaged presence, on the other, continues to typify many institutionally organized industrial documentary landscapes.[18]

As Kathleen Stewart proposes for the emergent social spaces of nostalgia, in documentary landscapes "resistance takes the form of making further inscriptions on the landscape of encoded things—inlays on the existing descriptions—in an effort to fragment the enclosing, already finished order and reopen cultural forms to history."[19] To illustrate the dynamics by which people inflect new meanings into existing models, I refer to notes taken in 1989 while working as a researcher and tour guide at Eckley Miners' Village, a state-owned-and-operated "open-air museum" near Hazleton, Pennsylvania. Eckley was a company town constructed in the mid-1850s, owned by a succession of coal operators, and finally donated to the state of Pennsylvania in 1972. There are a few coal mining families still living in the village, and they embody part of the museum's display.

In 1968 Paramount Studios produced the film *The Molly Maguires* at Eckley and utilized hundreds of local people as extras, construction workers, and chauffeurs. The film portrays the lives of Irish miners who formed a radical branch of the Ancient Order of Hibernians in the mid- and late nineteenth century. Scrapbooks, home movies, and memorabilia saved from the time of filming attest to the tremendous influence exerted by the movie on local historical consciousness. The remaining residents of Eckley recount endless narratives about hosting cast and crew in their homes. Former residents of Eckley identify where they came from as "the place where they made the Molly Maguires movie," and visitors converge on the village to encounter a film location as much as to experience a historical site. The museum, however, strives to downplay Paramount's intervention in the history of the town because it considers the film historically inaccurate, which it certainly is.

Nonetheless, film and place are inextricably linked in the consciousness of local residents. The year 1968 looms in the imagination as a pivot point between an era of collective struggle as a working coal patch and the textualization of the past by film and museum. In the complex battle waged over history, the museum has claimed and captured the period between 1854, the date of the town's original construction, and 1968, its reconstruction as a movie set. The residents of Eckley, for their part, view the film as the salvation of their community. Had the movie not generated the interest in the town that it did, many residents argue, Eckley would have been demolished and strip-mined like hundreds of other coal communities in the region. The film's production, which the museum views as irrelevant to the telling of Eckley's history, thus represents the most tangible *act* of cultural conservation ever experienced by the residents.

By the time Paramount's film crew left Eckley in August 1968, the town's physical appearance had reabsorbed the austere look of a mid-nineteenth-century coal patch. The antiquing of Eckley entailed removing trees from front yards, burying electrical and telephones lines, and standardizing the color of house facades. The studio also constructed several large structural props—a company store, mule barn, and massive coal breaker—all of which remain in the village today. The owner of Eckley's buildings endorsed these interventions to provide the film company with the dour look of a mining community "in the shadow of the coal breakers." Residents felt, and continue to feel, ambivalent about the antiquing of the town's fabric. They unhappily discovered that other mining families in the region began using Eckley as a visual baseline from which to calculate economic and social distance traveled since the bad old days of the nineteenth century. By comparison with Eckley's "restored" clapboarding and monochromatic facades, they reasoned, aluminum siding and television antennae represented visible material progress and the achievement of socio-aesthetic goals.

Almost immediately following the filming, Eckley's villagers heard rumors that the town was to become an open-air museum. Shortly thereafter, the state took control of Eckley and introduced new leases that prohibited residents from altering the outside appearance of homes. Local discussion and debate about the establishment of a state museum in Eckley initially registered the hopes and anticipation of residents for new employment opportunities. When these hopes never materialized, however, the film seemed less a salvation than a marker dividing time between one form of company control and another. Talking about the film then became an important emancipatory practice for people who felt surrounded and constrained by the power of the state. In short, popular memory in Eckley has appropriated and recontextualized the recent past by narrating and inscribing itself into the film's "script," or what might be better called its expanded and opened "ethnoscript."[20]

The actor Sean Connery played the film's lead role as Jack Kehoe, ringleader of the Molly Maguires. Never actually a miner as portrayed in the movie, Kehoe owned a bar in Girardville, Pennsylvania, which is currently operated by his great-grandson Joe Wayne. In 1978, the centennial of Kehoe's execution by the state, Wayne demanded and received an official pardon and exoneration for his great-grandfather from the governor of Pennsylvania. In the same year, Schuylkill County remodeled the courthouse in Pottsville where Kehoe was hanged. Wayne seized the opportunity to remove the block stones of the cell that imprisoned Kehoe, as well as the steel doors and iron shackles, all of which were installed, along with several framed portraits of Kehoe, in his bar as a "memorial" to family and organized labor.

These fragments of the collected past establish a direct and indisputable connection with the object of Wayne's fascination—his great-grandfather. As in all documentary landscapes, vernacular and institutional, the politics of Wayne's assemblage rhetorically declares what and whose memories are to be considered significant. In barroom conversation and debates about the Molly Maguires and their role in regional history, what is actively remembered about the past is a function of the social relationships established through talk. The character of social remembering in the bar depends largely on the knowledge and communicative strategies of the participants in conversation. Wayne's material "evidence," however, forcefully imbues space with a feeling that the past actually occurred as it is being imagined in the bar. Unlike Eckley's exclusively cinematic association with the Molly Maguires, Wayne's bar did physically shelter the rebels' notorious activities, which, according to local understanding, establishes the site's historical authenticity and its indelible significance to the American labor movement.

Social remembering in Wayne's "Hibernian House" bar constitutes an explicitly oppositional reading of the past as presented by film and museum. It rejects the film's depiction of the Mollies as a gang of terroristic thugs—"as far as I'm concerned, the real 'Molly Maguires' were the Pinkerton detectives," Wayne wryly comments—as well as the museum's silence on the role of organized labor in the region.[21] The bar destabilizes the museum's generic and categorical presentation of regional history by foregrounding Wayne's particular genealogy and ethnic ancestry. Since his genealogical background extends retrospectively to the "foundation of American labor," and because the United Mine Workers of America devalue ethnic particularism at the expense of class solidarity, the material objectification of Wayne's genealogy encompasses the diversity of patrons who identify with labor. In the starkly drawn prison portraits of Jack Kehoe that stare down from the dark walls of Wayne's bar, one sees not the vanquishing of a single individual, or representations of a collective other as in the Necho Allen, but sketches in the formation of a collective self. Whereas the function of the film in providing for the physical preservation of the town, and as an autonomous discursive space, figures most prominently in the minds of Eckley residents, Wayne wages war with the content of the film, expanding once again its ethnoscript. As for Eckley's lack of attention to organized labor, he simply states, "Most people who go up there come back down here."[22]

Museum, film, and bar, then, tell partial but intersecting stories about the past. Together they illustrate the fact that clashes frequently take place if not in the formation, then in the reception of heritage projects. Occasionally these skirmishes materialize strategic counter-memories of working-class life and make clear that, as Douglas Foley explains, "The great ideological struggle in advanced capitalism is not only over explicit ideologies; the struggle is also over one's mode of identity expression in an overly administered world of manufactured symbols and identities."[23] The meaning of the Molly Maguires and labor history in the anthracite region circulates among a variety of identity sites in this socially stratified locale. The challenge to cultural conservation as critical practice thus consists of conserving autonomous *spaces* that allow for the free expression of radically plural public cultures. Memory and counter-memory, model and inscription, script and ethnoscript interrogate, contest, shape, and destabilize one another. The questions for us become: whose texts do we sanction and to what end do we reorder them as "heritage"?

If the concept of heritage is to be reimagined as a shifting terrain of debate intersected by a variety of voices in dialogue about the past, we need to position ourselves on the borders between cultures where these voices can be heard.[24] Cultural workers (such as folklorists and anthropologists) in the institutional public sphere are more than likely already situated on the borders of their respective organizations. As Henry Giroux suggests for public educators generally, cultural workers practicing within the discursive frame of cultural conservation can facilitate "border crossings" between powerful institutions and the plurality of publics self-defined by class, color, and gender.[25] Such border crossing can recognize and present for discussion the limits and contradictions of specific cultural codes and representational practices. For example, workers in labor unions can be asked to consider the implications of having their industries situated in the imagery of the past and to act on the basis of such considerations. On the other hand, institutions will learn that the presentational norms encoded in vernacular labor displays privilege the experience of male workers, and the institutions can be encouraged to redress the silence of the vernacular sphere related to gender. Border crossing will always be partial, temporary, and intent on reforming the institution while safeguarding the autonomy of working-class counterpublics. Finally, we need to recognize heritage as a debate about cultural and material equity, about the right to cultural self-determinism, and about the need to assail the class, color, and gender blindness of America's dominant public sphere. Having recognized the importance of this debate for radical cultural democracy, we should endorse theory, critique, and practice as essential components in the emerging paradigm of cultural conservation.

NOTES

Many thanks to Mary Hufford and Kathy Kimiecik for their constructive comments on earlier drafts of this essay and to Paul Hanson, Bob McCarl, Bob St. George, and Bill Jones for conversations that helped me think through some of the essay's more contentious implications, not that they agree with what is expressed. I must also delimit the geographic scope of generalizations presented in this essay. My professional experience with issues related to heritage is limited to several (de)industrialized regions in Pennsylvania and Great Britain. Observations not specifically anchored to place by description or citation are connected to these social environments through experience.

1. See, for example, Richard Handler, *Nationalism and Politics of Culture in Quebec* (Madison: University of Wisconsin Press, 1988), "Ethnicity in the Museum," in *Negotiating Ethnicity: The Impact of Anthropological Theory and Practice,* ed. Susan Emley Keefe (Washington, D.C.: American Anthropological Association, 1989), 18–26, and "Who Owns the Past: History, Cultural Property, and the Logic of Possessive Individualism," in *The Politics of Culture,* ed. Brett Williams (Washington, D.C.: Smithsonian Institution Press, 1991), 63–74.

2. For a systematic analysis of the conceptual terrains occupied by "memory" and "history" with implications for the development of "heritage" discourses, see Pierre Nora, "Between Memory and History: *Les Lieux de Mémoire,*" *Representations* 26 (Spring 1989): 7–25.

3. I can think of no more pertinent example of this line of thought than Barbara Myerhoff's exquisite *Number Our Days* (New York: Simon and Schuster, 1978).

4. Scores of books and articles have been published in recent years on heritage preservation, the politics of culture, and within the framework of cultural studies. I list only some of the more salient works in each category. For folkloristic studies focusing on method and policy, see Ormond Loomis, coordinator, *Cultural Conservation: The Protection of Cultural Heritage in the United States,* Publications of the American Folklife Center, no. 10 (Washington, D.C.: American Folklife Center, Library of Congress, 1983); Burt Feintuch, ed., *The Conservation of Culture: Folklorists and the Public Sector* (Lexington: University Press of Kentucky, 1988); and Benita J. Howell, ed., *Cultural Heritage Conservation in the American South,* Southern Anthropological Society Proceedings, no. 23 (Athens: University of Georgia Press, 1990). For historical and anthropological accounts of heritage making in the Appalachian South, see David E. Whisnant, *All that Is Native and Fine: The Politics of Culture in an American Region* (Chapel Hill: University of North Carolina Press, 1983); Stephen William Foster, *The Past Is Another Country: Representation, Historical Consciousness, and Resistance in the Blue Ridge* (Berkeley: University of California Press, 1988); and Allen W. Batteau, *The Invention of Appalachia* (Tucson: University of Arizona Press, 1990). For superb ethnographic case studies of heritage politics, consult Handler, *Nationalism and the Politics of Culture in Quebec;* Virginia R. Domínguez, *People as Subject, People as Object: Selfhood and Peoplehood in Contemporary Israel* (Madison: University of Wisconsin Press, 1989); and Michael Herzfeld, *A Place in History: Social and Monumental Time in a Cretan Town* (Princeton, N.J.: Princeton University Press, 1991); and the articles in James Brow and Ted Swedenburg, eds. *Tendentious Revisions of the Past in the Construction of Community,* special issue of *Anthropological Quarterly* 63, no. 1 (1990). For critical insight into the formation of heritage scapes in Great Britain, see Robert Hewison, *The Heritage Industry: Britain in a Climate of Decline* (London: Methuen, 1987); Robert Lumley, ed., *The Museum Time Machine: Putting Cultures on Display* (London: Routledge, 1988); and John Corner and Sylvia Harvey, eds., *Enterprise and Heritage: Crosscurrents of National Culture* (London: Routledge, 1991). For an essay that signals a new turn in the analysis of cultural politics, that being policy development as it emerges from within a strongly articulated critical position, see Tony Bennett, "Putting Policy into Cultural Studies," in *Cultural Studies,* ed. Lawrence Grossberg, Cary Nelson, and Paula Treichler (New York: Routledge, 1992), 23–37.

5. "Cultural objectification" comes from Handler, *Nationalism and the Politics of Culture in Quebec;* the phrase "heritage as diversion" is from William Kelly, "Japanese No-Noh: The Crosstalk of Public Culture in a Rural Festivity," *Public Culture* 2 (Spring 1990): 65–81; the characterization of heritage as "protective illusion" is from Kevin Robins, "Tradition and Translation: National Culture in Its Global Context," in *Enterprise and Heritage,* ed. Corner and Harvey, 22; and the "suppression of unruly histories" is from Herzfeld, *A Place in History,* 47.

6. The studies by Domínguez and Herzfeld are clear exceptions to the generalization that research on heritage preservation has neglected popular re-

workings of cultural intervention by the state. Nevertheless, the generalization holds true. Also, I do not want to suggest that the studies focusing on institutional hegemony have been inappropriate or unenlightening. My point is simply that they have missed the methods and means by which institutional heritage projects are received and deconstructed by those being represented. Michel de Certeau, *The Practice of Everyday Life* (Berkeley: University of California Press, 1984), xiii, characterizes this type of appropriative use of the "makers" by the "users" as "secondary production." Of course, heritage workers located within institutions will reappropriate instances of secondary production only later to encounter forms of secondary production squared in this geometry of institutional strategies and popular tactics. The limits of maneuverability are reached with the exhaustion of autonomous and recalcitrant memories.

7. Craig Calhoun, "Indirect Relationships and Imagined Communities: Large-Scale Social Integration and the Transformation of Everyday Life," in *Social Theory for Changing Society,* ed. Pierre Bourdieu and James S. Coleman (Boulder, Colo.: Westview Press, 1991), 95–121. "Imagined communities" was introduced by Benedict Anderson in his well-known study *Imagined Communities: Reflections on the Origin and Spread of Nationalism* (London: Verso, 1983).

8. Arjun Appadurai's excellent analyses of the "deterritorialization" of identity through the development of such global cultural forms as tourist environments greatly influenced my thinking about industrial documentary landscapes. See his "Disjuncture and Difference in the Global Cultural Economy," *Public Culture* 2 (Spring 1990): 1–24, and "Global Ethnoscapes: Notes and Queries for a Transnational Anthropology," in *Recapturing Anthropology: Working in the Present,* ed. Richard G. Fox (Santa Fe, N.M.: School of American Research Press, 1991), 191–210.

9. Herzfeld, *A Place in History,* esp. chap. 1, draws the distinction between "monumental time" and "social time" in Greece. Monumental time is enshrined by the state as the period look frozen into buildings, ethnic costume, and local "tradition" through preservation policy. Social time is marked by interaction, improvisation, and the dynamics of social relationships.

10. Kenneth Burke, "Container and Thing Contained," in his *A Grammar of Motives* (Berkeley: University of California Press, 1969), 3–20. Hilda Kuper's now classic study "The Language of Sites in the Politics of Space," *American Anthropologist* 74 (1972): 411–25, first alerted me to this sort of reading of Burke.

11. The quotation is from a transcript of the radio program in Raymond Williams, *Resources of Hope: Culture, Democracy, Socialism* (London: Verso, 1989), 100.

12. John Bromley, *Lost Narratives: Popular Fictions, Politcs and Recent History* (London: Routledge, 1988), has made similar observations regarding the politics of retrospection in Britain.

13. John Urry, "Culture Change and Contemporary Holiday-Making," *Theory, Culture and Society* 5 (1988): 50. See also his chapter entitled "Gazing

on History," in his *The Tourist Gaze: Leisure and Travel in Contemporary Societies* (London: Sage Publications, 1990), 104–34.

14. The use of gender marked pronouns here is intentional. Vernacular museums in coal communities throughout Pennsylvania and Great Britain express the memory of work in extremely gender specific terms, usually through the artifacts of labor in the mine.

15. George R. Leighton, "Shenandoah, Pennsylvania: The Story of an Anthracite Town," *Harper's Monthly Magazine,* January 1937, 146–47.

16. Virginia Domínguez uses "collective other" throughout her insightful book *People as Subject, People as Object.*

17. The appropriation of "primitive art" by Western museums in the ninteenth and twentieth centuries deployed similar strategies of ethnic typification and erasure of the subject/artist. See Sally Price, *Primitive Art in Civilized Places* (Chicago: University of Chicago Press, 1989).

18. This observation refers to the relative absence of working people/indigenous people/local people in the planning stages of documentary landscapes versus the relative importance of their imagery after planning has occurred. Nancy Fraser, "Rethinking the Public Sphere: A Contribution to the Critique of Actually Existing Democracy," *Social Text* 25/6 (1990): 56–80, suggests this encourages the development of "weak publics" vis-à-vis heritage environments; that is, groups of people who can express an opinion only after the fact rather than participate in decision making during essential stages of concept building. "Strong publics," conversely, develop a discourse that "encompasses both opinion-formation and decision-making."

19. See Kathleen Stewart, "Nostalgia—A Polemic," *Cultural Anthropology* 3 (1988): 227–41, for a masterful theoretical elaboration of this point. The quotation is taken from p. 232.

20. Appadurai, "Global Ethnoscapes," uses the term *ethnodrama* to describe interplay between social identity and the seductions of the cinema in India. I prefer the term *ethnoscript* because it more aptly suggests the intertextuality of contested forms, such as the one just described.

21. Since my fieldwork in the anthracite region in 1989, Eckley Miners' Museum has attempted to introduce thematics related to organized labor.

22. Both short quotations are from taped oral interviews with Joe Wayne, recorded in his bar in Girardville, Pennsylvania, August 3, 1989.

23. Douglas E. Foley, "Does the Working Class Have a Culture in the Anthropological Sense?" *Cultural Anthropology* 4 (1989): 156.

24. Appadurai, "Disjuncture and Difference in the Global Cultural Economy"; Arjun Appadurai and Carol A. Breckenridge, "Museums Are Good to Think: Heritage on View in India," in *Museums and Communities: The Politics of Public Culture,* ed. Ivan Karp, Christine Mullen Kreamer, and Steven D. Lavine (Washington, D.C.: Smithsonian Institution Press, 1992), 34–55.

25. See Henry Giroux, "Border Pedagogy in the Age of Postmodernism," in *Postmodern Education: Politics, Culture, and Social Criticism,* by Stanley Aronowitz and Henry A. Giroux (Minneapolis: University of Minnesota, 1991), 114–35, and *Border Crossings: Cultural Workers and the Politics of Education* (New York: Routledge, 1992).

3

Traditional History and Alternative Conceptions of the Past

Alan S. Downer, Jr., Alexandra Roberts, Harris Francis, and Klara B. Kelley

History is not an objective chronicle of the events of the past as they actually happened. It is a historian's model of the past. This model is a reconstruction based on what survives in the documentary record, what portions of that record historians have discovered, what decisions historians make about which records to include as the basis for their analyses, and which analytical frameworks inform their analyses. History is actually a complex of relationships between the past and the present. This is hardly a revelation, since historiographers have made this point often. Historic preservationists and the federal and state officials, however, often act as if history were a complete or "objective" reconstruction of the past. This assumption leads preservationists to act as if everyone agrees on what is historically significant and therefore worthy of protection under the federal preservation program. Defining history only according to a Euro-American historical tradition severely limits what falls within the ambit of the federal preservation program.

We all carry "intuitive" definitions of history. Our definitions control what we consider to be of historic significance. Our intuitive definitions are constrained by our cultural backgrounds and our formal and informal education about the past. The formal training may be highly specialized, but even professional historians differ widely on what they consider historic and, for that matter, on what constitutes history.[1] The national historic preservation program is driven by "history," and determinations of historic significance must be made every day by federal and state agency staff and officials and the consultants who gather information for them. Those decisions relate directly to what gets protected and what does not. How history is defined is therefore a crucial issue, yet preservationists have not seriously scrutinized this issue.

Where individuals and communities are squarely or largely within the national cultural mainstream, the Euro-American academic historical underpinnings of the historic preservation program present few major problems. For communities outside the cultural mainstream, such as Indian tribes, which often conceive of the past in very different ways, this orientation may be totally inappropriate however.

This essay examines "history" at a very general level, especially as it relates to the federal historic preservation program. It introduces the concept of "traditional history" as an alternative conception of the past and an alternative basis for making determinations of historical significance.[2] It shows that traditional history is a valid and useful addition to the conceptual arsenal of the historic preservationist whose aim is to preserve the heritage of all the diverse cultures making up our pluralistic society. It is a useful tool for building the broader definition of preservation that the expression *cultural conservation* embodies. To make this more meaningful, we discuss present and future uses of the concept of traditional history on the Navajo Reservation. We provide the results of our consultations in several Navajo communities about the sorts of places they consider important to preserve. We also present a case study of how we used the concept of traditional history to protect these sorts of resources on Navajo land.

Defining History

The National Historic Preservation Act (NHPA) establishes federal policy to promote the preservation of the national heritage. This policy protects "historic properties." For the purposes of the law and mandated federal preservation programs, *historic property* is anything listed in or eligible for listing in the National Register of Historic Places.

A property may be eligible for inclusion in the National Register if it is deemed to be historically significant as defined in the National Register eligibility criteria, which state:

> The quality of significance in American history, architecture, archaeology, engineering, and culture is present in districts, sites, buildings, structures, and objects that possess integrity of location, design, setting, materials, workmanship, feeling, and association and (a) that are associated with events that have made a significant contribution to the broad patterns of our history; or (b) that are associated with the lives of persons significant in our past; or (c) that embody distinctive characteristics of type, period, or method of construction, or that represent the work of a master, or that possess high artistic values, or that represent a significant and distinguishable entity whose components may lack individual distinction; or (d) that have yielded or

> may be likely to yield, information important in history or prehistory (Code of Federal Regulations, Title 36, Section 60.4).

These criteria seemingly provide firm guidance on what should or should not be included in the National Register. Considerable professional and personal judgment, however, is actually required to determine what should be considered for inclusion. A property may be eligible if it has important historical associations with individuals, events, or trends. But who is historically significant? What is a historically significant event or trend? For that matter, what is history?

These are by no means trivial questions. We may all agree, for example, that George Washington was a historically significant figure, but would we all agree that General David Meade, a Washington subordinate, was a historically significant figure? The inhabitants of Meadeville, Pennsylvania, a town founded by Meade, would certainly say yes, but would a professional historian or historic preservationist? We believe that Meade probably is such a figure, but that is beside the point. We raise this question to illustrate the point that even within the mainstream of national culture, decisions about what is or is not historic are not simple and do not flow smoothly from the application of objective evaluation criteria to decisions on which everyone agrees.

For communities that are ethnically diverse, that are dominated by ethnic groups other than Anglo-American, or that possess entirely different cultural traditions, defining what is historic and applying the National Register criteria are considerably more problematic. Indeed, as we will discuss later, in dealing with some of these communities, preservationists must answer the question "What is history?" before they can consider questions about what is historic.

Webster's Seventh New Collegiate Dictionary defines history as:

> 1. an account of what has or might have happened, *esp.* in the form of a narrative, play, story, or tale 2.a) what has happened in the life or development of a people, country, institution, etc., b) a systematic account of this, usually in chronological order with an analysis and explanation; all recorded events of the past 3. the branch of knowledge that deals systematically with the past; a recording, analyzing, correlating, and explaining of past events 4. a known or recorded past (the strange *history* of this coast) 5. something that belongs to the past (the election is *history* now) 6. something important enough to be recorded 7. (Rare) a scientific account of a system of natural phenomena.

This definition clearly covers a range of concepts that do not fit many of our intuitive views of "history." Note there is no hint that the record of past events is accurate or true or that history constitutes a precise reconstruction of those events. This definition, when applied to the history of a people, refers to an account of a society's past that is generally accepted by members of that society—what happened, who was involved, and how that society came to be as it is today.[3]

Myth, legend, and history all chronicle the past and explain how the society's world came to be as it is. Myth typically revolves around supernatural beings with supernatural powers. Legend is centered on humans, although they often possess superhuman or at least unusual powers, and supernatural beings are often participants. History chronicles a past that involves humans endowed with no greater powers than people living today. While myth, legend, and history can be defined explicitly and differentiated analytically, they all serve the same essential purpose for societies. They all provide recountings of what went on in the past and how the society came to be as it is.[4] This perspective is a functionalist one.

For people who believe in supernatural beings, myth *is* history. Likewise for people who accept that humans have or had supernatural powers, legend *is* history. While every member of a particular society might not interpret myths and legends literally, they may find historical truth in these traditions at a deeper symbolic level. Accordingly, in such societies, the distinction between myth, legend, and history is not meaningful. Furthermore, while Euro-American analytical history is perfectly valid and useful in many contexts, in others it is not. When the goal is to preserve places associated with a society's past, reliance on a narrow, Euro-American perception of the past will exclude places important to the non-Euro-American community. Furthermore, oral traditions tend to "store" traditional history by associating particular stories with particular places, which therefore are very much a part of the "text" of the story. Failure to protect places associated with traditional history, then, jeopardizes the places *and* the entire traditional conception of the past.

We have adopted the term *traditional history* to refer to the history that members of an ethnic or other community tell about themselves in their own terms. A traditional history can encompass beings, acts, and events that are (in an analytical sense) plainly mythical or legendary, as well as oral tradition, oral history, and conventional history. The test of validity of a traditional history is not whether the recounting of events is accurate when taken literally (or as accurate as possible given the vagaries of document preservation and our analytical perspective, tools, and skills, etc.) but whether a particular reconstruction is culturally valid and accurate. If a society accepts the mythic and legendary elements either literally or symbolically and the reconstruction is culturally valid (that is, consistent with appropriate cultural standards), then it must be accepted as a valid reconstruction of the past, no matter what literally impossible or fantastic beings or events it incorporates.

The concept of traditional history is useful for many reasons. It is a conceptual and terminological bridge from diverse traditions to the existing historic preservation program. In critical preservation decisions, it avoids imposing on a community "etic" categories that may be meaningless for that community. It also avoids the problems that arise when places are categorized as "sacred," as places associated with traditional history have almost always been classed in the past, and the problems associated with trying to protect "religious" properties under the current federal preservation program and case law.[5]

The Concept of Traditional History and the Navajos

The concept of traditional history is more than just an intellectual curiosity or scholastic construct. In the United States, for example, there are many American Indian tribes or communities that still retain much of their traditional culture.[6] While it is true that many American Indians in the western United States wear cowboy boots and blue jeans, speak fluent English, drive pickup trucks, and have the same kinds of jobs that most other people have in the United States, these (and most other national cultural traits, however the list is selected) are often superficial signs of acculturation. From personal observation or experience we know that this is particularly true in the southwestern and western United States, and we suspect that it is also true of many tribes in the eastern United States, which have supposedly long been assimilated.

In the specific case of the Navajos, the apparent assimilation has little to do with the core way of life. Non-Navajo material culture has been incorporated into a basically Navajo way of life that has developed continuously and autochthonously from precontact roots. The 1980 U.S. Census reported that 92 percent of all Navajos speak Navajo as their language of choice.[7] While this figure seems far too high, it is nevertheless the case that most Navajos speak or understand Navajo. Over half of all Navajos still consult medicine people when they are ill. This practice is so prevalent that the Navajo Nation's employee insurance plan and at least one private health insurance company now cover consultations with medicine people.[8] In 1965 Chien Ch'iao found that most Navajo teenagers attending Bureau of Indian Affairs schools accepted the traditional Navajo theory of disease and curing. He also found that most feared witches and that this fear actually increased with age and length of time in school.[9] Leland C. Wyman concluded, "Their religion, or ceremonial system to use a more accurate term, was adhered to by the majority of Navajo in 1972."[10] This remains true today. These and other traditions do not persist as isolated cultural fragments. They are integral parts of an ongoing cultural system centered now, as in the past, in local communities of interrelated, extended families that raise livestock and crops on land to which they have inherited use rights.

We could cite more statistics and studies, but we think this is sufficient to demonstrate that Navajo culture retains its traditional core. Similar evidence could be provided for tribes throughout the southwestern United States.

Much Navajo traditional history consists of the stories of the origins of the present world, the Navajo people and their customs, Navajo clans, and various curing and other ceremonies, as well as family histories. As an example of traditional history, we summarize the Navajo Emergence story. Different versions vary in their details, as one would expect in an egalitarian society like the Navajos', where much oral tradition is passed down within the extended family or from medicine person to apprentice. The summary here consists mainly of what these versions have in common. Navajos say that this story is the "main stalk" from which all others branch.

The Emergence story recounts the adventures of the Holy Beings (supernatural beings), including First Man and First Woman, as they move up through a series of underworlds. Each time the Holy Beings moved from one world to the next, it was because their own misconduct or natural catastrophes forced them out. They brought with them, or re-created, certain parts of the world they had left behind, like the four sacred mountains that hold up the sky. They also added other things, so that each underworld is a progressively more detailed model of the Earth Surface World that the Navajos inhabit today.

Eventually, the Holy Beings emerged in the present Earth Surface World, where the First Pair created many things. The infant Changing Woman, one of the most revered Navajo Holy Beings, appeared on top of a mountain that now, together with the four boundary mountains and another near Changing Woman's birthplace, are known as the six sacred mountains that define and symbolize the traditional Navajo world. Changing Woman took up the creation where the First Pair left off. She gave birth to the Twins, who journeyed to the eastern home of their father, the Sun, who gave them the weapons to kill the monsters that roamed the earth's surface, preparing it for the future Navajo people. Changing Woman later created the progenitors of certain Navajo clans. Still later, the Sun persuaded Changing Woman to move to the western ocean, where she used the residues of her skin to create the progenitors of other Navajo clans. These people then journeyed eastward back across Navajoland to join others already there to become the Dine (Navajo) people.

Later, Changing Woman took two Navajo children and taught them the prototypes of all Blessingway ceremonies. The Blessingway ceremonies ensure continued harmony, renewal, and increase in the world, and many Navajos today consider these the most important of all ceremonies. Performing the Blessingway ceremonies also evokes in participants the Emergence story. Navajo traditional history, ceremonies, and traditional daily life are thus intertwined.

Traditional History and Places Navajos Consider Worth Preserving

In 1987 and 1988 the Navajo Nation Historic Preservation and Archaeology departments conducted a pilot ethnographic survey to identify types of places that Navajos want to see preserved.[11] From this project we learned the importance of places and landscapes in "storing" episodes of traditional history, as well as supplying locations and raw materials for traditional cultural practices. Places and landscapes of these types have been designated "traditional cultural properties" in the *National Register Bulletin Number 38*,[12] although "sacred places" is a closer translation of the Navajo term.

We worked with 13 of the 109 chapters (local units of government) in the Navajo Nation. In each chapter we asked chapter officials, medicine people, and other community elders to identify specific places that they think should be preserved and to tell us of any other, more general preservation concerns. These people identified 164 places in the thirteen chapters. We think these interviews revealed most *types* of places that people care about but only a small proportion of all the places themselves. The atomistic passing down of traditional history and the dense web of traditional associations attached to virtually every kind of natural and cultural "thing" on the earth's surface mean that individual Navajos differ widely in the traditions they know. One must therefore interview many people in exhaustive detail to approach a complete inventory.

The 164 significant places they identified include such conventional historic places as buildings (old Bureau of Indian Affairs buildings, early trading posts) and prehistoric archaeological sites not conventionally associated with Navajo tradition. The largest category of significant places, however, consisted of those associated with traditional history and practices, and most lack evidence of human use. Among the places commonly identified were the location of events in the Emergence story and the origin stories of various ceremonies, as well as the origin places or homes of various clans. Hilltops where people place offerings and pray for mental and physical well-being were often named, as were hilltops and springs where people offer sacred stones and prayers for rain. Still other significant places were where people gather medicines and other materials for curing and other ceremonies, including old cornfields where they gather sand for sandpaintings and other religious uses and offer prayers for rain and plentiful crops. Cairns, where one places a stone or stick after saying a prayer, were also named, as were places where curing ceremonies have been performed, former homesites, corrals, sweathouses, and family graves. Also included were certain prehistoric ruins that figure in Navajo origin stories and early Navajo settlement areas (often identified by landmarks rather than by archaeological remains). Collectively, these traditional cultural places make up three-quarters of the places identified during this project.[13]

By identifying culturally important places, people also revealed the basis of their importance. One basis is the feeling of unity with the land. Historically, Navajo families have put their labor into their land base, which has in turn sustained them with crops and livestock. Even today, when livestock and crops only supplement the livelihood of most families, the land remains a haven from which even poverty and unemployment cannot dislodge the family. Furthermore, as Navajo life materially, socially, and even ideologically converges with life in the United States in general (at least the way of life of rural poor people), Navajo traditional history and the land where it happened have come to symbolize the ethnic distinctiveness of the Navajo people.

The four or six sacred mountains of the Emergence story symbolize the land base of the Navajo Nation as a whole. Particular landmarks, homesites, gravesites, and prayer-offering places symbolize the land base of individual extended families, embody family history, and validate the family's right to use particular lands. The locations of certain events in the Emergence and ceremony origin stories, in the clan origin stories, and in more recent community history symbolize respectively the entire Navajo Nation, the particular clans, and communities.

Finally, the places that provide raw materials for traditional activities, especially ceremonies, are linked indirectly to traditional history even if they are not locations of traditional historic events. The use of the places helps perpetuate ceremonies, where elders often tell the associated traditional history. Such use also preserves "intangible" traditional practices.

One of the surprising results of our study was not that as much as three-quarters of the places significant to Navajos are associated with traditional history and practices but rather that Navajos consider so many other types of places significant, including the historic buildings mentioned earlier. Although some Navajos devalued these as monuments to colonialism, others seemed to view them as symbols of twentieth-century Navajo communities, networks of dispersed rural families that share these central public places.

The landscape, therefore, stores Navajo traditional history. Stories or traditional practices are associated with particular places. Visits to places or mention of their names often prompt people to tell about traditional history. These places, in turn, are bound together by traditional history and practices into larger landscapes. It is the landscape, rather than a single place, that stores a whole story. Preserving individual places without reference to the surrounding landscape therefore is not enough. Nor, for that matter, is the purely physical preservation of the landscape. People must also continue to tell the stories and maintain the practices that make the landscape significant in terms of traditional history. They must be able to keep visiting the places, gathering the materials, and performing the ceremonies.

Nearly all Navajo traditional cultural places have strong "sacred" qualities. Before the publication of *Bulletin Number 38,* preservationists would probably have dismissed most of these places as "religious," which would have automatically excluded them for consideration in the listing of the National Register of Historic Places.[14] While *Bulletin Number 38* represents a tremendous advance, it still preserves, although in some ways radically redefined, the categorical exclusion of religious properties.

While emphasizing the "sacred" qualities of the places they identified, the Navajos we interviewed also stressed that the entire traditional Navajo homeland, even the entire earth's surface, is sacred. One place is no more sacred than any other, although places have different kinds of "power." In traditional Navajo belief, everything in the natural world contains an apparently anthropomorphic inner form that "makes it alive," and these things all interact to make larger systems or wholes (the traditional Navajo conceptualization of the ecosystem). People chose to tell us about certain places because those places have stories about them that contribute to their power. In fact, the common statement "A story goes with that place" seems to be almost a gloss for "The place has special power." We can most strongly bear witness to these beliefs among Navajos, but listening to other American Indians convinces us that they hold these beliefs too.

While recognizing differences in the power in various things and processes in the world around them, these American Indian communities rarely distinguish categorically between sacred and secular along the lines of the liberal, democratic philosophy that underpins the U.S. Constitution and legal system. Members of such communities would probably find this distinction meaningless, especially since some might see the Constitution as an origin myth, the legal system as a system of rituals to perpetuate the world according to the origin myth, and the liberal, democratic philosophy a closer analogue to unorganized traditional tribal religions than are the "organized" religions from which the Constitution separates the state.

Asking such peoples to make this distinction requires a cross-cultural decision making based on merging values that may have meaning in only one of the cultures. The result is some sort of transcultural decision that is meaningless in at least one of the cultures. Typically, the decision is based on the values of the dominant culture, so it has no merit to the traditionalist. Finally, using this distinction in preservation programs will result in either indefensible, ad hoc decisions or exclusion of a "traditional" community's most important places because of their "sacredness."

AT&T and Peaks Ranch Traditional Cultural Properties

One must consider traditional history when dealing with preservation issues in traditional communities. Recognizing traditional history as grounds for eligibility in the National Register forces one to identify the full range of historic properties important in the traditions of local communities. Identification, however, is only the first step in protecting and managing cultural resources. Once identified, traditional cultural properties must be considered in exactly the same way that more conventionally historic properties are.[15] Traditional cultural properties must be considered in the federal review process established by Section 106 of the National Historic Preservation Act, as implemented by the Code of Federal Regulations, Title 36, Chapter 7, Part 800. The Navajo Nation Historic Preservation Department (HPD) represents the Navajo Nation in the federal Section 106 process. In addition, the Navajo Nation Cultural Resources Protection Act[16] establishes the Navajo Nation historic preservation officer's authority to review all projects on lands of the Navajo Nation. Traditional cultural properties may be affected in ways that conventional historic properties may not be. Activities that may have "no effect" or "no adverse effect" (an adverse effect that can be effectively mitigated) on archaeological sites may have unacceptable impacts (adverse effects) on traditional cultural properties. Normally one can only assess such effects by talking with traditionalists.

Until the mid-1980s, however, the various review and approval processes lacked guidelines for dealing with traditional cultural properties. The guidelines clearly applied mainly to archaeological sites and historic buildings. Recognizing this deficiency, the Advisory Council on Historic Preservation (Advisory Council) and the National Park Service (NPS) issued guidelines for including traditional cultural properties in the federal preservation program.

In its draft *Guidelines for Consideration of Traditional Cultural Values in Historic Preservation Review*, the Advisory Council stated its policy is to "seek full consideration of traditional cultural values in the review of Federal projects under Section 106."[17] The guidelines focus on nonarchitectural properties, the values of which lie in the "roles they play in maintaining the cultural integrity of a particular social group."[18] The guidelines show federal agencies how to (1) identify historic properties that may be eligible for inclusion in the National Register of Historic Places because they are valued in traditional culture, and (2) consider potential effects of agency undertakings on such properties by consulting knowledgeable members of the social group to which the properties are culturally significant.

More recently, the NPS issued the *National Register Bulletin Number 38*, which details specific procedures for identifying traditional cultural properties that may be eligible for inclusion in the National Register. It tells how to identify traditional cultural properties by collecting ethnographic data, since many (perhaps most) such properties cannot be identified by standard archaeological or historical research or by reference to the literature.

Federal and Navajo Nation legislation, regulations, and guidelines can thus help the HPD protect Navajo traditional cultural properties from the effects of undertakings both in and outside Navajo land. One recent and relatively "easy" case exemplifies the use of these various tools to protect the traditional cultural value of a Navajo traditional cultural property affected by a federally licensed undertaking.

Early in 1989, a contractor working for AT&T contacted the HPD about an environmental assessment for a below-ground fiber optic cable between Flagstaff, Arizona, and Las Vegas, Nevada. The environmental contractor was contacting all Indian tribes whose lands would be affected by the cable installation to determine whether the project would affect any traditional cultural places.

Part of the cable line crosses ranch lands on the San Francisco Mountains in Arizona that the Navajo Nation had recently purchased and leased. The San Francisco Mountains are the farthest west of the four sacred mountains that symbolize the limits of the traditional Navajo homeland. The HPD told the contractor that, in addition to surveying the right-of-way for archaeological sites, the contractor must consult knowledgeable members of the nearest Navajo community about the project's possible effect on the traditional significance of the San Francisco Mountains and measures that might be necessary to "mitigate" any such effects.

AT&T had the Navajo Nation Archaeology Department conduct the archaeological survey. Several months later, the HPD received the archaeological survey report for review and approval. The report identified several prehistoric archaeological sites and recommended measures to keep the project from affecting them. The report also stated that no traditional cultural properties were identified in the project area, but it offered no ethnographic data to support this conclusion.

The HPD approved the construction of the cable line across the ranch on two conditions: (1) the line must avoid the archaeological sites, as recommended in the survey report, and (2) the company must consult knowledgeable members of the nearby Navajo community of Cameron about the potential effects of the undertaking on the traditional significance of the San Francisco Mountains.

After several meetings and some deliberations, AT&T agreed to the ethnographic consultation. For convenience, AT&T asked the HPD to consult the Cameron people on its behalf. Alexandra Roberts of the HPD started by contacting the president and secretary of Cameron Chapter to tell them about the project and to find out who else should be consulted about it. The chapter officials recommended two prominent medicine men and scheduled an initial meeting between Roberts and the chapter president.

Roberts explained the scope of the proposed undertaking in detail to the chapter president and why the HPD wanted to determine whether the undertaking would affect the traditional significance of the San Francisco Mountains. The president said that the two medicine men were the only appropriate people to answer questions of a religious nature. His only concern was whether the project had gone through the proper approval process in the Navajo Nation capital. If part of that process included identifying "religious" and other traditional concerns, individual medicine men should be consulted, not local political leaders. (Officials of other chapters, however, might not respond in the same way.)

After meeting with the chapter president, we contacted one of the two medicine men at his home. With the medicine man's son interpreting, we described the project in detail and asked him whether it would affect the mountain. The medicine man and his wife first explained that six mountains define that Navajo world, and they are among the holiest places of the Navajo people. To dig into one of them without talking to it first is to harm it, and harming the mountain risks bringing harm to all people. Before construction, one must talk to and bless the earth that the construction would disturb. The earth then would protect the cable and ensure its proper operation. He agreed to perform the blessing the next morning at the proposed construction site.

Illustrating the role of traditional history in ceremonies, the medicine man also said that he must tell the story of the mountain to place it in the context of Navajo history and to make us understand why he would sing the blessing. He told the story after the first conversation. We tape-recorded it at his request. The next morning, the medicine man, his wife and son, AT&T representatives, Roberts, and ranch employees gathered at the proposed construction site. Before the blessing ceremony, the medicine man continued the historical account that he had started the day before, and this was also tape-recorded. The blessing ceremony itself (a version of the Blessingway ceremonies mentioned earlier) included a series of prayers for the earth (both the specific area to be disturbed and the earth as a whole), for the fiber optic cable to ensure that it carries information well and that its products are helpful to the Navajo people, and for each of the individuals present at the ceremony. By first paying respect to the mountain, this blessing lessened (or negated) adverse effects of the proposed construction on the mountain.

The Section 106 review process, as applied in this case, first identified conventionally defined historic properties (archaeological sites), considered effects on them, and avoided those effects (by avoiding the sites). Second, the process identified traditional cultural properties (which preservationists are belatedly acknowledging as "historic properties") and mitigated adverse effects on them. Navajos were consulted as tribal and federal law and regulation require. In sum, federal and tribal legislation combined in this case for a successful consultation process that treated traditional cultural properties in the same way that more "conventional" historic properties are treated.

We admit that not all cases are as simple and straightforward as this one was. The process of ethnographic consultation, of identifying less well-known traditional cultural properties, of locating the individuals who know about them, and of devising ways to treat any properties that an undertaking might adversely affect, can be long and complex. Furthermore, the Section 106 review process does not guarantee that such properties will receive any more protection than any other kind of historic property receives. The end result of the process therefore may not be as positive as it was in this instance.

To ensure that traditional cultural properties are identified at an early stage in project planning and development, the HPD has developed a policy and measures to identify traditional cultural properties in that early stage. The HPD offers cultural resource consultants (archaeologists or ethnographers working with the archaeologists) a checklist of information to request when interviewing Navajos about a project area. The HPD policy requires cultural resource consultants to make a good-faith effort to identify concerns about impacts on traditional cultural properties by interviewing chapter officials, residents of the project area (if any), and other knowledgeable people recommended by the officials and residents about traditional cultural properties that the proposed project might harm. They must also ask about what, if any, measures should be employed to protect or lessen adverse effects on those places. Archaeological and anthropological consultants must obtain permits from the HPD to conduct cultural resource investigations, and such permits may require use of the checklist. Permits also require consultants to review literature about traditional cultural properties along with their archaeological records search. Cultural resource consultants receive annually updated guidelines and standards from the HPD regarding all aspects of cultural resource investigations on Navajo lands. For some proposed undertakings, because of their nature or location near a particularly sensitive area, the HPD may require a separate, intensive ethnographic program to identify concerns about traditional cultural properties and measures necessary to avoid, minimize, mitigate, or negate any adverse effects on them.

These measures combine to help locate traditional cultural properties and incorporate their treatment into project planning. The regular use of these varied measures will meet the intent of tribal and federal protection laws. It is important to remember, however, that these measures come into play only after a specific undertaking is proposed in a specific location. At this stage it is difficult to protect large traditional cultural places by moving the entire undertaking and to deal with the undertaking's impact on whole landscapes. The most effective ways to consider and, one hopes, minimize the impact of development on traditional cultural properties are continued research and identification of such places throughout the traditional Navajo homeland and the development of a comprehensive historic preservation plan that covers all types of historic properties. These are long-term goals toward which the HPD continues to strive.

Conclusion

Traditional history is an essential concept for extending the national historic preservation program to cover the full range of properties that are "historic" to different communities in our pluralistic society. Its use is critical to avoiding the traps inherent in a reliance on a Western historical perspective. Perhaps more important, this concept does not rely on vague constitutional assurances of freedom of religion to protect places that have powerful "religious" associations. If such places are also significant in the traditional history of a community, they can receive full consideration and equal protection, even though the community does not normally make the constitutional distinction between sacred and secular. The places of concern to such people can then receive the full consideration afforded to more conventional historic properties, as well as protection that they have not typically received in the past from either federal agency officials or the federal courts (when their relief has been sought).

Dealing with places important in traditional history raises some issues that preservationists do not usually face, namely, reliance on ethnographers and ethnographic primary data collection. In fact, however, dealing with such resources in the context of, for example, the Section 106 project review process can be the same as dealing with other cultural resources. On the Navajo Reservation, we have demonstrated that it is practical and possible to incorporate ethnographically identified, traditional cultural properties in the review process—to protect such places without undue burdens on project sponsors.

In short, we have discovered it is possible to find the same sorts of accommodations and to resolve apparently intractable conflicts between development and preservation of traditional cultural properties in exactly the same way that these issues and conflicts are resolved with more conventionally historic places. We believe that widespread application of these approaches will ensure proper consideration of these vitally important resources, without systematic adverse impact on equally vital development projects, although sacrifices on both sides are inevitable. Preservation and development can coexist so that meaningful elements of culture are preserved and essential development projects still go forward. In the future, traditional Navajo culture can continue to exist while Navajos obtain the benefits and amenities available to the rest of us living at the end of the twentieth century.

NOTES

1. David Hackett Fischer, *Historians Fallacies: Towards a Logic of Historical Thought* (New York: Harper Torchbooks, 1970).

2. The term *traditional history* crops up occasionally in the ethnographic literature and in the "gray literature" of cultural resource management and social impact assessment. Although the implicit meaning in those works is very close to our interpretation of the term, nowhere, as far as we can tell, was the term explicitly discussed and defined until Alan S. Downer, Richard Begay, Harris Francis, Klara Kelley, and Alexandra Roberts, *Navajo Nation Historic Preservation Plan Pilot Study: The Identification of Historic Properties in Six New Mexico Chapters of the Navajo Nation* (Window Rock, Ariz.: Navajo Nation Historic Preservation Department, 1988). We have adopted their usage here.

3. Ibid.; Alan S. Downer, Stella Clyde, Harris Francis, Klara Kelley, Alexandra Roberts, and Loretta Werito, *Navajo Nation Historic Preservation Plan Pilot Study: The Identification of Historic Properties in Seven Arizona Chapters of the Navajo Nation* (Window Rock, Ariz.: Navajo Nation Historic Preservation Department, 1988); Alan S. Downer, *Anthropology, Historic Preservation, and the Navajo: A Case Study in Cultural Resource Management on Indian Lands* (Ph.D. diss., University of Missouri, Columbia, 1989).

4. Bronislaw Malinowski, "Myth in Primitive Psychology," in *Magic, Science, and Religion,* ed. Bronislaw Malinowski (New York: Doubleday, 1954), 93–148.

5. Downer et al., *Seven Arizona Chapters of the Navajo Nation;* Downer et al., *Six New Mexico Chapters of the Navajo Nation;* Downer, *Anthropology, Historic Preservation, and the Navajo;* Alan S. Downer, "Management of the Sacred, 'Sacred Places' in Cultural Resources Management and Historic Preservation: An Example from the Navajo Nation," in *Proceedings of World Archaeological Congress II,* ed. Brian Reeves (London: Unwin Hyman, forthcoming); Alan S. Downer, "'Sacred Places' and Cultural Resource Management," in *Management of the Sacred,* ed. Robert Laidlaw (Sacramento: California State Office, U.S. Bureau of Land Management, 1987).

6. Although we use *traditional* in a way that may seem to imply that it refers to something static, like all aspects of culture it is constantly changing. *Traditional Navajo culture* refers to a core of old and stable cultural practices and values, but how old and how stable is not a subject for discussion here. Certainly traditional Navajo culture in 1990 is different from traditional Navajo culture in 1950, or 1910, or 1880, or 1800, or 1770. The real issue is whether differing cultural traditions will result in differing definitions of what history comprises and, accordingly, what must be deemed historic. Even though *tradition* is not a term subject to complete or precise specification, it is essential in understanding different perceptions of the past and what impact those perceptions have on what should be preserved.

7. Navajo Nation, *Navajo Nation Overall Economic Development Plan: 1985* (Window Rock, Ariz.: Economic Planning Department, Division of Economic Development, 1986).

8. "Aid Agency Pays for Navajo Cure," *The Independent* (Gallup, N.M.), December 12, 1987, 1–2.

9. Chien Ch'iao, "Continuation of Tradition in Navajo Society," in *Academia Sinica,* Institute for Ethnology Series B(3) (Taipei: Institute for Ethnology, 1971), 91–94.

10. Leland C. Wyman, "Navajo Ceremonial System," in *Handbook of North American Indians (Southwest),* vol. 10, ed. Alfonso Ortiz (Washington, D.C.: Smithsonian Institution, 1983), 356.

11. Downer et al., *Seven Arizona Chapters of the Navajo Nation;* Downer et al., *Six New Mexico Chapters of the Navajo Nation.*

12. Patricia L. Parker and Thomas F. King, *Guidelines for Evaluating and Documenting Traditional Cultural Properties,* National Register Bulletin, no. 38 (Washington, D.C.: National Park Service, Department of the Interior, 1990).

13. Throughout this essay we use *traditional cultural property* and *traditional cultural place* interchangeably to refer to places with important associations in traditional history or culture. *Traditional cultural property* is the term used by the National Park Service in *Bulletin Number 38.*

14. Downer, *Anthropology, Historic Preservation, and the Navajo.*

15. Downer, "Management of the Sacred."

16. Navajo Nation, *Navajo Nation Cultural Resources Protection Act,* Navajo Nation Council Resolution CMY-19-88 (Window Rock, Ariz.: Navajo Nation Council, 1988).

17. Advisory Council on Historic Preservation, *Guidelines for Consideration of Traditional Cultural Values in Historic Preservation Review* (Washington, D.C.: Advisory Council for Historic Preservation, 1985).

18. Ibid.

4

Federal and Neighborhood Notions of Place: Conflicts of Interest in Lowell, Massachusetts

Douglas DeNatale

Lowell, Massachusetts, lies in space at the confluence of the Concord and the Merrimack rivers and in time at the confrontation between corporate plans and individual dreams. Founded by corporate investors in the 1820s, Lowell claims several distinctions. It has been identified as the site of the first large-scale industrial manufacture in the United States and as America's first planned city. In 1942, more than a century after the city's founding, the architectural historian John Coolidge observed, "The outstanding achievements of Lowell are its [corporation-built] housing and its city planning." Similar views have been voiced by more recent social historians.[1]

At the time of Coolidge's writing, Lowell was long past its heyday, when foreign and national dignitaries came to tour the city's well-ordered mills and boardinghouses. It was deep in the grip of a twenty-year economic decline that would persist for another two decades. During the 1980s Lowell's emergence from this painful period of economic and demographic stagnation garnered an intense new wave of outside interest. For the most part, the Lowell of the 1980s was lauded as an innovative model of urban revitalization through government intervention.

Historic preservation played a key role in this transition, through the efforts of two federal agencies: the Lowell National Historical Park, established in 1978 as one of the nation's first urban national parks; and the Lowell Historic Preservation Commission, established to develop and oversee a general historic preservation plan for the city. Working in cooperation with Lowell's civic authorities, these agencies established programs and managed preservation efforts that transformed the city's physical fabric, created new social spaces and interactions, and helped elevate the self-esteem of the city's inhabitants. The process of revitalization also revealed key issues for cultural conservation, involving the interplay of cultural pattern and physical landscape.

My observations here derive from a yearlong folklife survey conducted in Lowell in 1987 and 1988 by the American Folklife Center and cosponsored by the Lowell Historic Preservation Commission. The Lowell Folklife Project examined the interrelationship of government-sponsored revitalization efforts and the present-day cultural dynamic of Lowell's neighborhoods and public places. From the perspective of the American Folklife Center, Lowell offered a unique opportunity to test some of the lessons learned in its earlier New Jersey Pinelands study—this time in an urban setting.[2]

Even as our common image of wilderness can prevent us from accounting for, and working with, the human portion of an ecosystem, our awareness of cities as the most technically complex of human creations may prevent us from fully acknowledging the organic relationship between city form and cultural expression—leading us to credit the architect and investor, instead of cultural expectations and group performances, for the origins of city construction. "Cities have . . . two recognizable cultural landscapes," suggests Amos Rapoport, "a high-style order based on the schemata of small groups, including professional designers, and a vernacular order expressing more widely shared (and sometimes very different) schemata."[3] Rapoport's observation can be expanded to include the multiplicity of vernacular orders that may exist in an urban environment, as well as the temporal layering of the cultural patterns formed from those orders.

Rapoport and other cultural geographers argue not only that the urban landscape is a product of human behavior but also that human behavior is, in a sense, stored in the landscape: "The environment can . . . be said to act as a *mnemonic* reminding people of the behavior expected of them. It takes the remembering from the person and places the *reminding* in the environment."[4] From the perspective of the urban planner, the most successful urban places are overt and easily legible texts that can be deconstructed by anyone encountering them for the first time. For example, Tony Hiss has characterized New York's Grand Central Terminal as "a sort of introductory course (or, for old-timers, a refresher course) in how to join the choreography of New York City."[5]

In reality, most urban places are arcane texts narrowly available to esoteric communities—whether these be Wall Street stockbrokers or Khmer refugees. No individual can master all the places of a city. Yet the ability to move intelligently through the multitude of orders particular to any one city separates the urban native from the outsider. In Lowell, the evocative noun *blow-in,* which is employed to suggest any newcomer's lack of connectedness with the landscape, reflects an implicit understanding of this relation. Urban expressive traditions abound with accounts of first encounters with alien places, such as transportation terminals. For Lowell's newly arrived Umbelina Figueira, for example, a return trip to Portugal was less daunting than one across town. "It's too far to go on, on the streetcar," she recalls complaining to her mother.[6]

If the urban landscape is a product of multiple orders of behavior in space and a layering of multiple patterns in time, then any programmatic intervention with the aim of cultural conservation must take both these dimensions into account. Lowell provides a telling case study in this regard. The government agencies involved have explicitly interpreted the past by restoring the downtown area's physical fabric to evoke nineteenth-century social space, while adapting these spaces to late twentieth-century needs. Sensitive to the potential effects on the city's older housing districts, the authors of Lowell's historic preservation plan carefully delineated the boundaries of the city's preservation district.[7] At the same time the larger social effects of the readaptive use of the city's nineteenth-century physical fabric have been channeled by the historical relation between Lowell's nineteenth-century corporate entities and past cultural processes. Though the underlying notions were very different, late twentieth-century federal notions of place were infiltrated by nineteenth-century corporate notions encoded in Lowell's urban landscape.

The orientation of Lowell's present landscape has been shaped fundamentally by the particular configuration of its natural topography. Early nineteenth-century Lowell was bounded by the curving arc of the Merrimack River to the north and the mirroring sweep of a transportation canal built to circumnavigate a fourteen-foot drop in the Merrimack River to the south. It was the immense waterpower potential of the site that attracted outside investors, who purchased the canal and almost all of the large diamond-shaped tract of land between the canal and the river. The large mill complexes powered by the company's canal system became concentrated along the two eastern sides of the diamond, where the greatest potential waterpower was created by the greatest differential in elevation. The corporation boardinghouses at the heart of the renowned "Lowell System" of closely supervised female labor were likewise drawn in perpendicular ranks adjacent to the mills at the eastern end of the canal district.

Lowell's corporate founders conceived of the city as an enlightened manufacturing center, where large-scale industry would not create the social ills of European manufacturing districts. In a personal reminiscence, one of the city's founders wrote that "the operatives in the manufacturing cities of Europe were notoriously of the lowest character, for intelligence and morals. The question therefore arose, and was deeply considered, whether this degradation was the result of the peculiar occupation or of other and distinct causes." The Boston Associates, the enterprise incorporated to built Lowell's mills, concluded that the segregated place of European manufacture, not the nature of textile work, was the cause of such ills.[8]

Instead, the Boston Associates planned an integrated city of mills, housing, and a commercial district running parallel to the river. The unusual diamond-shaped plot presented the industrialists with an engineering dilemma however. John Coolidge noted, "In the ideal scheme the two elements [town and factory] were conceived together. They balanced about the central axis of the main street. But when geography made such a balance impossible, it was the town which was sacrificed."[9]

Lowell's consciously planned development was therefore concentrated at the eastern end of the canal district. In an economic sense, this resulted in a value gradient within the core area of the canal district that reflected the corporations' reliance on waterpower. The western portion of the corporation's plot of land at the shallow, upper end of the waterpower system was relatively useless to them. The unbalanced nature of the landscape resulting from economic considerations became apparent when the day laborers who built the canals and mills—for the most part Irish immigrants—established a squatters' settlement, first known as the Paddy Camps and later as New Dublin and the Acre, within the canal district at the western edge of the mills.[10]

The Irish squatter community was a clear vernacular assertion of place. At first the mill corporations tolerated the Acre as a transient phenomenon because the space had little value to them. Later they came to terms with its presence because they found it advantageous to use Irish labor to undercut the position of the rebellious Lowell "mill girls." The Irish immigrants represented disorder and filth, mayhem and immorality for the Yankee population of Lowell. A typical newspaper account of the 1840s derided the "odoriferous region . . . denominated 'the acre.'"[11] Yet the Irish settlement also contributed an essential element toward a more balanced urban landscape, in which a multitude of orders would redefine the monolithic company town.

The Irish were followed by other immigrant groups that established their own neighborhoods, such as the French-Canadian "Little Canada," in the western end of the canal district. Social historical research suggests that these neighborhoods were not a mechanical creation of ethnicity but a transitional accomplishment of association. Frances Early has documented the process by which the French-Canadian population, at first dispersed throughout the city, coalesced through personal networks into the area that became Little Canada. When a secondary wave of Irish immigrants arrived in Lowell during the late 1800s, they did not restock the Acre but clustered in an outlying area that became known as the Grove. In contrast, when immigration quotas for Portugal were readjusted in the early 1960s, a secondary wave of Portuguese immigrants were drawn to the declining Back Central area, where they are largely credited with revitalizing the Portuguese neighborhood to such an extent that it probably presents a more uniform ethnic character now than it did during the previous period of Portuguese immigration.[12]

The absentee landlords who controlled the land in the core canal district on which the early immigrant communities coalesced had little regard for vernacular notions of place. Even so, by pooling their resources, Lowell's immigrants found ways to create new public places in their churches and their social clubs, which asserted a vernacular sense of other landscapes.[13]

The control asserted by corporation and landowner attenuated as Lowell's later neighborhoods expanded beyond the inner canal district with the development of streetcar suburbs. An outer ring of neighborhoods maintained ethnic association at the same time that they signaled economic mobility. Here there was greater latitude for individuals to shape their domestic environment.[14]

The composition of the older core neighborhoods shifted with outward migration. For example, Irish migration from the Acre cleared space for the Greek community. Over time, the older core neighborhoods, particularly the Acre, gained a reputation for being the entry point for new immigrants to Lowell, though there were significant exceptions to this pattern, including the Portuguese and Polish communities and even a later secondary Irish migration.

I have outlined the nineteenth- and early twentieth-century dynamic between Lowell's corporate and vernacular landscape in broad, paradigmatic terms, without recounting evidence of the processes of competition, complicity, and cooperation that accompanied the establishment of a multitude of vernacular orders. In broad terms, the cityscape received by the present can be read along a number of different axes. The industrial order of Lowell's textile past placed the planned commercial world of the mills to the east and the world of the immigrant workers to the west. Another axis defined the core neighborhoods within the canal system as the entry point for immigrant workers and the ring of outlying neighborhoods as their desired destination. Each of these is an idealization based on a complex past, but each plays an important role in orienting the spaces of the city for its present inhabitants.

Lowell's fundamental reliance on textiles left it vulnerable to changing conditions and subject to a long economic depression that lingered from the 1920s until the late 1960s. During this period Lowell suffered such an erosion of its self-image that "Low Hell" became one popular nickname for the city. There was a corresponding erosion of a sense of place, to such an extent that few local students could name the canals that were once the heartblood of the city.[15] Lowell's self-image became a central concern to those seeking ways to bring about its revitalization. Patrick Mogan, a local educator who was a central figure in these efforts, observed:

> We found out that, as someone said, "people that had no past have no future." . . . We had to look into what our composition was, what our city was, and find out if there was any positive thread on which they could give a decent future and a decent chance to our kids. . . . Fortunately, on looking into it, we found out that Lowell was a living exhibit on the process and consequences of the American industrial revolution. What we were was a very important part of the story of the United States. So we had no reason to consider our background and what we were as negative. We had every reason to look at it as positive.[16]

The creation of the national park in Lowell was the eventual outcome of successful lobbying that had begun essentially as a local effort.

Lowell's preservation plan focused on the city's "way of life" as its focus, finding in the expressions of the present a manifestation of the past. One of the missions set by the Preservation Commission was "to tell the human story of the Industrial Revolution in a 19th century setting by encouraging cultural expression in Lowell." At the same time, the Preservation Commission was well aware of the potential for social disruption by federal efforts: "The recognition of Lowell as a National Park can either enhance or splinter these traditions. While the impact of economic revitalization, in-migration of middle income professionals, and the visitor-oriented emphasis of the National Park Service are welcome, the challenge to understand and absorb this change is great."[17]

In seeking a balance between federal intervention and local autonomy, the plan restricted the preservation district to Lowell's nineteenth-century core within the canal district. During the first ten years of the commission and the park, physical rehabilitation work concentrated on the eastern, commercial and industrial end of the original, diamond-shaped tract of land—in effect recapitulating its nineteenth-century development and economic value gradient.[18]

One effect of this has been to reinforce a perfected image of Lowell's ethnic past, with the public agencies helping to validate existing public ceremonies of symbolic ethnicity. As William Flanagan put it, "If you think of Lowell not as a city but as a microcosm of the U.S., it opens its door to immigrant groups and they keep coming and one group moves up and out and a new group comes in."[19] Within the preservation district, the surviving core neighborhood of the Acre has been reinforced as an epitome district, to use a term coined by Grady Clay. Clay notes, "Special places in cities carry huge layers of symbols that have the capacity to pack up emotions, energy, or history into a small space. . . . places where one may observe formal and informal rituals, symbolic activities: the organization of folk festivals ranging from parades to inaugurations, from unveilings to auctions to rallies to funerals and swearings-in. . . . The beginning point—historically and at the moment—is a special sort of epitome district."[20] Over time, it is the multiethnic population of the Acre that has become its defining characteristic, and its symbolic role in the life of the city has been formalized as a transient area that acts as a conduit for new immigrant populations.

The success of Lowell's revitalization during the 1980s, fueled in no small part by an expanding regional electronics industry, brought about its own new wave of immigration after a long period of declining population. A dramatic influx of Southeast Asians during the decade followed earlier waves of Azorean Portuguese and Colombian and Puerto Rican Hispanics. Lowell's population regained its historical peak of over a hundred thousand by the decade's end, largely due to the influx of Southeast Asians, who may now constitute as much as a fifth of the city's population.[21]

These new populations have been differentially welcomed to the extent that each group fits vernacular notions of the human story of the industrial revolution in Lowell. In a sense, the revitalization process founded on historic preservation has heightened the dependency of twentieth-century orders of relation between cultural process and physical landscape upon a formally interpreted past. While eager to embrace the forms of cultural expression among the newer groups, Lowell's federal agencies have themselves been guided by the need to draw parallels to the nineteenth-century development of ethnic enclaves. In one example, the Preservation Commission funded the creation of a garden along the banks of a canal in the Acre, which contained plants representing Lowell's various ethnic groups. The project drew a bitter response in the local paper from Joe and Lina Tymowicz, whose own dramatically idiosyncratic garden synthesized from elements in Lina's Sicilian heritage faced the prospective site. In this case, a constructed civic memorial to symbolic ethnicity confronted an emergent personal cultural landscape of the present.[22]

Within the preservation model it has been possible to validate the cultural expression of new groups but not always to comprehend them in a manner that has gained public sanction. During the summer of 1989 the Olmstead-inspired design for a city-sponsored pocket park in the Acre drew the criticism of a community organization, which submitted an alternative plan based on Southeast Asian motifs developed in consultation with Cambodian community leaders. A prominent feature of the proposed design was a sculptured head, a common motif in Cambodian parks to represent the culture hero Pram, who cut off his own head rather than suffer dishonor. Though supported by the commission, the design was vehemently rejected by the council subcommittee, which declared it a presumptuous claim to public space by an upstart community. One councilman is said to have declared, "I'll be dammed if I let some cut-off head be put up in the Acre."[23]

The historic preservation model has proved a powerful tool for revitalizing Lowell's urban landscape, but its focus on the city's physical fabric has at the same time enmeshed its realization in the logic of the past as embodied in the physical landscape. Parenthetically, in the wake of the region's more recent dramatic economic downswing, Lowell once again was threatened by an overreliance on a dominant industry. As it has increasingly recognized the limitations of basing its cultural mission on notions of symbolic ethnicity, the Preservation Commission has increasingly turned to the notion of folklife—a body of emerging vernacular traditions—as a more appropriate model for relating physical landscape and cultural expression. Following the American Folklife Center project, the commission established a folklife center in conjunction with the expansion of its preservation work in the western canal district and hired a folklorist to serve as the commission's cultural affairs director. The ultimate effects of this readjustment remain to be seen.

Lowell's experience illustrates the cultural creation of landscape, the power of landscape in current cultural relations, and the need for reworking the preservation model to comprehend these as a connected whole. If the urban landscape is understood as an accretion of social relationships rather than as the product of architectural imagination, then conservationists cannot overlook the social stance implied in emphasizing physical fabric over contemporary cultural process.

NOTES

1. John P. Coolidge, *Mill and Mansion: A Study of Architecture and Society in Lowell, Massachusetts, 1820–1865* (New York: Russell and Russell, 1942), 8; see, for example, Thomas Bender, *Toward an Urban Vision: Ideas and Institutions in Nineteenth Century America* (Baltimore: Johns Hopkins University Press, 1975).

2. Mary Hufford, *One Space, Many Places: Folklife and Land Use in New Jersey's Pinelands National Reserve* (Washington, D.C.: American Folklife Center, Library of Congress, 1986).

3. Amos Rapoport, "Culture and the Urban Order," in *The City in Cultural Context,* ed. John A. Agnew, John Mercer, and David E. Sopher (Boston: Allen and Unwin, 1984), 55–56.

4. Amos Rapoport, *The Meaning of the Built Environment* (Beverly Hills, Calif.: Sage Books, 1982), 15, 80–81.

5. Tony Hiss, "Experiencing Places," *New Yorker,* June 22, 1987, 45.

6. Interview with Manuel and Umbelina Figueira by Barbara Fertig, Lowell, Mass., November 9, 1987, Lowell Folklife Project Papers, item number LFP-BF-F1109.A, American Folklife Center, Library of Congress, Washington, D.C. (hereafter materials from the Lowell Folklife Project will be referred to by item number). See also interview with Richard Taffe by David Taylor, Lowell, Mass., September 17, 1987, LFP-DT-R006.

7. Interview with Sarah Peskin, Lowell Historic Preservation Commission, by Doug DeNatale, Lowell, Mass., November 5, 1987, LFP-DD-R039-42.

8. Quoted in Coolidge, *Mill and Mansion,* 13.

9. Coolidge, *Mill and Mansion,* 23–24. See also Margaret Terrell Parker, *Lowell: A Study of Industrial Development* (New York: Macmillan, 1940), 72–73.

10. Bender, *Toward an Urban Vision,* 101; George F. O'Dwyer, *The Irish Catholic Genesis of Lowell* (Lowell, Mass.: Sullivan Brothers, 1920), 8; Brian C. Mitchell, *The Paddy Camps: The Irish of Lowell, 1821–61* (Urbana: University of Illinois Press, 1988).

11. *Advertiser* (Lowell, Mass.), August 19, 1851.

12. Frances H. Early, "The Settling-In Process: The Beginnings of Little Canada in Lowell, Massachusetts, in the Late Nineteenth Century," in *The Little Canadas of New England,* ed. Claire Quintal (Worcester, Mass.: French Institute, Assumption College, 1983), 33–34; *Sun* (Lowell, Mass.), April 17, 1988; interview with Francisco Corvalno by Barbara Fertig, Lowell, Mass., November 18, 1987, LFP-BF-A007.

13. See Rapoport, "Culture and the Urban Order," 56–67.

14. See Sam Bass Warner, *Streetcar Suburbs: The Process of Growth in Boston, 1870–1900* (Cambridge, Mass.: Harvard University Press, 1962), for an overview of the creation of streetcar suburbs; Parker, *Lowell,* 87.

15. Interviews with Lowell National Historical Park rangers by Doug DeNatale, Lowell, Mass., April 7, 1988, LFP-DD-R070, LFP-DD-R072; interview with Patrick J. Mogan by Doug DeNatale, Lowell, Mass., November 5, 1987, LFP-DD-R035.

16. Interview with Patrick J. Mogan by Doug DeNatale, Lowell, Mass., August 27, 1987, LFP-DD-R008.

17. Lowell Historic Preservation Commission, *Preservation Plan* (Lowell, Mass.: Lowell Historic Preservation Commission, 1980), 2.

18. Interview with Sarah Peskin, Lowell Historic Preservation Commission, by Doug DeNatale, Lowell, Mass., November 5, 1987, LFP-DD-R039-42.

19. Interview with William and Dorothy Flanagan by Martha Norkunas, Lowell, Mass., August 17, 1987, LFP-MN-R015.

20. Grady Clay, *Close-Up: How to Read the American City* (Chicago: University of Chicago Press, 1973), 38–39.

21. Interview with Larry Flynn, Gateway Cities Program, by Michael Bell, Lowell, Mass., November 2, 1987, LFP-MB-R001-3.

22. Interview with Joe and Lina Tymowicz by Tom Rankin, Lowell, Mass., September 11, 1987, LFP-TR-R040-43.

23. Personal communication.

5

Cultural Conservation of Place

Setha M. Low

In this essay I argue that cultural conservation is inseparable from the conservation of place. Certainly part of our mandate for preserving cultural resources is based on the notion that the environment is valued and encodes important elements of our biophysical, social, and cultural history. Place *is* space made culturally meaningful, and in this sense it provides the context and symbolic cues for our behavior. Place, however, is not just a setting for behavior but an integral part of social interaction and cultural processes. An understanding of place cannot be separated from how people live their lives or from the historical moment and sociopolitical institutions that structure those lives.[1] Further, place links local identity and its specificity with the globalization and interdependency of the modern world. Without place conservation, the contexts for culturally meaningful behaviors and processes of place-making disappear, cutting us off from our past, disrupting the present, and limiting the possibilities for the future.

It is hard to imagine cultural behavior without its culturally appropriate place. It can occur; we all create makeshift facsimiles of an ideal world. But try to picture Pueblo cultural life without the richness of Pueblo landscape and architecture or the difficulty of socializing your children without a home. The concept of place signifies this embeddedness of person, space, and action. Place-making, the symbolic appropriation of space, is an ongoing human activity that is fundamental to human well-being. Not having a "place" in society, at least in the United States, has resulted in legions of homeless people whose sense of social identity and personhood has been radically altered by the loss of a home, where basic place-making activities most often occur.

We grieve when we experience the loss of place. Bereavement has been well documented for the residents of the West End of Boston[2] who lost their community to urban redevelopment and for the Appalachian inhabitants[3] who survived the Buffalo Creek flood. Other studies document the breakdown of social and family ties that were the underpinnings of economic survival among poor residents in center city slums and relocated residents' sense of social loss when trying to create new suburban networks in Lagos, Nigeria;[4] London, England;[5] and Lima, Peru.[6] The loss of place is not just an architectural loss but also a cultural and personal loss in terms of what we as a society provide as meaningful environments of human action and expression.

Place is the site of social and cultural reproduction and, as such, must be considered as part of the cultural conservation mission. Marxist geographers discuss place in terms of the reproduction of labor and argue that "conflicts in the living space are . . . reflections of the underlying tension between capital and labor."[7] But place reproduces more than labor. Places have use values that are quite special and indispensable.[8] A person's home in a particular place provides access to friends, school, workplace, and shops; and a home has emotional and symbolic meanings and connections that characterize place attachment.[9] Within the home, social relations are maintained and reproduced through everyday patterns of activities, feelings, and preferences. The disruption of place, then, does more than destroy the sites of labor reproduction; it also limits people's ability to reproduce their social world and everyday lives. If we do not provide supportive environments or at the very least allow them to exist, we can actually eliminate the social and cultural diversity we are trying to preserve.

The practice of place conservation, however, is complex and often problematic in that place is (1) politically as well as culturally constructed, (2) pluralistic, reflecting a diversity of cultures, and (3) constantly changing, since cultures are dynamic and fluid, and therefore can not be frozen in time and space without endangering future cultural expressions. The moment a move is made to conserve a place, a number of alternative political, social, and cultural uses of a location may be eliminated, and the ramifications of all such choices must be carefully examined and evaluated. Questions emerge, as they have in other essays in this book, about who is to judge the importance of a cultural resource and who benefits or suffers in the conservation or eradication of that resource. Even more important, the planning and design processes that are developed to implement place conservation introduce problems and conflicts. Some of the ways that conserving places presents new challenges and solutions for cultural conservation advocates are outlined in this essay.

The Political Challenges to Place Conservation

One important concern when discussing any kind of cultural conservation is that such labels and concepts as culture or ethnicity are politically as well as culturally constructed and manipulated for a variety of ends. When we define the *cultural* of cultural conservation, we are dealing not with static, definable attributes that can be measured or codified but with definitions and identities that are negotiated, fluid, and context dependent. Whether a group takes on a class-related identity (e.g., working class) or a culture-related identity (e.g., Italian-American) or whether some groups are considered political entities at all certainly influences what is construed to be the meaning of a place. The political importance of a neighborhood can change, depending on how the residents present themselves and their concerns to the various players involved. Sociopolitically constructed ethnic labels, such as black, African American, Jamaican, or Haitian, evoke different meanings and responses for New York City officials and planners and are actively manipulated by the community in neighborhood descriptions and media coverage. Within the politics of place, however, poor people's neighborhoods are always the most vulnerable because the local constituency does not have the political and economic power to struggle against the definitions and decisions of governmental officials and private entrepreneurs.

Further, processes of cultural hegemony (that is, the preeminence of one cultural group's ideas and values over another) maintain the control of middle-class, white values over the very definitions of what can be considered a relevant group with the power to give its own meanings to local environments. Governmental officials, land use planners, landscape designers, land developers, private entrepreneurs, and the myriad of professionals who are involved in the creation and destruction of place are trained within an academic paradigm and ethos that privileges "mainstream" middle-class ideas about place and group. These professionals not only dictate how a place should look but also designate which group's inscriptions of place might be considered valid.

An example from a recent lecture I gave illustrates this point. An environmental design professional who lived on a "multiethnic" block remarked that she could not understand why the facades of the houses were so chaotic. She wanted to know if she could do something to encourage the local residents to "unify" their look. She mentioned that she did not mind cultural diversity but that she was concerned because it made her block "a mess." The designer, its seems, considered herself culturally and socially sensitive to her local neighborhood, but she challenged the rights of her neighbors to express their individuality if it threatened a homogeneous "cultural" identity. She argued that cultural definitions of place were acceptable as long as they were ordered rather than chaotic—an aspect of her taste culture.

A more powerful example of middle-class values dominating definition of place is found in urban renewal that used government authority and subsidies to attract large-scale private investment in areas that were too poor to attract investors.[10] City officials and planning professionals viewed the neighborhoods of poor and low-income residents, who were often black and not represented in city government, as a drain on city revenues and as a "blight" or "slum" that should be "cleaned-up." Yet the social science literature documents that these neighborhoods were important sources of social and economic support for the residents.[11] The perspective of the planners and officials that these places needed to be "cleaned-up" justified the dismantling of poor neighborhoods and the loss of 10 percent of white and 20 percent of black housing units in the central city, with consequences that we are still trying to deal with today.[12]

Another political issue is whether planning and design reinforce traditional power relations and conflicts of race, class, and gender, as well as cultural inequality. These inequalities are expressed in the built environment through decisions that allocate space to those with political or economic power, while at the same time those without power lose their communities through development processes that favor one group over another or vested interests. The urban gentrification that has occurred in Society Hill, Philadelphia, is a prime example of how planning decisions restructure the use as well as the allocation of space, reforming and reconceptualizing neighborhoods without considering the deleterious impact of these changes on poor or disenfranchised residents.

In the case of Society Hill, upper-class residents formed a coalition with interested members of the banking community and city government in a concentrated effort to revitalize the area through preservation-based actions starting in the late 1950s.[13] Tours of Elfreth's Alley and other historic preservation activities brought attention to the wealth of historic buildings that could be available for renovation. The rhetoric of preservation was supported by government subsidies for slum clearance of low-income neighborhoods and new housing construction that displaced local businesses and manufacturers as well as Italian-American, African-American, and Puerto Rican–American residents. Further incentives, such as so-called dollar houses that were offered only to middle- and upper-middle-class buyers who could demonstrate the financial ability to restore the houses, accelerated the changing social composition of the neighborhood. Within twenty years, the area was heralded as successfully gentrified, having become an upper-middle-class residential enclave surrounded by new offices, fancy restaurants, and historic preservation and tourist sites. The original neighborhood where working-class and low-income families could live, shop, and work was totally eradicated through the combined interests of investors, bankers, city planners, and governmental officials who generated tax dollars and increased tourist revenues in this gentrification scheme.

The consolidation of power groups to renovate a low-income or working-class urban area has been repeated in other well-known cases, from the Inner Harbor, Federal Hill, and Otterbein in Baltimore to downtown Manhattan. The process of gentrification has many forms, but the basic theme is one of sociopolitical inequality to control the destiny of a neighborhood or piece of land. In New York City, Lower East Side Manhattan residents who want to remain in their neighborhood and retain its working-class array of shops, workplaces, and low-cost housing have formed coalitions of local housing organizations in an attempt stall the gentrification efforts. Yet developers, speculators, and middle-income people are the potential buyers for city-owned properties, and with each sale there are fewer homes for low-income residents.[14]

Another political issue concerns our roles as professionals working with local communities. There are significant differences between professional and popular control of conservation and design in that the professional community of planners, designers, historians, and social scientists who provide the knowledge base for design do not necessarily value the same places that the local community does. Although design and planning education trains professionals to be spokespersons for local communities, it also espouses a set of professional culture beliefs and practices that limit communication and understanding. This breakdown in communication often goes unnoticed because the two groups use the same words and appear to speak the same language. But the images that each group collectively holds of what a particular built form might look like may have almost no relation to each other. A community interpretation of a water element may read as a children's play area, while a professional interpretation of a water element may be an *beaux-arts* fountain for a civic plaza. Students in a design studio may spend considerable time asking local residents what would be appropriate landscape elements, yet when the students return to their studio, the pressure of what is professionally appropriate becomes more important. Students thus learn to design for their colleagues and professors rather than for the community.[15]

John Dorst's recent analysis of the impact of postmodern modes of cultural reproduction on place suggests that in the example of Chadds Ford, the image or idea (of the designer, historic preservationist, or resident trying to preserve Chadds Ford "as it was") becomes the reality of place. Chadds Ford is not one place but an ideological discourse and an assemblage of texts about the struggle to create an "authentic" Chadds Ford. Place thus becomes a cultural production, and its preservation depends on presenting it as a representative display, with all the "duplicity of any specimen."[16]

Dorst describes this process of representation in terms of "postmodern hyperspaces" that are constructed to behave like surfaces, so that the place becomes a "tour of surfaces"[17] that have no depth. Within this postmodern reality the meaning of place and place conservation becomes separated from the locality and the lives of the people affected. The professionals and elite residents who share their interests deconstruct and reconstruct a world of images rather than deal with the reality of local lives, and they thus maintain a stranglehold on the cultural reproduction of place in Chadds Ford.

What is the solution to the dilemma that professionals face as they go about the business of reading local communities? How should they handle the powers conferred on them? Mary Hufford offers another example of the conflict and dilemmas that professionals and, in this case, activists face. She points out that grass-roots activists often seize on environmental and preservation strategies for saving places that really need to be saved but not as historic or natural resources. For example, preservationists in her community in Arlington, Virginia, are trying to keep a developer from tearing down nearly six hundred affordable housing units to build condominiums. The preservationists are trying to save the units by having Buckingham Village declared a historic landmark, since it was built in the 1930s to provide affordable housing for government workers and in some ways is still fulfilling its historic aims. While the buildings satisfy a number of criteria for this designation, affordable housing is the real community value people are trying to save. There is, however, no language and no set of strategies available to preserve the housing other than using the historic preservation designation.[18] What are the consequences of designating the housing a historic monument? What does this designation do for the people who live there? Will it in some way change the fragile ecology that still provides affordable housing? The strategies of the professional, often joined by grass-roots activists, as in the case of Arlington, or by conservative upper-class forces, as in the case of Chadds Ford, still have considerable impact and "voice" in the social construction of place. But we must continue to question how these strategies limit the voices of other participants who view the local situation differently.

The Challenge of Pluralism

The culture of a place is never singular but is made up of a cultural mosaic built on a multiplicity of histories, voices, and peoples. Whenever we talk about cultural conservation, we must ask the question "Whose culture?" or "Whose tradition or history?" to make clear to others what or about whom we are talking. As I have mentioned in the discussion of cultural hegemony, some of these voices are never heard. Particularly in urban America it is difficult to think of a place as having a dominant culture because of the complex nature of urban society. Yet the expression of this plurality is difficult to achieve, especially in terms of place, where the demands of contrasting taste cultures may dictate very different scenarios that are often mutually exclusive.

An example of mutually exclusive land uses is the conflict over the adaptive reuse of the Manayunk Canal buildings in Philadelphia. The city and outside entrepreneurs wanted to use these buildings for restaurants and boutiques to attract tourists and new residents, while the local neighborhood wanted to use these sites to attract light industry back to the area. The traditionally close relationship of home and work was an important aspect of the community for Manayunk residents, who had walked to work for more than two generations. Light industry, however, did not fit in the image of Manayunk as a tourist attraction with quaint stores and restaurants lining the once functioning canal that city planners and private entrepreneurs saw as "the solution" to Manayunk's economic decline. The demands of the local neighborhood were overlooked in the final planning process because industry was incompatible with gentrified shops and amenities. A pluralistic image of Manayunk was never generated because of the different and conflicting physical programs of each scenario.

Similar issues have arisen in conflicts over waterfront redevelopment, where "historic" or locally important waterfront sites are redeveloped to preserve the site but at the same time create the kind of place that specifically caters to a mobile, professional, middle-class culture. Planning and design redevelopment projects have a tendency to reduce rather than maintain cultural diversity. They also reduce the spectrum of cultural experience by designing for a targeted group of people or for a particular "look." An example of how diversity is limited is found in the similarity of harbor developments in Boston, Baltimore, and New York, which despite their regional external character contain the same shops, restaurants, and services, thus attracting the same tourists and middle-class locals regardless of the location. By targeting tourists and their preference for a "middle-class" experience, the otherwise economically invigorating projects limit the cultural diversity that is presented as well as the population invited to participate. A new kind of "placelessness" is being created that communicates a "classness," which is not specific to any physical or cultural location but invites and responds to a particular kind of people.

One very telling case of how redevelopment projects limit cultural diversity was observed after the creation of the Inner Harbor in Baltimore. Baltimore is a city of ethnic neighborhoods, with long traditions of outdoor festivals and parades. Before the Inner Harbor these festivals took place in the streets and parks of the local sponsoring neighborhoods. In this arrangement everyone in the local community could attend, and outsiders were invited to join in by visiting for the day, purchasing foods and local crafts, and learning more about the residents and their distinct ethnic or neighborhood culture. As part the Inner Harbor project, a large shed, or "festival hall," was constructed as a site where local festivals and commercial "shows" (the auto show or boat show) could take place. An expensive parking lot and booths were also provided. In the following year local neighborhoods were encouraged to use the new shed, but this changed the nature of the festivals. Taking the festival out of the streets of the neighborhood and placing it in a structure identified with the middle-class, tourist center of the city affected who would attend. The festivals seemed to become part of the middle-class entertainment of the Inner Harbor area rather than celebrations that renewed the vitality of the local neighborhood.

Neighborhood cultural plurality can exist, but there may be tensions in its maintenance. This can be seen in such places as Adams-Morgan, a popular area in Washington, D.C. Adams-Morgan is made up of a variety of cultural and class groups, loosely held together by a central shopping and entertainment area focused on the intersection of Columbia Avenue and Eighteenth Street. Recently there were a series of local fights and upheavals, accompanied by looting and destruction, that were said to be caused by conflicts between the poorer Hispanic and African-American residents and the middle-class establishment. The Tenants Hold-Out Organization defended the residential rights of poorer residents in this gentrified neighborhood. For the moment, then, Adams-Morgan does present an alternative to a gentrification scenario that allows only one upwardly mobile group to dominant what was once a cultural mosaic.

The Challenge of Cultural Change

The problems of politics and plurality refer to privileging one culture over another or not including all cultural groups in the determination of place design and planning. There is, however, another even more serious problem facing us, especially in terms of conserving place: the reality that culture is not static but is always changing. Cultural groups are fluid; even the values and beliefs of traditional societies change dramatically over time. When a place is designed, cultural elements are fixed in the physical environment that may have already changed and no longer represent the people who live in or use that environment.

Many of our important historic preservation projects to save a valued building or landscape freeze the taste culture to an environment that may have little to do with the current population's cultural needs. Dolores Hayden's projects within the Power of Place, an organization that works with local communities in Los Angeles to help the residents preserve those parts of their neighborhood that have meaning to them, try to remedy this privileging of one group over another.[19] Her success in commemorating the homestead of Biddy Mason, an African-American working woman who struggled to gain her freedom from slavery, and turning the site into a public history and art project is an example of the kind of conservation that responds to local concerns and images.

Another kind of example is from a project in Oley, Pennsylvania, where an architect, William Ryan, and I worked with the local community and architectural historians to try to determine what about the eighteenth-century German stone farmhouses was distinctive and important to preserve for the local residents. We used an ethnosemantic technique to bring together the perceptions of the architects and residents so that what was most culturally meaningful could become the basis for new designs and plans for the community. The findings indicated that the details of the houses, their materials, windows, and tiled roofs were the critical "Oley" features and that new designs were possible as long as they retained consistency of materials and details. Still, the question remains: how do we conserve place through planning and design while acknowledging that culture changes and that the groups whose cultures are being expressed will change as well? I find this dilemma ironic in that as we work to help a community save some aspect of the local environment, we are also precluding other choices that may better accommodate the future. Many of the most bitter fights over cultural conservation in communities are about the dialectic between the past and the future control of culture.

The Cultural Aspects of Design

Grappling with these issues has led to cross-disciplinary thinking and such alliances as the Cultural Aspects of Design Network, a group of social science and design researchers and practitioners dedicated to bringing cultural issues to the attention of the design and planning fields. We are proposing new solutions to some of these problems that focus on cultural as well as aesthetic issues for design and planning. Since design and planning decisions can both create and solve place conservation problems, we are suggesting new approaches that incorporate culturally appropriate design to maintain the integrity of culturally meaningful places.

One kind of solution to the problems of cultural plurality of place design and planning is a new set of methodologies that incorporate the cultural mosaic of communities. "Cultural mosaic" is used here as a conceptual alternative to the "melting pot." It suggests it is possible to create, support, and foster a healthy diversity of cultural groups in such a way as to respect and give power to each part of the community and its values.

Randy Hester, a landscape architect working in North Carolina and California, has developed a methodology for working with rural towns that includes the townspeople in the data collection and analysis phase so they can identify their own "sacred spaces."[20] These sacred spaces then become a focus for redesigning and renovating the community; the identified spaces are preserved and highlighted in the town masterplan, thus conserving the culturally meaningful elements for the community.

Another methodology that deals with cultural plurality is constituency analysis,[21] used in a planning project of Farnham Park in Camden, New Jersey. Developed as part of a landscape architecture studio at the University of Pennsylvania, the methodology involves segmenting community members into subcultures, that is, groups that have differing opinions and value orientations on issues related to redesigning the park. The community was divided into over ten distinct groups, and plans were developed for their individual needs and desires. The final phase of the project integrated the different plans through a political negotiation process. The benefit of the method was that subcultural diversity was maintained throughout the planning process instead of being lost in the first phase, when one group would normally have been selected to represent the whole.

Cultural symbols can also be used to maintain a sense of cultural identity in the design and planning of a neighborhood. One example is the redesign of buildings and sidewalk details in Philadelphia's Chinatown, where pagodas are found atop telephone booths, Chinese gates mark the entrance to the area, and buildings by the postmodern architect Robert Venturi have Chinese detailing on their balconies and entrances. Symbols can add an important dimension to a project without necessarily excluding other uses of the space. Although they are not a permanent way to preserve a place, they provide an intermediate level of cultural conservation and local community spatial identity.

Local cultural adaptation—in other words, design that provides cultural meanings through means that are ecologically or socioculturally adaptive—is another method for dealing with place conservation and cultural meaning. Cultural groups often transplant elements from their native environments to new locations that have preexisting cultural traditions and incompatible environments. In some cases the newly introduced cultural elements can have a deleterious effect on the environment, such as the desire to have water-dependent grass lawns in Tucson, Arizona. A local cultural adaptation that responds to both the ecological problem of water shortages and the desire to maintain the cultural symbol is green rock front lawns or cement front lawns painted green. These clever adaptations of the original symbolic form suggest how cultural forms can survive even in hostile surroundings.

Conclusion

By way of summing up I would like to emphasize three points. First, place is an inseparable part of cultural conservation, but it entails planning and design that generate a new set of problems to be considered. Second, those problems—the political, pluralistic, and changeable qualities of culture and cultural groups—must be addressed to produce more informed place conservation decisions. Third, there are solutions, albeit small ones, that groups are working on, including some suggestions from the Cultural Aspects of Design Network.

NOTES

I would like to thank Mary Hufford, Joel Lefkowitz, and Laurel Wilson for their comments and suggestions for revising this essay.

1. Margaret Rodman, "Voices of Place" (Unpublished manuscript, 1991).
2. Marc Fried, "Grieving for a Lost Home," in *Urban Condition,* ed. Len Duhl (New York: Basic Books, 1963); H. Gans, *The Urban Villagers* (New York: Free Press, 1963).
3. Kai Erikson, *Everything in Its Path* (New York: Simon and Schuster, 1976).
4. Peter Marris, *Family and Social Change in an African City* (Chicago: Northwestern University Press, 1962).
5. Michael Young and P. Willmott, *Family and Kinship in East London* (London: Routledge, 1957).
6. Susan Lobo, *A House of My Own* (Tucson: University of Arizona Press, 1983).
7. David Harvey, "Labor, Capital, and Class Struggle around the Built Environment," *Politics and Society* 6 (1976): 289.
8. John Logan and Harvey Molotch, *Urban Fortunes* (Berkeley: University of California Press, 1987).
9. Irwin Altman and Setha M. Low, *Place Attachment* (New York: Plenum, 1992).
10. Logan and Molotch, *Urban Fortunes.*
11. Carol Stack, *All Our Kin* (New York: Harper and Row, 1984).
12. Logan and Molotch, *Urban Fortunes.*
13. Sharon Zukin, *Landscapes of Power* (Berkeley: University of California Press, 1991).
14. Delmos Jones and Joan Turner, "Housing and the Material Basis of Social Reproduction," in *Housing, Culture and Design,* ed. S. Low and E. Chambers (Philadelphia: University of Pennsylvania Press, 1989), 13–30.
15. Setha M. Low, "Professional Culture," *Resources in Education,* ERIC Report 219290 (1982), 2–19.

16. John D. Dorst, *The Written Suburb* (Philadelphia: University of Pennsylvania Press, 1989), 48.

17. Ibid., 106.

18. See Mary Hufford, "Buckingham Village: Pieces of a Dream," *Washington Post,* August 13, 1991, C8.

19. Dolores Hayden, "Using Ethnic History to Understand Urban Landscapes," *Places* 7 (1990): 11–37.

20. R. T. Hester, *Planning Neighborhood Space with People* (New York: Van Rostrand Reinhold, 1984).

21. Setha Low, "Social Science Methods in Landscape Architecture Design," *Landscape Planning* 3 (1982): 137–48; Setha Low, "Anthropology as a New Technology in Landscape Planning," in *Proceedings of the Regional Section of the American Society of Landscape Architecture,* ed. J. Fabos (Washington, D.C.: American Society of Landscape Architecture, 1981); Setha Low and William Ryan, "Noticing without Looking," *Journal of Architecture and Planning Research* 2 (1985): 3–22.

6

Powerful Promises of Regeneration or Living Well with History

Roger D. Abrahams

In 1802 George Washington's adopted son, George Washington Parke Custis, produced an agricultural fair in Arlington, Virginia, in which he called for all of those attending to wear homespun clothing.[1] This reference to past ways of life might be seen as an act of pure nostalgia were it not for the fact that, like George Washington, Custis was deeply interested in scientific agricultural practices and was exploiting the occasion of the fair to bring farmers together to discuss the newest experiments in animal husbandry and crop technology. The homespun touch was his way of voicing the need to maintain the ideals of the old ways in searching out the new.

In asking everyone to dress in homespun, Custis was reminding his neighbors and friends of the continuing need for self-sufficiency. Finding a way of symbolically bringing the old ways together with new technologies to maintain the vigor and resourcefulness of these descendants of settler people has been high on the agenda of many activist Americans ever since. That is, those who are conservative in the true sense continue to search out ways of deploying old ways to serve new ends.

This is the legacy of American folklorists, conservationists, and preservationists, those concerned with maintaining the variety of life forms generated about us. We all share so many attitudes and approaches to the past and future that it seems very strange we have not sought to make common cause on environmental issues before now. Although we share concerns, many of our assumptions regarding the sacred character of our mission remain unexamined in our common work. In a world of diminishing resources, this situation calls for immediate attention. Not only have we all been accused of paying excessive attention to the frayed edges while problems in the present go unattended, but we stand accused of political and social naivete as well.

Americans have long regarded the gross national product as the index of our progressive vitality. As an agricultural nation, we cast the aura of sacred trust on the land itself, the territory, and its productivity. Among conservationists—and here I include folklorists—there is now a widespread sense that these resources are far from inexhaustible and that popular perceptions of the earth as an inexhaustible resource need to be altered. To bring about such a change, however, we need to examine our own continuing adherence to the idea of the sacrality of the land.

Such an examination is all the more important because in other parts of the world, as close as Canada and as far away as Sri Lanka, nationalistic movements are calling for separation from past political alliances, which broaches the possibility of ethnic cleansings in those territories. We must recognize how closely allied our conservationist style of thought is to such zealous movements, especially insofar as both are grounded in nostalgia for a past that might never have existed.

Nostalgia often leads to a conflation of culture and territory, imputing natural virtue to traditional practices as well as to vernacular buildings and landscapes. On the basis of a putative natural connection with the land and the past, claims of legitimacy and authenticity seem to emerge "naturally" from having hunted and gathered, tilled the land, or tended the flocks in a certain terrain over an extended period of time, leading to the development of some kind of natural legitimacy for control over that territory.

That those who have lived in these ways have rightful claims to pursue their lives in their accustomed manner is not at issue. That they should receive due honor for enduring is beyond debate. That indigenous peoples should be so honored on the basis of some imputed natural right should be approached with greater caution. My remarks should be taken as suggestions for those involved in developing cultural conservation policy who might meaningfully question past practices of our combined disciplines.

Folklore is especially susceptible to visions of a prelapsarian world that might somehow be recaptured, in spirit if not in detail. As other essayists in this volume observe, we are far from alone in this mind-set. This vision suggests that at some point a fall from grace, a cataclysmic disjunction occurred, after which life was forever altered. To account for, and perhaps counter, the complexity of the modern world, an earlier stage of existence is posited in which things were simpler, more humane, and more manageable. This world before the fall provides a convenient fiction against which contemporary values and practices may be compared and criticized.

Insofar as conservationists are commonly called upon to recompose the past through their materials, it has been too pedagogically useful to place matters of yore in a kind of timeless world, one dominated by the features of life we now suppose we have lost. Nostalgia then emerges for members of an audience who are connected with each other through the experience of common loss, not through any ongoing and present cultural achievement itself. People thus may be united as well by a sense of disgust with predecessors who have passed on an inheritance of historical disruption and forfeiture. One unfortunate byproduct of such thinking is a feeling of betrayal, of having somehow lost a birthright, with little recognition of what that legacy would have been. This depiction of the past draws on the "victimage" model of explanation, tying to the past through the sins of the forebears, a perspective that calls somehow for a kind of expiation of sins without the sinning. Worse still, using the imagined community of such a prelapsarian world as a basis for constituting contemporary lifeways is to risk essentializing, vulgarizing, and virulently stereotyping the people we have decided have maintained some of these communitarian lifeways.

Folklorists, along with historic preservationists, have inherited from the Romantics a taste for the fragment and the ruin. Insofar as one of our tasks is to educate the public, we attempt to devise strategies of presentation that do justice to the materials and to the peoples we set out to study and understand. Questions of authenticity constantly plague us as we seek proper ways to convey messages inherent in historic materials about a world we have lost. Just as folklorists wonder how best to present traditional performers in various settings—the concert stage, the workshop, festival, or some other fabricated intimate setting—so historic preservationists debate whether to scrape and paint, how faithfully to replicate past technologies when reconstructing an artifact, and so on. Similarly, in preserving and presenting patches of wilderness, nature conservancies must decide which visions of nature and attendant rituals to accommodate—those of scientists, hikers, hunters, or a mixture of all of them.

A problematic assumption shared by conservation professionals is that the more "natural" materials are made to seem, the more they will make their own "messages" manifest. That is, we work in the penumbra of the Romantic notion that the basic lessons of life may be better understood if we open our own natures to what is natural "out there." In folklore the idea of "induced natural context" has evolved into a festival presentational technique; that is, festival producers devise settings in which traditional performers and nontraditional audiences are better able to imagine themselves in the "natural" milieux for these performances.[2] We see similar efforts in living historical museums, park-centered public presentations, and buildings that are restored and maintained as landmarks.

Essentially, this appeal to a reconstruction of the natural context was developed from one of the basic fictions of antiquarian representations, what we might call "the mystique of the fragment." In one widely reported legend an object or great tradition is saved at the last moment from obliteration by one of the founders of the field. This potsherd, evocative ballad, or snatch of a fiddle tune forever after opens a window onto antiquity.

This saved-from-the-fire story has provided a good deal of interest for fieldworkers in any of our disciplines, for through its retelling, the merry scientist-adventurer is transformed into that special kind of culture hero, the historical rescue worker who finds, captures, and preserves some feature of that expired time we call history. This discovery narrative provides the background for carrying out what Barbara Kirshenblatt-Gimblett has called "eleventh hour ethnography"[3] or jaws-of-destruction fieldwork. Important features of natural and cultural life are constantly disintegrating, in this view, from the callous neglect of those in power (always a careless lot). The trope also has provided the standard arguments for funding salvage projects, not only in folklore, ethnography, and archaeology but also in historic preservation and natural conservation.

The found fragment,[4] then, becomes the launching point for a discovery narrative that argues for further searches. It is a compelling story, one that has proven extraordinarily useful in persuading local, state, national, and even international governing bodies to sponsor our basic field research and in representing our findings to the general public. It also places our professions in a position to authenticate ways of preserving and presenting the past. Such a past connects people in the future to those features of history that inform notions of ourselves as citizens of this nation and this world.

Not all questions of folklore, much less historic preservation and environmental protection, emerge out of the search for national identities, however. Far from it, a good deal of our work in common seems to emerge in direct reaction to the commercial dimension of state-formation and to the technologically driven alterations of the environment, natural and social, that arise so regularly in powerful nation-states.

Even in such a case, the terms of the argument are dictated by the power distribution and redistribution that occurred under the construction of modern nation-states. Indeed, if the disciplines share any philosophic predisposition, it is a reaction against the excesses of centralized power, as modern national entities impose hegemony through technological development and the trade engendered by this technology. In reaction, an antimodernist[5] argument arises, one that emphasizes the unnaturalness of these developments and the need to retain the more humane features of traditional lives, including certain simpler technologies of the past.

In this argument nature and traditional culture are conflated. Folklore, as the general term for face-to-face performances and handmade objects, becomes naturalized, a direct outgrowth of the land and the native language. Such a formulation of our contemporary situation tends to idealize and dehistoricize specific eras in the past, imposing a kind of forced sacrality on the land and placing indigenous peoples in the category of protectors of the land simply because they happened to stay on it against all odds.

Europeans have thus repeatedly cast American Indians in the role of protectors and worshipers of the environment, seizing on the purported sacred status of Mother Earth as a way of projecting these antiprogressive sentiments.[6] Even when a specific historical period is seized on as the model of the good life, the era itself is dehistoricized, recast as if it were some prelapsarian time. Dehistoricizing exacts a price, especially when dealing with materials that are supposedly historical. As essayists elsewhere in this volume make clear, such an exoticizing move is part of a process of deep stereotyping, one that is deleterious even when the stereotyping seems positive—as in the yeoman farmer as opposed to the hayseed, the independent mountain man as opposed to the hillbilly.

In a Rousseauistic mode, societies before their first contact with Europeans, especially societies of hunter-foragers, are made to represent an edenic life-style, in which problems of property ownership and the attendant alienation of product from process is avoided. Alternatively, the European Middle Ages are endowed with certain communitarian features, especially as portrayed in the customary relations on the manor, in the monastery, or, most recently, in the early marketplace.[7] Throughout the nineteenth century, the American frontier was also characterized nostalgically and linked to the ways of Indians or pioneers. In its latter form, it is still referred to as "The Age of the Homespun"—an era during which the pioneer homestead was seemingly self-sufficient.[8]

In these recastings of the past, commercial and industrial development come to illustrate the human pride that goeth before a major fall. We thus become "our own worst enemies," unique among species for "fouling our own nests," especially under industrial conditions. This version of edenic thinking establishes an era in national history before human degradation prevailed, during which the bounties of nature provided the necessary materials for the self-sufficient life and people got along nicely on very little.

By a process of dismaying simplification, these arguments from nature valorize anything claiming an indigenous heritage. Such simplistic argumentation, under the name of essentialism, has become a source of constant concern in the cultural critique because of its ahistorical stance and its historical uses for the purposes of landgrabbing and genocide. Moreover, it threatens the pluralist political position. The obvious xenophobic turn of such a brand of populism is patent, one that promotes the "get off of my property" argument.

In some cases the naturalizing of indigenous language and culture is a rhetorical device employed, as in say Catalonia or Quebec, to achieve social or cultural equity for groups denied political access. These oppositional Romantic nationalistic arguments rely on the strategies of late eighteenth-century and early nineteenth-century nation-builders, who sought to undermine the megalithic governmental structures that emerged during that era of empire. In more thoroughgoing cosmopolitan contexts, these separatist strategies suggest that an overly complex society is in need of simplification and that one way of doing this is to sanction local autonomies.

But separatist movements, by accepting the land-and-language bases of the arguments for political autonomy, also embrace the exclusionist and potentially xenophobic dimension of their goals. Their perspective rests on a notion of the natural as being god-given, self-correcting, systematic, good. It fails to recognize that there have been many ideas about what is "natural," just as there have been various modalities of judging authenticity. Such matters involve a good deal of cultural construction and are deeply embedded in criteria of the beautiful, good, and clean, and the ugly, bad, and contaminated. This good, clean rendering of the past relies on a great deal of artful forgetting.

In effect, separatist movements depend on that special mode of thinking that Fredric Jameson has called "nostalgia for the present," a yearning for a world that never really existed and therefore was not there for the losing.[9] In a very deep sense, American society not only constantly reinvents the past to engender nostalgia but also, under present media conditions and the ever-mounting value placed on entertainment services, promises the recovery of an infinite reservoir of images and gestures. As Arjun Appadurai has usefully noted, "The past . . . has become a synchronic warehouse of cultural scenarios, a kind of temporal central casting to which recourse can be had as appropriate, depending on the movie to be made, the scene to be enacted, the hostages to be rescued."[10]

Moreover, as the countryside is depopulated of agricultural workers, the very notion of the country and its agrarian past becomes suffused with these nostalgic meanings. The countryside itself comes to represent the lost world; we search in its geographies for evidence of the kind of humane effort in clearing the land and breaking the sod that bear up under our notions of the morally vigorous life. So much of our work is predicated on the sense that the rural community is somehow harmonious and self-sufficient and that in the countryside, even in the face of depopulation, we might recover that sense of wholeness, even as we establish a sense of continuity to a meaningful, morally informed past.

Common sense tells us that popular culture throughout the West invents representations of the past that are subject to nostalgic deployment, even in drawing on topographies or objects or texts put together "back then." To this extent we need to share the postmodern reflexive sensibility and, with it, to recognize the limitations of including any marginal people or people of color as *folk*. With the folklorist Susan Stewart, one can argue that "our task [is] to pose a critique of temporality that is deeply aware of the constraints of periodization and any other construction we may place upon the past."[11] With her, one can recognize the inherent prison-house of such temporality implicit in the words *folk* and *lore*, even as we have seen the liabilities of using *primitive, savage,* and *barbarian.*

As bourgeois substitutes for *the peasantry*, terms like *folklore* and *folklife* ought not to be accepted uncritically. All such terms emerged as part of a modernist and progressive rhetoric that sought to expose the vulgar errors of the past or, alternatively, as an element of the rejection of such modernism, in which a cultural advocacy began in the nineteenth century and attempted to identify and preserve practices and products that derived from a simpler, less commoditized culture. Some of our key concepts, especially tradition and authenticity, are built on a bedrock of Renaissance, Enlightenment, and Romantic notions that have remained convenient fictions in carrying out our discussion, but fictions nonetheless.[12]

The invention of the idea of "the folk" is often attributed to Johann Gottfried Herder, who developed the argument on local and national character into a sociopsychological theory tying language and lore to a people living in a particular topography. As Isaiah Berlin said of this development, "Herder virtually invented the idea of belonging." Just as people must "eat and drink, to have security and freedom of movement, so too they need to belong to a group." Building on this thought, Berlin proceeded, "Deprived of this, they felt cut off, lonely diminished unhappy. Nostalgia, Herder said, was the noblest of all pains. To be human meant to be able to feel at home somewhere, with your own kind."[13] These ideas he associates with the spirit of the folk and nation, as manifest in the language, the customary practices and beliefs of a people united through the common historical experience, and their involvement with the particularities of the terrain.

This yoking of land, language, custom, and indigenous peoples, however, is an invention of various European monarchs in early modern Europe that was launched some time before Herder and the onset of Romantic nationalism. From the mid-sixteenth century onward, one European nation after another saw antiquarianism arise as one dimension of royal and scientific initiative. With the development of the print technology as it was put to use by early modern monarchs, publication in the vernacular came to provide a principal technique for asserting monarchical hegemony.

Monarchs found it useful to inventory the ancient practices of the realm, using them for a variety of purposes in promoting their powers and particularly as a means of unifying communities and individuals with a variety of historical experiences, language forms, and cultural backgrounds. These monarchs were themselves schooled in the international codes of diplomatic and social interaction of the time, but they found it useful to bestow royal favor on certain dimensions of countryside practices. In this way the mystique of native genius was imposed on the terrain, sacralizing not only the land but also its occupants and their products.

To be sure, those who had remained in the countryside and continued as laborers became native exotics at this point, admired for their indigenous status but regarded as backward and possibly dangerous because of their possible irredentist claims on the land—for the monarchs were seldom natives of the nation they were committed to making sacred. Nevertheless, monarchs were able to argue that they ruled sacred ground and that this property might be taxed and be used by them in various ways. Asserting divine right of kingship, monarchs rationalized their protection and expansion of the realms they came to personify.

Under such conditions a fracture between past and present is felt. Early in the Renaissance, when this objectification first took place, the prospect of mass literacy came to be seen as an effect of a cultural intervention that severed the past from the present. At this point the distinction between oral and written cultures became an important feature of the discourse on culture. As Elizabeth Eisenstein has argued in her magisterial study of the effect of print technology on early modern European history, by permanently preserving what had been ephemeral—that is, oral or scribal—print stabilized culture itself and the past. Recorded in print, the past became available for purposes of collection and comparison.[14]

At this point the past seemed all the closer, since it might be recaptured through a close study of those objects, including manuscripts, produced in prior times; but the past also became a time that was continually receding from the contemporary world and was thus ever-more shrouded in the realm of the strange and the mysterious unknowable. The very act of producing a sense of an emergent present distanced intensely from the past introduced the formative elements of that greatest of modern cultural ailments, nostalgia.

This sense of a present moving away from an ever-receding past was dramatized early in American history when George Washington Parke Custis called for homespun clothing. To be sure, this was during a period when Americans regarded consumption of nonnative products, especially cloth, as unpatriotic. Moreover, what has come to be called "the Jeffersonian ideal" of agrarian self-sufficiency connotes a "middle state" mediating between the savagery of the wilderness confrontation and the refined and too often decadent practices of urbanized populations. This position was outlined for Europeans by the Englishman Richard Price, who was widely read and followed in the United States. As Price argued, when a state was able to produce "an independent and hardy YEOMANRY," the result was a citizenry "trained in arms . . . clothed in homespun—of simple manners—strangers to luxury—drawing plenty from the ground—and that plenty, gathered easily by the hand of industry."[15]

While assuming the usefulness of this middle way, few called for the usages of the past, whether in agricultural practice or in the cities. To the contrary, George Custis's sheepshearing involved an attempt to introduce new, more scientific techniques into the practices of his neighbors. Nor should it in any way be regarded as involving a celebration of nature or the natural.

The United States differed from Europe in its nationalistic movements precisely with regard to its attitude toward the past and the landscape. To be sure, in this country the power and beauties of nature were discovered and embroidered before culture and tradition were endowed with the kind of value they have today. Indeed, for much of the first half century of our national history, Americans seemed to agree that one could exist very nicely without traditions and the detritus of past thinking. Nature itself would put us in our proper place socially, politically, or cosmically. It was neither useful nor appropriate for Americans to appeal to tradition or to follow custom. As the authors of *The Federalist* put it, "Is it not the glory of the people of America, that whilst they have paid decent regard to the opinions of former times and other nations they have not suffered a blind veneration for antiquity, for custom, for names, to overrule the suggestions of their own good sense, the knowledge of their own situation, and the lessons of their own experience?"[16]

Americans would substitute natural laws and common sense for traditions. In place of the cultural debris of the past, represented to Americans by the ruins that attracted so much of the attention of those taking the Grand Tour of Europe, Americans had natural wonders by which they might give themselves moral perspective. If Europe had its monuments and was able to commune with the past in achieving feelings of the sublime, in "Nature's Nation," as Thomas Jefferson called the United States, Americans had an ancient landscape on which God's messages were inscribed.

Following this line of thought, Americans developed their own Grand Tour, featuring visits to such sublime vistas as the Natural Bridge, the Mammoth Caves, the Catskills, Niagara Falls, and later Yellowstone, Yosemite, and other natural spectacles of the West. As John Sears has noticed in his study of nineteenth-century tourist practices, these sites served as stations in a secular pilgrimage and, like such sites in the Old World, were soon surrounded with specialists in framing the experience and providing the visitor with an articulated moral gaze that enabled everyone to experience the same kind of moral uplift.[17]

By this move, early architects of our national consciousness denied our need for a sense of tradition. If this country was to assert its place among nations, it was going to do so by creating a tradition of the new. This newness would build on monuments dated before the advent of humans in a land "as old as the flood" and in need of "no ornament or privilege which nature could bestow," as Ralph Waldo Emerson put it.[18]

In spite of Emerson's call for a worship of unadorned nature, Americans were as drawn to the spectacle of these natural wonders as Europeans were to the architectural wonders of Egypt, Greece, and Rome. Without the grandeur and sublimity of the celebrated American vistas, the rest of nature came to be as dispensable as European custom and tradition had been in the creation of the tradition of the new under the doctrine of progress. Nevertheless, in an inventory of the notable features of America and Americans, these natural wonders asserted themselves, evoking the attitudes that engendered our modern conservationist and environmentalist stance.

Europeans shaped national identities from indigenous cultural resources long before such resources drew Americans' attention. Not until the 1840s did some Americans begin to make a call for a national culture based on the same principles as those of the European Romantic nationalists, who looked for the genius of a national people in the language, the lore, and the landscape. When this feeling emerged, it was cavalier agrarians in the South, such as William Gilmore Simms, who launched this argument, saying that "no nation of our magnitude—sprung from such famous stocks—having such records of the past—having such fears of the future—with our boldness of design—can long remain without its *Genius loci!*"[19]

The American Revolution itself, replayed in parades and other festive formats, became a primary resource for the self-conscious construction of American culture. It was the experience of revolution itself, then, not the native genius of the landscape or the language, on which the first American customary practices were constructed.[20] The national holidays, the Fourth of July, New Year's Day, and Election Day, provided the occasions for celebrations that borrowed from the vocabulary of traditional festive practices, now wearing the garb of new achievements in the face of the Old World and its old ways.

The overt rejection of traditions did not, in fact, reflect a total dismissal of Old World patterns of thinking and doing things, even in the area of self-conscious public celebrations. This was clear, for instance, in the choice of May 1, July 4, and January l as the dates on which the parades, the muster of the guards, and the shooting of the cannons replayed the successful

Revolution. These were the traditional times of celebration in the Old World as well, even if the May Pole was now transformed into the Liberty Pole. Just as in Europe, every piece of land in the United States bears witness to a series of struggles, not only over ownership but over meanings as well. One of the aims of preservationists is to maintain the site in such a way that it reflects the struggles that made them—and continue to make them—that way.

The movement to preserve representative historic buildings, wilderness areas, and early agricultural sites owes much of its energy and bearing to the present retreat from urban, industrial, and commercial blight and from the social and psychological stresses produced by this modern condition. With this in mind, let us reflect on our methods and motives for conserving selected pieces of the past.

In a polity that espouses cultural pluralism, some folklorists and preservationists have become advocates for those who have been politically and culturally ignored in the past. Through discovering and celebrating the genius of the best of the performers and craftspeople in small groups connected somehow to a place or a distinctive way of life, we alert the public to the presence of alternatives to officially sanctioned forms of cultural expression.[21] It is here that terms like *folklore* and *folklife* have proven rhetorically useful.

If advocacy for the dispossessed and underappreciated is our motive, however, we need to think critically about how our categories, criteria, theories of culture, and strategies of presentation advance or inhibit this goal. Could our efforts to realign power, resting on the constructed natural relationship between a homeland and language and lore, invite the very kinds of irredentist responses that have led to unending boundary disputes, litigation, and war? Who falls into the crevasse when we assign primacy to old and pure strains of land-based vernacularity?

With other social scientists we have tended to regard the small face-to-face group, or community, as the site of production of all legitimate culture, whether *community* refers to a village or a gathering of elites. Yet this canonical notion of community, one of our major conceptual tools, is ill-suited to multicultural settings and too often leads to a privileging of traditional over emergent, though equally vernacular, forms. In a world where cultures of all sorts are constantly transforming under creolizing conditions, all of us concerned with cultural conservation need to do more serious observing and theorizing to understand better or legitimize this process and its products.

People dispossessed in an urban setting have always constituted the greatest challenge for social theorists in the West, even when these populations produced forms of expressive life that are hallmarks of cosmopolitanism. Think of how gypsy music and dance, such as czardas or flamenco, have been accepted wherever cafe society sprang up but how feared and loathed gatherings of Rom have remained. It is in the midst of the urban confluence of cultures that performance traditions have repeatedly emerged out of the confrontation between the new and the old. Thus, for example, African-American forms and performers interacting with other cultural impulses constantly produce new and challenging forms of expressive greatness. Yet performers from these black traditions, fitting so nicely into the market economies of urban peoples, become target populations for the rejection of marketplace values. If we wish to empower urban citizens against the forces of cultural homogenization, we need to move beyond theories that posit culture as a display of communities linked to specific locales.

How may the view that cultural formations come together in dialogical arrangements in urban and mercantile environments translate into a national cultural mission? How shall we represent and protect the great African-American traditions emerging from Rio, Buenos Aires, Trinidad, New Orleans, and Chicago without sanitizing their points of origin in confrontational milieux? Indeed the forms of competitive performance—samba, tango, jazz, calypso, tap dancing, blues, hip-hop, and rap—that surface in such cosmopolitan centers become ways in which those cities symbolically represent themselves. Insofar as they are confrontational and aggressive at their point of origin, however, they are feared by the populace in general. Consider, for instance, the widely publicized reaction against rap music over the past decade. Even on the plantation, before even in the Delta towns and in cities like Memphis, Chicago, Rio, and Buenos Aires, black performances and white imitations came together in a symbiosis that affected entire generations of performers.[22]

I think we stand on weakest ground at the very point at which we seem to have the greatest approval of the public. Whether we derive our politics from the pastoralists—wishing to maintain the vision of America as rural and to keep our entertainments around the hearth or in the barn—or from the cosmopolitans—who recognize the passion of the city and look to the concert hall or the museum as the appropriate place for cultural performance—we may use our politics to distance ourselves from the contagion we continue to find at the marketplace. Perhaps we feel cleaner and purer in excoriating the traders and purveyors of commodities. In doing so, however, we selectively rewrite our past, overvaluing the importance of place at the expense of choice and mobility. I fear that we take so many of these places to our hearts precisely because we have been and continue to be such a reckless and restless people. As such, are we not fastening on these places out of nostalgia, embracing the values of hearth and home, of family and community stability that are noticeable in their absence elsewhere in our lives?

The land itself has always been invested with meanings, but not the same ones by everyone. What was once a hunting ground for some became a farm or a factory site for others. Our foreparents, no matter what the color of their skins, did not necessarily value the land for its natural plenitude. Many saw it as property, the basis of the family fortune, or just a commodity to be converted into cash at the appropriate moment. The family farm and other kinds of homeplaces have achieved greater significance in story and song than they ever had in the lives of earlier Americans.

Most Euro-Americans came to this country to experience greater liberty—a sense of freedom made palpable because America was an outpost of commercial culture from the very beginning. Even the yeoman farmers that made up a large proportion of the early Republic were hardly tied to the land in anything other than the economic sense of a place to make a living. Many families, like that of Laura Ingalls Wilder, moved from the little house on the prairie to a sod house on the plains, from sod to log to clapboard houses, from the prairie to the big woods and even into the great desert, when a new territory opened up or when the neighborhood seemed to get too populated.

Farming and cattle herding were tied to national and international markets. Little care was evinced for the land itself. If they were not in the land game just to establish a claim and then sell it and move on, yeoman farmers in any case were neither peasants nor freeholders in the European sense; they were futures traders, looking to find the cash crop that would advance them and their families in the world, even as it permitted them to experience life choices at their fullest. This was, in fact, the message of the "middle way"—that the American agriculturalist was self-consciously working to find a way in which both productivity and manufactory could be entered into without falling into either savagery or oversophistication.

Staying on the go may be liberating, but it also produces a feeling of loss, of leaving one place to find a new one. The very idea of home is under constant negotiation, featured in some of the central fictions we enact about ourselves, though not in all that enduring a fashion. The little log cabin in the pines really was a halfway house, no matter how we might wish otherwise. Having a home base seems more important in baseball and square dancing than in family life.

Having choices and making them is the American way, not only at department stores and malls but also in flea markets and swap meets, not only in theme parks but also in national parks and other kinds of green zones. If the American creed rests on an abiding belief in optimizing choices and maintaining the possibility of such alternatives, then choice infuses our notions of liberty. One way of acting on our liberties is to ensure that the rights of others may be maintained as ways, potentially, of spicing up our own lives down the road.

A central task of the cultural conservationist is to lay bare the presuppositions underlying cultural advocacy and to reveal the interests served by such presuppositions. The argument that any conservation program should be carried out for generations to come should be mounted with caution, for this is the way that hereditary elites and imperialists traditionally have argued.[23] Acknowledging a common purpose, we cannot give over either reason or disciplinary insight to the sentiment of the moment. We will be laughed at, and rightly so, if we do not recognize the tissue-thin quality of our notions of the past and admit that here we fashion a golden veil through which we interpret nature and culture. Among the things filtered out by this golden veil are the links between our cherished pasts and the aspects of commercialism against which we battle. We owe it to ourselves, and to those who come after us, to be honest about it.

NOTES

Thanks are due to Archie Green, Bob Cantwell, Dan Ben-Amos, Dorie Noyes, Xan Griswold, Laurie Shapiro, and Bob St. George, who helped me work out these ideas, and to Mary Hufford and Jim Hardin for editorial advice. John Roberts's work in progress, "African American Folklore in a Discourse of Folkness," assisted me in thinking through some of the implications of imposing the concept of folk on any self-identified group, but especially those who do not identify themselves with the land and who do not carry out their primary expressive exchanges around the hearth.

1. For descriptions of this event, see Wilhelmus Bogart Bryan, *A History of the National Capitol from Its Foundation* (New York: Macmillan, 1914), 596–97; and Rodney H. True, "The Development of Agricultural Societies," in *American Historical Association Annual Report 1920* (Washington, D.C.: American Historical Association, 1925), 300. Deborah Kodish first brought these to my notice and allowed me to see her manuscript in preparation, "Watson, the Father: The Origins and Ideology of the American Agricultural Fair." My thanks to her.

2. The term and the concept come from Kenneth S. Goldstein, *A Guide for Field Workers in Folklore* (Hatboro, Pa.: Folklore Associates and the American Folklore Society, 1964). See also his "The Induced Natural Context: An Ethnographic Folklore Field Technique," in *Essays on the Verbal and Visual Arts*, Proceedings of the American Ethnological Society, ed. June Helm (Seattle: University of Washington Press, 1967), 1–8. It grew out of his pioneering early work as a fieldworker and was adapted by producers of folk festivals beginning in the late 1960s.

3. Barbara Kirshenblatt-Gimblett, "Problems in the Historiography of Jewish Folkloristics" (manuscript in preparation). She suggests alternative names, "the ethnographic phantom" or "the open grave." This is a trope that has successfully suffused Romantic argumentation, in connection with the major archaeological finds, and enters folklore studies at their very inception, with the rescue of the Percy Folio manuscript from being used to start fires. It could also be called the "letter in the bottle" argument, insofar as the found object appears to carry messages from afar.

4. The notion of the evocative fragment, a commonplace feature of the rhetoric of high Romanticism, permeates the discussion of the place of the past in our poetic imaginations. For interesting recent discussions of this and related ideas concerning the scarce evidence of tradition and its relations with souvenirs, mementos, miniatures, and related phenomena, see the work of Susan Stewart, especially her chapters on "The Miniature" and "Objects of Desire" in *On Longing: Narratives of the Miniature, the Gigantic, the Souvenir, the Collection* (Baltimore: Johns Hopkins University Press, 1984), 37–69, 132–70, and her chapters on ballads and related text types in *Crimes of Writing: Problems in the Containment of Representation* (New York: Oxford University Press, 1991), 66–131.

5. The term is elaborated in T. J. Jackson Lears, *No Place of Grace: Antimodernism and the Transformation of American Culture, 1880–1920* (New York: Pantheon, 1981).

6. For this putative Indian worship of the earth in maternal form, see Sam Gill, *Mother Earth: An American Story* (Chicago: University of Chicago Press, 1987).

7. For a consideration of the draw of the manor and the monastery, see Lears, *No Place of Grace.* The early marketplace has been introduced into this mix through the work of Mikhail Bakhtin, especially his *Rabelais and His World,* trans. Helene Iswoldsky (Cambridge, Mass.: MIT Press, 1968). For some interesting work developing and modifying Bakhtin, see Peter Stallybrass and Allon White, *The Politics and Poetics of Transgression* (Ithaca, N.Y.: Cornell University Press, 1986); and Jean-Christophe Agnew, *Worlds Apart: The Market and the Theater in Anglo-American Thought* (Cambridge: Cambridge University Press, 1986), 17–56.

8. The term *age of homespun* used in this moralistic sense is associated with the nineteenth-century popular preacher Horace Bushnell. For a survey of his use of the idea, see Theodore Hovet, "Horace Bushnell's 'The Age of Homespun' and Transcendental Symbolism," *American Transcendental Quarterly* 55 (1955): 5–18. The ideal of self-sufficiency is treated at some length in relation to pioneer bees and frolics in the second chapter of my *Singing the Master: The Development of Afro-American Culture on the Plantation* (New York: Pantheon, 1992). The subject is complex and not appropriately waged in this forum, but it should be noted that there was a division of thought on the subject in early America, as there had been in Europe—one, attached to the poetic argument of the pastoral eclogue, made leisure a virtue, was given voice by the shepherd, and placed a heavy symbolic burden on natural fecundity of a

land; the other, attached to the georgic, made labor a virtue and placed the farmer in the privileged position of commentator on life.

9. Fredric Jameson, "Nostalgia for the Present," *South Atlantic Quarterly* 88 (1989): 517–37; see also Arjun Appadurai's notion of the "social imaginaire," in his "Disjuncture and Difference in the Global Cultural Economy," *Public Culture* 2 (1990): 4–5.

10. Appadurai, "Disjuncture," 4; this subject is at the center of Susan Stewart's work, especially in *On Longing,* and *Crimes of Writing.*

11. Susan Stewart, "Notes on Distressed Genres," *Journal of American Folklore* 104 (1991): 27, reprinted in *Crimes of Writing.*

12. I provide an overview of this history in "Phantoms of Romantic Nationalism in Folklore," *Journal of American Folklore* 106 (1993): 1–37.

13. Nathan Gardel, "Two Concepts of Nationalism: An Interview with Isaiah Berlin," *New York Review of Books,* November 21, 1991, 19. My thanks to Dan Ben-Amos for bringing this interview to my attention.

14. Elizabeth L. Eisenstein, *The Printing Press as an Agent of Change: Communication and Cultural Transformations in Early-Modern Europe* (Cambridge: Cambridge University Press, 1979), 43–162.

15. Richard Price, *Observation on the Importance of the American Revolution* (London, 1785), 57–58, quoted in Leo Marx, *The Machine in the Garden: Technology and the Pastoral Ideal* (New York: Oxford University Press, 1964), 105.

16. James Madison, *The Federalist Papers,* vol. 14, ed. John C. Hamilton (Philadelphia: J. B. Lippincott, 1906), 136.

17. John F. Sears, *Sacred Places: American Tourist Attractions in the Nineteenth Century* (Oxford: Oxford University Press, 1989).

18. Ralph Waldo Emerson, "The Young American," in *The Collected Works of Ralph Waldo Emerson,* vol. 1 (Cambridge, Mass.: Harvard University Press, 1971), 244.

19. William Gilmore Simms, quoted in Michael Kammen, *A Season of Youth: The American Revolution and the Historical Imagination* (Ithaca, N.Y.: Cornell University Press, 1978), 25.

20. Susan G. Davis, *Parades and Power: Street Theater in Philadelphia* (Philadelphia: Temple University Press, 1986).

21. The process of canonical privileging of certain forms of traditional expression is described nicely by Stewart, "Notes on Distressed Genres," 5–32, for those genres seized on during the eighteenth century and deployed to produce "natural" and "naive" literary effects: the ballad, fairy tale, proverb, and fable.

22. See the last chapter of my *Singing the Master.*

23. See Barbara Kirshenblatt-Gimblett, "Mistaken Dichotomies," *Journal of American Folklore* 101 (1988): 143.

Part 2

Protecting Biocultural Diversity

7

Thailand's Tourism Paradox: Identity and Nationalism as Factors in Tourism Development

Erve Chambers

Tourism has become one of the largest industries in the world. For some Third World and lesser developed countries, international tourism has become the major source of foreign exchange, outstripping these countries' agricultural and industrial production. These trends are expected to continue and intensify as the populations of the more economically fortunate nations continue to age, increasing the number of high-income employed and retired individuals who have both the means and desire to travel. Although it is only beginning to receive attention as a serious research subject for social scientists, tourism has clearly become a major economic and cultural force in the modern world. In both its negative and positive impact, international tourism development has come to play a major role in issues related to cultural and environmental conservation.

The paradox described in this essay can be generalized to global issues related to tourism and conservation. On the one hand, tourism helps draw international attention to a country or region's cultural and environmental resources—beaches, forests, people, and their traditions become prized commodities worthy of protection, in terms of both their function in promoting and preserving national or regional integrity and their value in attracting international visitors. On the other hand, like most industries, large-scale tourism development poses considerable threat to the very resources on which it depends. The potentially negative effects of tourism include rapid environmental degradation, the introduction or escalation of social and health problems, and the alteration and disruption of distinct cultural traditions. Recent attempts to mitigate the cultural and environmental risks associated with tourism have included strategies that focus on community or local participation in tourism development (usually labeled "appropriate," "alternative," or "sustainable" tourism) and initiatives that both capitalize on and seek to protect environmental resources (such as "nature" or "eco" tourism). For the most part, these models of tourism planning have been developed in the West, and little serious attention has been devoted to assessing their applicability to non-Western contexts. In anthropology, a discipline that might be expected to contribute much to such an effort, response to the issues posed by international tourism has been minimal, and where anthropologists have considered alternative approaches to tourism planning, their approach has tended to be partisan and uncritical.

Malcolm Crick is correct in arguing that most of the anthropological research devoted to tourism has come about as an afterthought, is biased toward negative instances, and treats tourism as a singular impact, without adequate regard for other historic or contemporary influences on the communities we study.[1] We go to distant places to study something else, discover that the tourists have already arrived, and cloak our disappointment in brief and summary articles of disdain. There are notable exceptions, but in the main anthropologists have devoted nowhere near the sustained attention to tourism that they have to other indexes of cultural change and economic development.

Given these limitations, it might be considered premature to ask how social inquiry can be *applied* to problems in tourism development and planning. This would be the case if we held that application can only follow the laying of a solid base of empirical research. In this case, however, it is more likely that such a base will be established as a direct result of applied work and the inevitable contradictions that arise as we attempt to shape our inquiries to practical ends. Recent publications indicate that this process has already begun and that there is a clear relationship between attitudes toward tourism development and the framing of tourism research.[2]

A major contribution of anthropological research to the problems posed by international tourism lies in its focus on ethnographic inquiry and the attempt to represent those "local voices" that are least likely to be considered in most other approaches to the topic.[3] This contribution appears most consistent with the advocacy of tourism strategies that are deemed to be "appropriate" or "sustainable" by virtue of their attention to local-level experiences and initiatives and that promise to be ecologically responsible in their concern with relationships between culture and the environment. There are, however, dangers to limiting our inquiries in such a way. One is that removed from the full range of concerns faced by tourism planners and developers, our representations are easily ignored. Another is that the models most likely to shape our inquiries, such as those of appropriate development or ecotourism, remain susceptible to ethnocentric interpretations. What is appropriate or even ecologically reasonable in one cultural setting might not be so in another. In their furthest extreme, our good intentions carry with them the potential of modern intellectual imperialism.

This essay follows four years of intermittent research in Thailand. Most of my work has been devoted to ethnographic research, with the original aim of better understanding the impact of tourism on "hill tribe" peoples in the northern provinces of Chiang Mai and Mae Hong Son. This research has expanded to include consideration of the effects of international tourism on relations between these northern provinces and the Thai central government and an attempt to place tourism in the even broader contexts of Thai identity and political economy. Although space permits only a cursory discussion of some of these issues, I argue here that inclusion of these perspectives is a vital component of tourism research.

Thailand's Tourism Boom

In 1986 Thailand inaugurated its Year of the Tourist, a campaign to encourage international tourism on a larger scale than the country had previously enjoyed. The promotion was designed to draw attention to Thailand's cultural heritage and recreational resources, in anticipation of increasing visits by families. It was hoped that success would lessen the country's reliance on solo male travelers, who came to Thailand primarily to participate in the sex trade.[4] The 1986 campaign surpassed its planners' expectations and has been followed by similar annual promotions. The rate of growth in international tourist visits has exceeded 20 percent each year for the past four years, and family visitors have begun to account for a respectable share of the total visitor count. Tourism has replaced rice as Thailand's principal "export" industry, becoming the country's major source of foreign currency. The success of Thailand's promotion has drawn the attention of other Southeast Asian countries. Both Malaysia and Indonesia have recently inaugurated their own Year of the Tourist campaigns.

Although nearly all visits to Thailand begin in the capital of Bangkok, the tourism boom has resulted in unprecedented growth of the tourist sector in the country's northwestern and southern provinces. These regions were less prepared to accommodate larger numbers of tourists, but a rapid development of facilities and accommodations virtually transformed the most popular tourist destinations in a matter of a few years. Significantly, at the beginning of the fourth year following the Year of the Tourist, the Tourism Authority of Thailand did not announce a new theme campaign but decided to devote that year's effort to solving some of the environmental and cultural problems associated with rapid tourism development.

In the northwest of Thailand tourism is centered on the city of Chiang

Mai, described traditionally and in tourist brochures as the Rose of the North. Much of the present-day tourist appeal of Chiang Mai rests with the region's ethnic diversity. The province is populated by several distinct hill people, whose handicrafts (or reasonable facsimiles) are readily available to tourists in the city's popular night market. Coach and walking tours to hill tribe villages are advertised throughout the city. The growth of the trekking industry in Chiang Mai is remarkable. When I first visited the area in 1986, I counted less than twenty agencies offering treks. Three years later I was able to identify more than seventy such agencies. Competition among the agencies to provide unique trekking experiences among "remote tribes not visited by tourists" has become intense.

Tourism development in the south of Thailand is largely limited to beach and island resort areas. Again, the impact of tourism development is readily apparent. In some areas close to Bangkok, such as Pattaya, the community infrastructure seems close to collapse. Water and electricity shortages, suffered much more intensely by the local population than by tourists, have become commonplace. The Gulf of Thailand is so thoroughly polluted along the Pattaya coastline that swimming is discouraged everywhere except in the pools of luxury hotels. Other popular beach areas, such as the islands of Phuket and Samui, are developing so rapidly that some beach areas are almost unrecognizable from one year to the next. The increasingly high costs of land, rents, and food have forced much of the local population from this prime real estate and made many others dependent for their livelihood on marginal employment in the tourism sector.

For these local populations the potential benefits of tourism, such as opportunities for small-business enterprise and employment, are minimized by competition with outside investors and job-seekers. Much of the capital accumulated as a result of Thailand's recent economic boom has been invested in land speculation and tourism development. Additional capital has been supplied by foreign investors, although not as intensely as in some other popular international tourist destinations. While large-scale tourism development does provide increased employment opportunity, the most desirable positions are seldom available to locals, who generally lack the training, education, or personal contacts that would permit them to compete with applicants from Bangkok's professional elite, whose education has generally exceeded middle-level career opportunities.

Although public demonstrations are rare in Thailand, recent tourism development has given rise to protests in both the northwest and the south. In Chiang Mai local groups banded together to halt the construction of a cable car to the top of Doi Suthep, a significant Buddhist mountain retreat. They have been less successful in their efforts to control new hotel and condominium construction in the city. In the south, some residents of the island of Phuket and other Thai have demonstrated repeatedly against the development of a new tourist complex that would encompass much of the remaining "free" beach available to island residents.

The government of Thailand recognizes both the benefits and problems that have accompanied this phenomenal spurt in tourist activity. Its success in promoting tourism has come to endanger the very resources on which the industry depends. How the Thai confront these problems will be of considerable interest. Their success will depend in some part on their willingness to profit from the experience of other nations, but it will also hinge on their ability to shape their responses to their unique circumstances.

The Regional Impact of Tourism

Compared with other forms of international commerce, tourism is an intensely personal and rapid medium of exchange, distinguished by the diffuse nature of its investments. It serves to transform human and environmental resources into specific kinds of commodities, sometimes in association with other major social and economic changes and sometimes in contradistinction to those other changes. Thus, a significant community ritual might become transformed into a tourist display, or a locally important marine industry might be forced into competition with increased recreational use of a beach front. Before social research can be useful to planners, or even of much legitimate benefit in the ongoing debate concerning the human costs of international tourism, we need to be able to refine our ability to perform at least two tasks. First, we must be able to separate the impact of tourism from that of other change and development activities. Ethnography is probably the key to this ability, because it is the one approach in which the activities particular to tourism can be directly identified and observed over time. Second, we need to recognize that ethnographic research on tourism is not easily generalized from one setting to the next. The ethnography of communities is not likely to lead us far in this regard.

Even within Thailand the impact of tourism in the northwestern mountains poses different problems and possibilities than it does in the southern coastal areas. Much of the research on tourism among Thailand's ethnic minorities treats tourism as a singular effect visited on relatively isolated people.[5] This research almost invariably fails to offer any means to separate the effects of tourism from the effects of other development activities in the region. Tourism, because it involves face-to-face interaction, is simply the most visible (and to some observers the most unseemly) of the social and economic effects on these regions. Yet it is possible that it is also among the most benign of influences—certainly more benign than, for example, the Vietnam War and its aftershocks throughout this region of Southeast Asia and almost certainly more benign than the large-scale resettlement and agricultural experimentation currently being visited on the minority hill people.

It can be argued that tourism in these regions is in many cases a positive factor in conserving cultural identity and promoting some degree of appreciation for Thailand's minority people. International tourism has, for instance, dramatically increased the visibility of the hill people—a cultural minority who are not indigenous to the region, who almost never hold title or recognized claim to the lands they have settled, and who have in the past been systematically discriminated against by the ethnic Thai. In a sense tourists have, out of their interest in the hill people, helped make them a valued part of the imagery of Thailand.[6]

I will offer two simple observations in this regard. The first is that, since the Year of the Tourist campaign five years ago, there has been a noticeable shift in the amount of positive attention paid to the hill people by Thailand's media. They have become the subjects of popular music, they have been featured with a degree of fairness in television soap operas and dramas, and they (or ethnic Thai dressed like hill people) have been regularly employed in television advertising. As never before, the unique dress, appearance, and experience of the hill people are beginning to take shape as a part of the Thai national identity.

My other observation comes in the form of a small irony. Increasingly concerned over the possible impact of tourist treks among the hill tribes, the Tourism Authority of Thailand recently issued a pamphlet for visitors. One piece of advice was to refrain from giving hill people items of clothing, because such gifts only encouraged them to abandon their traditional dress. Yet, in my experience of the region, it was in the more remote and less likely to be visited villages that one was most likely to encounter people wearing Grateful Dead T-shirts and Nike running shorts. Traditional dress was far more likely to be seen in areas that were heavily visited—the people themselves had correctly perceived their unique finery as valuable commodities and representatives of worth in this strange market.

In the northwest of Thailand, people, their customs and appearances, are a major tourism resource. Because the region is vast and the commodity is both sentient and readily available, this area might be described as a "frontier zone" of tourism development. As such, it is comparatively open to entrepreneurship that requires little capital investment, making it possible for previously marginalized people to commoditize themselves and realize significant profit from the exchange. In this respect a kind of "trickle down" economy does seem to be operating in the region. The capital-rich investors who supply the new first-class hotels to Chiang Mai certainly realize the greater share of profits from the tourist industry, but there is substantial opportunity for others to benefit as well.[7]

Tourism shows a different face in the south of Thailand, where the major commodity is a physical environment that is limited to the carrying capacity of suitable beach recreation areas. Here competition to develop beach resorts, capitalized largely by Bangkok and foreign investors, has pushed most of the local population to the periphery of the tourist market. Although there are increased opportunities for service-related employment, wages are low and more than offset by the rapidly rising costs of shelter and food. Local populations bear the brunt of the shortages of water, electricity, and other community services. The situation of ethnic minorities in the south is especially revealing. There has been little effort to draw tourist attention to the distinct Muslim communities of the south or to the scattered aboriginal groups, such as Thailand's "Sea Gypsies." Dependent on the sea for much of their livelihood, many of these people have been displaced by large-scale tourist development.

A lesson to be derived from this comparison is that the commoditization of culture, so often decried by observers of international tourism, might deserve a second look. Without discounting the dangers tourism often poses to community values and social structure, the commoditization of tradition that is peculiar to ethnic tourism can in some instances accord these people previously unrecognized value in their lands and can to some degree shield them from many other undesirable consequences of the nearly inevitable modernization with which they are faced.

Ecologies and Buddhism

Modern, liberal Western ideology extends special status and a protectionist ethic to both the environment and ethnic minorities. This tendency has developed in association with Western rationality and is consistent with a belief in linear progress and social reformation, as well as with a Christian perspective that awards stewardship of the earth to humankind. To the extent that contemporary concerns for the impact of tourism are driven by these same ideologies, we miss important steps in the assessment of these problems across cultures. For example, a recent advertisement for a new edited volume on ecotourism stated that although the case studies for the book were devoted to Latin America and the Caribbean, "its analysis applies worldwide."[8] This cannot be true.

Thailand is a Buddhist nation. Thai attitudes toward the environment and toward cultural minorities are more complex than they might at first seem. On the one hand, Buddhism is a religion that espouses reverence for all forms of life as well as tolerance of human differences. On the other hand, Buddhist belief in long and inevitable cycles of prosperity and decline and in the concepts of individual karma and merit shifts its cultural and environmental concerns in directions that do not fully correspond to Western belief.

In Thailand most popular complaints concerning tourism and its association with environmental degradation focus on aesthetic rather than ecological issues—shrines and beaches littered with garbage, even rapidly biodegradable garbage, are more likely to be held as examples than are the less visible pollutants and environmental degradation that can be associated with increased population densities, overuse of natural resources, and the construction of luxury tourist facilities. There are, of course, professionals in Thailand who are vitally concerned with these issues, but I doubt the general public fully shares their view—and this is due not so much to a lack of exposure to the problems as to the fact that, in contrast to much of Western thought, the idea of a degenerating and decaying environment is neither an alien nor an altogether alarming concept.[9]

The relationship between ecology and religion in Thailand may be even more difficult for Westerners to appreciate because of Thailand's unique historical circumstances. As the country began to modernize along Western lines at the turn of the nineteenth century, Thailand's King Mongkut adopted the policy of deliberately maintaining institutional separation between Western science and Thailand's Buddhist faith.[10] This policy established a powerful precedent for maintaining separation between the two ideologies, leaving the promise of technological development to Western science and responsibility for cultural preservation to Buddhism. Areas of inquiry and concern where, at least in the Western view, technology and culture coincide, as they do in modern ecology and cultural conservation, are likely to be expressed much differently in Thailand than they are in Western nations.

Similarly, in terms of human populations, the Buddhist doctrine that closely links fate with individual merit and reincarnation contrasts sharply with Western beliefs. The minority people who seem most vulnerable to tourist development, the hill people of the north and ethnic minorities in the south, are not as a rule Buddhists. Their governance and their protection, however, are entrusted to a sovereign Buddhist nation. I am not certain what the Buddhist position is in this regard, although I do know that in popular Buddhist faith such intangibles as luck and material demonstrations of reverence figure strongly in any final measure of human worth. To each their own life, and to each their own destiny. The cultural minorities of Thailand have been able to maintain their uniqueness partly because of the Buddhist doctrine of noninterference. By the same token, as threats to their uniqueness come increasingly from outside the nation, to some extent as a result of tourism, Buddhist attitudes provide little motivation for actively defending these people.

Robert C. Lester describes two other aspects of Theravada Buddhism, practiced in Thailand, that suggest significant differences in attitudes toward social and environment change.[11] First, Theravada Buddhism emphasizes individual moral development, arguing that the improvement of individuals is the prerequisite to social betterment. Second, popular Buddhism has a tendency to favor development and to approve of economic growth, because prosperity is the basis from which one is able to perform those acts of merit essential to individual religious development.

Does this mean that Buddhism is an obstacle to planning for an ecologically responsible approach to the problem of tourism? It does, I believe, only if the ecology we imagine is based solely on Western principles. Religion and politics are closely linked in Thailand.[12] There is precedent for an alliance between Western scientific approaches and technological development, but when development impinges on matters of culture, these advantages seem to wane. Regarding the protection of both human and natural resources, it seems likely that religion will play a significant role in defining the terms of an appropriate ecology.

The Bureaucratization of Tourism Planning

Thailand has a highly centralized government, with most of its public activity and nearly all of its authority emanating from Bangkok, the capital.[13] Tourism development in the United States, while encouraged by federal agencies, is left largely to local governments and chambers of commerce. In Thailand nearly all matters of tourism development are in the hands of the central government, which decides what regions of the country are to be targeted for development, how they will be promoted, and in great part who will participate. This centralized base of power largely accounts for the Tourism Authority's successes over the past several years.[14] It also poses fresh problems as the country begins to face the consequences of tourism.

Thailand's government bureaucracy is not only centralized but also highly balkanized. There is comparatively little precedent for cooperation between government agencies. This poses a distinct problem in dealing with such issues as the environment and cultural minorities. The northern hill peoples, for example, are subject to the policies of a great variety of central government agencies concerned with such matters as internal and external security, narcotics control, education, health, forestry, and tourism. Cooperation and joint endeavors between these agencies are rare.

It might seem that a solution to these problems would be to encourage greater local participation in such matters as tourism development, but such a solution is not likely to be easily realized. The traditions that continue to support centralization of decision making are too numerous to recount here, but a single example might be helpful. In very real terms, not so many decades ago and even today in symbolic terms, the Thai have maintained that the ownership of their land is vested in the monarchy rather than held as inalienable private property. Any attempt to "localize" control over natural and human resources will have to consider, among other things, this still vital relation to central authority.

One argument for sustainable development is that communities know how to manage their local resources better than central authorities do. This model has recently been introduced in Thailand in the form of "social forestry," one of several responses to the rapid depletion of the country's rain forests. So far, social forestry is still in an experimental stage and limited to work in a few model communities. A comparison of the issues related to deforestation and tourism would be useful, because they involve many of the same actors in issues pertaining to land tenure, resource exploitation, and cultural differences. There is a relation, for example, between the northern hill peoples' increased interest in tourism as a revenue source and the government's attempts to discourage them from practicing slash and burn agriculture, which Thai authorities tend to view as destructive to the country's forest reserves.

Regarding tourism and local control, it is worth noting that the traditions of local communities do not always equip them to cope with the changes accompanying rapid development. Western or Thai, the visitor to many remote hill villages will be impressed first by the amount of industrially manufactured garbage strewn about these villages. The traditional response to waste was efficient enough—throw it off the porch to feed the animals below. Unfortunately, although this practice continues, no one has yet found an animal that can thrive on mounds of plastic bags, film containers, and cigarette filters.

While Thai national tourism policy and planning are centralized, there is also a strong tradition in the country for local independent action in implementing national policies.[15] What this implies for tourism development is that the central government can, through the manipulation of transportation routes, promotions, and investments, be successful in directing tourism to particular areas of the country, but it is relatively helpless to control the rate or kind of growth that occurs once a tourist area becomes popular. In this respect the country is clearly victimized by its own rapid modernization. The relative independence of local governments (extending, in the past, all the way down to the *muang*, or village) was encouraged both by distance from the capital and the prior existence of many parts of Thailand as semi-independent principalities.[16] Modernization, including the effects of rapid tourism development, has helped erode the barriers that insulated these localities from Bangkok's influence. The irony of this situation is that effective local control over those resources that are most endangered by activities like tourism is likely to come about only as a result of increased national involvement in local affairs.

Nationalism and Tourism

Sometimes it is rewarding to ask naive questions. A question I have routinely asked while traveling in Thailand's provinces is, "Do you think tourism is good or bad?" The answer I usually get is that tourism is good for Thailand but not necessarily good for the places tourists visit. There are important distinctions here. First, most informants regard the "good" of tourism not simply in economic terms but also in relation to Thailand's increased status in Southeast Asia and the world community. Second, most of the people I have talked with regard themselves not only as Thai and responsible to the nation but also as closely linked to other regions or ethnic claims. These relationships are often seen as oppositional. Because tourism has become such an important part of Thailand's development, it provides a mirror for the society as a whole, reflecting in myriad ways what the Thai people think about themselves.

Tourism development is closely linked to Thailand's continuing struggle to assert its nationhood, in relation to both its own populace and its place among other nations. Here it is important to keep in mind that although Thailand has been around a long time, its arrival as a modern nation-state is comparatively recent. With the exception of Bangkok, most of the now popular tourist destinations in modern Thailand were, until the end of the nineteenth century, quasi-independent or tributary states of Siam. The incorporation of these states into modern Thailand is a process that is politically accomplished but symbolically incomplete. Tourism encourages these populations to reassert their uniqueness, and it also helps define the ways in which the central government attempts to incorporate regional symbols into a Thai national identity. To some extent, tourism and the taste and interests of international tourists are helping redefine what it is to be Thai.

As mentioned earlier, tourism has recently contributed to public demonstrations and protests, each of which has reflected regional dissatisfaction with central authority. It is likely that there will be similar confrontations in the future. One reason is because tourism actually has had a considerable impact, but I think another reason is because tourism is a comparatively "safe" issue to protest—it is safe because the tourists are not Thai (or, rather, the tourists likely to get the blame are not Thai). What this suggests to me is that complaints about tourism often carry the weight of a more general public dissatisfaction with the uneven development and distribution of resources that is typical of Thailand's rapid modernization. Complaints about tourism are representative of a larger unrest concerning issues that are less safe to protest. To the extent that this is true, it becomes even more difficult to arrive at an understanding of the actual impact that can be attributed directly to tourism development.

Here again it is important to recognize the central government's major role in tourism development. In the provinces international tourists are in effect seen as emanating from Bangkok, and the relationships of visitor and host are often subtly cast in these terms. This is a historical as well as contemporary relationship. Its precedent was established before the turn of the past century by treaties with Western nations that guaranteed Bangkok's cooperation in assuring the access and protection of Western travelers to provinces, which at the time were barely under the control of the central government. For more than a hundred years foreign travelers to Thailand's hinterlands have thus served as emissaries of a somewhat reluctant but accommodating central government. Over the past several years tourism has also come to play a major role in establishing Thailand's relationship with its neighboring states. It is a spearhead in the Thai government's attempt to solve some of the problems of mainland Southeast Asia through economic cooperation and development rather than armed conflict. Thailand is currently actively encouraging joint tourism development projects with Burma, Laos, and Vietnam. There is a potential for considerable advantage in these exchanges, both for the cash-poor countries on Thailand's borders and for Thailand, which is well positioned to serve as the hub for travel throughout Southeast Asia. There is also increased risk to these countries, especially their environments and cultural minorities, as they open their doors to tourists.

Still, it must be kept in mind that initiatives such as these do hold the possibility of lessened hostilities in this politically fragile part of our world. Thailand offers a model in this respect. Increased economic reliance on tourism has become a major factor encouraging political and regional stability. Active representation of the interests of those people who are most likely to suffer the effects of tourism must take into account the now vital role tourism plays in the country's continuing process of nationalization.

Conclusion

To the extent that we treat international tourism as a wholly modern, unique, and purely "foreign" phenomenon, unconnected to a host country's historical development, we are tempted to oversimplify the means by which solutions can be found for those aspects of tourism that do harm the environment and human cultures. Moreover, to the extent that we judge the effects of tourism to be largely the same wherever they occur and focus on those effects that seem clearly harmful, we are likely to neglect those indigenous responses that are most promising of a solution.

My argument is that we cannot fully appreciate the importance or measure the risks of large-scale tourism development in Thailand until we understand that it is about more than building big hotels, making some money, and exploiting the environment and its people. It is also about belief and articles of faith, about traditions of control and allegiance to authority, and about how these are reproduced in a people's relation to their land. It is also about identity and nationhood, about fundamental struggles to determine what it is to be Thai, and in a very real sense about a commonly held, even if differently realized, desire for peace and relative prosperity.

NOTES

1. Malcolm Crick, "Representations of International Tourism in the Social Sciences," *Annual Review of Anthropology* 18 (1989): 307–38.

2. Elizabeth Boo, *Ecotourism: The Potentials and Pitfalls* (Baltimore: World Wildlife Fund, 1990); Benita J. Howell, ed., *Cultural Heritage Conservation in the American South,* Southern Anthropological Society Proceedings, no. 23 (Athens: University of Georgia Press, 1990); Barbara R. Johnston, ed., *Breaking Out of the Tourist Trap,* special issue of *Cultural Conservation Quarterly* 14, no. 1 and 2 (1990).

3. Crick, "Representations of International Tourism," 307–44.

4. Linda K. Richter, *The Politics of Tourism in Asia* (Honolulu: University of Hawaii Press, 1989).

5. Eric Cohen, "The Impact of Tourism on the Physical Environment," *International Asianforum* 10 (1979): 5–38; Edith T. Mirante, "Hostages to Tourism," *Cultural Survival Quarterly* 14 (1990): 35–38.

6. Several distinct minority people, such as the Hmong, Karen, Lahu, Meo, Akha, and Lisu, are commonly linked by the "hill tribe" designation. It is of interest to note that tourism reinforces the distinctiveness of these people among themselves, if only in the way tourists are encouraged to "collect" visits to as many different groups as possible. This process serves as a partial corrective to the tendency of the ethnic Thai to regard the hill people with increased disregard for the ethnic distinctiveness of the several groups.

7. There are any number of provisos to this attempt to point to some of the potentially positive features of ethnic tourism. For example, much of the control over tourist visits to hill villages is in the hands of tour groups based in Chiang Mai, and villages that chose to participate in tourism are subject to the heavy-handness of some urban tour guides. Competition among the tour groups for access to unique trekking experiences has clearly put some villages at risk and endangered groups as well as individuals.

8. *Cultural Survival Quarterly* 14 (1990): 19.

9. Jeffrey A. McNeely and Paul Spencer Wachtel, *Soul of the Tiger* (New York: Doubleday, 1988).

10. Yoneo Ishii, *Sangha, State, and Society: Thai Buddhism in History* (Honolulu: University of Hawaii Press, 1986).

11. Robert C. Lester, *Theravada Buddhism in Southeast Asia* (Ann Arbor: University of Michigan Press, 1973).

12. K. M. de Silva, Pensri Duke, Ellen S. Goldberg, and Nathan Katz, eds., *Ethnic Conflict in Buddhist Societies: Sri Lanka, Thailand and Burma* (Boulder, Colo.: Westview Press, 1988); Bardwell L. Smith, ed., *Religion and Legitimation of Power in Thailand, Laos, and Burma* (Chambersburg, Penn.: ANIMA Books, 1978); Somboon Suksamran, *Buddhism and Politics in Thailand* (Singapore: Institute of Southeast Asian Studies, 1982).

13. John L. S. Girling, *Thailand: Society and Politics* (Ithaca, N.Y.: Cornell University Press, 1981).

14. James Elliot, "Politics, Power, and Tourism in Thailand," *Annals of Tourism Research* 10 (1983): 377–83.

15. Voradej Chandarasorn and Likhit Dhiravegin, "Policy Implementation in the Thai Public Bureaucracy," *Southeast Asian Journal of Social Science* 15 (1987): 96–106.

16. David K. Wyatt, *Thailand: A Short History* (New Haven, Conn.: Yale University Press, 1984).

8

Managerial Ecology and Lineage Husbandry: Environmental Dilemmas in Zambia's Luangwa Valley

Stuart A. Marks

These days some Africans are arguing that they have been following the wrong models of development. These models were either borrowed from or imposed on them by the industrialized states in the Northern Hemisphere. Along with this argument has come the recognition that ultimately they as Africans are responsible for their choices and that development must become based on the cultural strengths of their own peoples.[1]

I frame my essay on the contentious issue of wildlife in central Africa within this realization. Europeans, Americans, and increasingly Africans trained in Northern institutions see this wildlife primarily as a "world" resource, as a stock commodity, and seek to incorporate it into their own myths and harness it for their own purposes. They have intervened repeatedly as the numbers of large mammals have declined perceptively, beginning with the active European conquests of central African territory in the 1880s. Northerners have subsequently sought hegemony over "the wildlife problem" and its continuing resolution.

I wish to illustrate this issue by discussing perspectives from the statements of two proponents, one a Northerner and the other a more localized talent. Both were contemporaries; both now belong to history.[2] Having known and talked with both men, I find admirable points about each and wish to make neither a hero or a villain. They never met as far as I know; had they had that opportunity, the exchanges would have been decidedly one-sided, given the breeding and bearing of the Northerner. Yet others of similar inclinations met, clashed, fought, and suffered casualties without resolving their differences.

At issue are cultural traditions, ways of perceiving and acting in the world, and ideas about life and livelihoods, about participation and place, and about who is involved and how. I propose no resolution other than to suggest a groping for a more inclusive vocabulary and the beginnings of more conciliatory behaviors.

Managerial Ecology

The Northern engagement with wildlife in central Africa began in the nineteenth century. Those attitudes and behavior were embedded in their struggles to replace the slave and ivory trades with more "legitimate" commerce while taming the landscape and its people for Christianity and administrative control.[3] I begin here with Sir Julian Huxley, for he articulated the "modern synthesis" of "the wildlife problem" in the 1960s. The basic components of his model are still accepted by most Northerners today. His words describe this mode, which I label managerial ecology.

In 1960 Sir Julian Huxley was sent by the United Nations Educational, Scientific, and Cultural Organization (UNESCO), an international body that he helped establish as its first director-general, to review and make recommendations on the wildlife sanctuaries in eastern and central Africa.[4] For Northern scientists and resource managers, a major environmental crisis was pending beyond that of the imminent political independence of former colonies. Wildlife, "of enormous potential importance if properly used," was "gravely diminished . . . threatened in the immediate future." Detractors from an "ideal natural state" were many; most were endemic to the African environment. Huxley mentions the "alarming increase in organized poaching, [and] the equally alarming increase in population." These factors, together with state-of-the-art methods for controlling tsetse flies and diseases in livestock (removing wildlife from vast areas through shooting), administrative inclinations toward technological and agricultural development over practical endeavors with wild animals in their naturals habitats, the monetization of "tribal" economies, and the rapid rise toward all-African governments, were adversely stacked against the survival of the continent's natural endowments of fauna and flora. Despite the gloomy pessimism of those times, Huxley's outlook was "tempered optimism," an optimism based on an increasing worldwide interest in nature and ecological science. Ecological science would dictate "the proper approach to the practical problems involved."

The situation in central Africa was salvageable "provided that the conservationists can induce African governments and the African public to understand and follow the ecological approach." Huxley sought to frame this problem in objective terms: "The ecological problem is fundamentally one of balancing resources against human needs, both in the short and in the long term. It must be related to a proper evaluation of human needs,

Figure 8.1. Sir Julian Huxley. (Photo by W. Suschitzky; courtesy of UNESCO)

and it must be based on resource conservation and resource use, including optimum land use and conservation of the habitat."[5] Ecology was "the science of interrelations." For Huxley and others like him the balance in those relationships was oriented toward the past, was against indigenous thoughts and acts, and was equivalent to the new synthesis of Northern ideas about how nature worked. His belief in the universality of Northern criteria for rationality remained unshaken.

Basic to Huxley's model was an "original ecosystem," which "has suffered vast damages at the hands of man." There were two main variables, habitat and wildlife, with reciprocal dependencies. In the past millennium African occupation of this habitat had "unconsciously transformed and largely degraded the habitat" in a process that, within the last one hundred years, had been "great[ly] and alarming[ly] accelerate[d]" under European/Northern influences. To avoid disaster, "we must learn to control the process"—to "plan the future of the habitat." Wildlife was "no longer merely a local matter." "What is needed," he maintained, "is a bold official conservation policy based on scientific research, backed by world opinion and furnished with adequate finance."

Habitat control remained the key to the preservation of wildlife. The lock sought on habitat degradation was the proliferation of national parks. "They give some guarantee of permanence," Huxley asserted, "since they are established by legislation, and can only be abolished by further legislative action."[6]

Huxley thought that as a "resource of unique value," wildlife through the "proper management of wild lands can yield a large crop of wild meat as well as numerous ancillary animal and plant products." The importance of "proper management" was to reduce "poaching"—whose abolition had become the compelling goal, for it, "like the slave trade," was "profitable, highly organized, extremely cruel, and quite ruthless." Huxley's litany against "poachers" is long and elaborate, disclosing more about his apprehensions than about poachers' enterprise. "One of the numerous urgencies in the situation is," he believed, "the need to change the attitude of Africans to conservation in general and wild life in particular, and to help them to understand its value to themselves and their countries."[7] The attitude of "most tribal Africans" toward wildlife, characterized as "either a pest to be destroyed or simply as meat on the hoof to be killed and eaten," could "be changed only by satisfying the region's natural meat-hunger." "In particular, once local Africans understand that organized game cropping can provide them with more and probably cheaper meat than organized poaching, and that illicit individual shooting is killing the goose that lays the golden eggs, they will begin to see wild life, and all the measures designed to conserve it, in a very different light."[8]

I could continue with Huxley and others during the 1950s and 1960s. Many of these ideas were expressed somewhat earlier by Sir Frank Fraser Darling and implemented later by a disastrous Food and Agriculture

Organization of the United Nations (FAO) Conservation Project in Zambia.[9] My point is that Huxley and Darling synthesized an enduring paradigm during the uncertain political and economic climate of the late 1950s. Among its planks were the application of universal principles and knowledge ("science") controlled largely by Northern practitioners, state management and control supported by revenues from tourism, wildlife "cropping," safari hunting, and its edicts enforced by a large corps of protectors (in local idioms, "the animal police"). Despite recent "superficial" changes, such as the nationalization of the civil service in state wildlife departments, ideas about local participation, and revenue sharing for development projects, these same planks remain in vogue. Search through any recent development document, and one finds the ubiquitous vocabulary of managerial ecology, with its emphasis on "control," "objectives," "strategies," "monitors," "production," "indicators," and "sustainable"—all metaphors from the industrialized/Northern, if not bureaucratic, world.

This African world is held together largely with Northern funding and by consultants whose status stems from their research "there" or indigenous staff with education and experiences "abroad." This framework of government, education, and influential lobbies provides the structures upon which rests a particular construction of what wildlife is about. This construct is energized by the monetary flows of the Northern tourists and research trades, their consuming interests, and foreign aid. In this view, wild animals are found in designated landscapes (national parks, game reserves, wildlife management areas), where they are displayed and interpreted by staffs of corporations holding rights delimited by states and are cared for by a corps of professionals who have their own theories about what is going on in the "natural world." Individuals outside of those sanctioned networks, whose values and actions are informed differently, are summarily dismissed. With the state's environmental bureaucracies staffed by managerial ecologists, it has been difficult for other voices to be heard.

Lineage Husbandry

In 1966–67 I was a neighbor of Luben Kafupi, even then an elderly man and one Huxley would have readily dismissed as a "poacher." Kafupi lived in the middle of Zambia's Luangwa Valley, a tsetse fly–infested place where it was impossible to raise domesticated livestock (just the type of habitat Huxley was hoping to preserve). As an elder of his lineage and as the village headman (a statutory role sanctioned by the state) for his kin, he survived by participating in shifting cultivation and being a local healer. Kafupi further contributed to the well-being of his family and lineage by killing game and participating occasionally in labor migration to obtain wages (to purchase cloth and pay for school fees and taxes). When I asked him why he hunted and killed local animals, he replied:

> My maternal grandfather, a great hunter, visited me in a dream telling me to find a gun and begin hunting. When I told my maternal uncle about his dream, he advised me to go and purchase a [muzzle-loading] gun in Serenje District. For this I used money earned while working in Wankie [then Southern Rhodesia]. When I returned, my uncle called all of our relatives together. Each elder in my lineage, there were three men and several women, put three white beads on a string and tied them around my gun. My maternal uncle as senior member of the lineage pronounced the following blessing: "Uwaice uyu akwate imfuti. Ayokwendo mutende muchonde. Ayokwipaya inama kulya palupwa." [This youngster now has a gun. May he be protected in the bush and kill animals so the lineage may eat.] Before dispersing, we put other white beads into a *nkombo* [a special gourd with a long handle and an opening for offerings] and it was named and dedicated to my late ancestor.[10]

Kafupi's reasons for hunting were similar in content and contexts to others'. Through the idiom of an ancestral call (dream summons), an individual established a claim to an essential lineage task of providing meat and protection to relatives.[11] Elders (soon ancestors) acted as "gatekeepers" to such claims, allocating their dependents among various activities. An aspiring hunter proved himself by coping with real and imagined dangers in the natural and supernatural worlds and with the petty jealousies and rivalries of those in his social world. In the process he ventures stories about his prowess that became aspirations for his nephews. When successful in killing animals, the hunter distributed portions of the carcasses in accordance with normative expectations; otherwise, he could expect various "afflictions" that he must overcome to continue his activities.

Among local hunters in the Luangwa Valley, prescriptions for successfully overcoming failures of various kinds, interpretations of events, knowledge, awards, incentives, recognition of ancestral guidance, and affiliation within a social field all are expressed within a particular cultural framework (cognitive domain). This framework, or paradigm, I call *lineage husbandry*. It is difficult, maybe impossible, to capture the essence or translate the meanings of *lineage husbandry* into English without undue slippage of contexts and without using a prejudicial vocabulary. Consider the inference that managerial ecology is based on "science," rationality, detailed "objective" observations, and experimental methods. Counterpoised against such positive attributes, the distinctive and different idioms

Figure 8.2. Luben Kafupi, November 1988. (Photo by the author)

of "local knowledge" are often translated as based on magic, superstition, unfounded assertions, and mysticism. As a consequence, I resist further translation here.

The Present Predicament

In 1988–89, while studying environmental and cultural changes in the Luangwa Valley, I again spent some time with Luben Kafupi. He was twenty-five-years older, his vision had dimmed, and he had been succeeded in his role as village headman by a younger nephew. He had not hunted for years, but his role as traditional healer had expanded. In his old age Kafupi was patronized by many whose afflictions were not amenable to Northern medicines. During the twenty-five-year interim his access to wild animals and to other essentials for life had become increasingly scarce and uncertain.

Measures to save the wildlife through the application of managerial ecological practices had created a "commons" situation of open access, depressing wildlife populations throughout the valley. The Luangwa Valley had been carved into three "spheres of influence," each under a different variant of managerial ecology. Each of these spheres had its own Northern manager, its own sources of external funding (one was patronized by a zoological society, and the others received bilateral aid), its own coterie of consultants and experts, and its own connections to Northern institutions for educating their staffs. Although the managers of these spheres espoused the same vocabulary in discussing what they were about—participation, local management, community development, improving rural life—none of these "goods" had percolated down to make a perceptible difference at the village level. My conversations with Kafupi and his neighbors, together with my observations, reveal that their standards of living had progressively declined since we first had met in the 1960s.

Yet Kafupi had successfully passed on his traditions to his sons, grandsons, and nephews, as was evident in my conversations with them. My interviews with local hunters elsewhere in the valley showed not only the survival of local hunting traditions connected to kin and place but also a widespread distrust of government initiatives and hostility toward development initiatives.[12] Their concerns were that supposed guardians of the game (the wildlife scouts together with their bosses) were guilty of killing off more wildlife than the hunters did. These guardians had used their power and prerogatives, including weapons and vehicles supplied by well-intended foreign aid, to enable them to have continued access to the diminishing stocks of game. Once the game was secured, the proceeds went to augment the progressively decreasing standard of living of individual civil servants. Moreover, they had used their authority to abuse local men and women.

To be sure, there were "commercial poachers" as well. Their connections in towns made their rural expeditions for elephant and rhino possible. Some locals had found these outsiders to be more dependable than the government for delivering such essential goods as cooking oil, clothes, money in exchange for their knowledge and skills in showing where the "game" is.

Toward a Resolution

I have discussed wild animals in Zambia's Luangwa Valley as both a resource and a source of conflict between government and local residents. My ethnographic and historical research suggests two frameworks for depicting this dilemma; both have variants, and neither is independent. Techniques, ideas, and actions within one framework have developed often in response to those within the other. *Managerial ecology* is concerned with wildlife as commodities (stocks), and its survival is dependent on Northern finance, expertise, technology, and "universal" knowledge. It is linked with tourism, wildlife cropping, safari hunting, and a large corps of protectors to assure revenue for government. *Lineage husbandry* is dependent on local knowledge and use, local subscription, and specific cultural forms, and it is place- and kin-based. Since there has been no agreed upon accommodation between the two camps, both have been hard on the resources. "Poaching" is pandemic. The problem remains how to link the two frameworks in words and deeds to conserve the tangibles and the intangibles of wildlife about which both are concerned.

I frame my intuitions this way. Wildlife is a cultural construction. Despite the commonplace assertion in the humanities and social sciences that no "objectively prescribed animal" exists and that physical nature is endowed with multiple, socially constructed realities, I find such flexible ideas scarce among my biological (ecological) colleagues. The shape wildlife takes at any given moment is more than the tangible aspects of an individual species or "resource," the normal discourse for biologists. My perspective begins with the realization that wildlife "problems" are not so much mistaken assessments of nature as they are miscalculations and errors of access and human relationships. In central Africa the rural groups most affected by past wildlife "constructions" were never consulted and today still are not, given the isolation of formal bureaucracy and the distance between where policy is made and where it is implemented. Bureaucrats and technicians often approach "problems" as if they were without history. Neither invests the time to research why their theories may be inappropriate in a different cultural or environmental context. Rural inhabitants are likely to be just as parochial in their views and behavior. As societies in the Northern Hemisphere have changed from a rural, agricultural base to an urban, postindustrial one, they have forgotten how their attitudes toward wildlife and each other have changed.[13] Since most of us live in a hierarchical society, any discourse about wildlife tends to be about social relationships. Whom can we exclude from our Garden of Eden, and how can we keep "others" from trespassing on valuables that help sustain our life and livelihoods, if not our identities?[14]

Wildlife in any culture's vocabulary contains a treasure trove of symbols (for Northerners, try "wilderness"), prescriptions ("habitat improvements"), rituals ("hunting seasons"), stories ("articles in learned journals"), and livelihoods ("career ecologists"). Wildlife is not so much about "things" as it is about processes and "beings." How can these cultural aspects be used to enhance understanding among traditions, if not disciplines?

Although its essence is embedded in a different vocabulary if not landscape, lineage husbandry serves many of the same functions and values that managerial ecology does. It recruits and legitimizes its members, it provides them with a language for discussion and action, and its symbols make sense while providing some answers.

If cultural conservationists are to use such ideas to design institutions and a consensus that enhances the relationships between communities of people and other animals, then they must invent and use a different vocabulary.[15] Such a vocabulary must incorporate the ideas of diverse individuals participating in the creation of social relationships whose values are shared by all. It must overcome the suspicions embedded in the earlier vocabulary and in the polarization of groups. Such a vocabulary may be woven from such root metaphors as "belonging," communication, intrinsic worth, kinship, trust, equality, and compassion. It begins with specific perceptions and place and with the recognition and worth of others. For such enabling language to become a resource for both managerial ecologists and lineage husbands, together they must craft a more inclusive and pluralistic world for other people as well as for other forms of life.

NOTES

1. H. G. Ward, *African Development Reconsidered: New Perspectives from the Continent* (New York: Phelps-Stokes Institute, 1989).

2. Luben Kafupi survived longer than Sir Julian Huxley. Kafupi died and was buried outside the village bearing his name in March 1991.

3. See, for example, Harry H. Johnston, *British Central Africa* (London: Methuen, 1897); and C. R. S. Pitman, *A Report on the Faunal Survey of North-*

ern Rhodesia with Special Reference to Game, Elephant Control, and National Parks (Livingstone, Northern Rhodesia: Government Printer, 1934). Wildlife exploitation had begun much earlier in the nineteenth century by Boer and European hunters and traders. See William Cornwallis Harris, *The Wild Sports of Southern Africa* (London: Henry G. Bohn, 1852); and R. Gordon Cumming, *A Hunter's Life in South Africa* (London: John Murray, 1850), among other period texts. Since their arrival at a much earlier time, African have used wildlife for may purposes.

4. Julian S. Huxley, *The Conservation of Wildlife and Natural Habitats in Central and East Africa* (Parish: UNESCO, 1961). Phrases in quotes are from this volume; the more extensive quotes are cited by page number.

5. Ibid., 13.

6. Ibid., 60.

7. Ibid., 92.

8. Ibid., 92–93.

9. Frank Fraser Darling, *Wildlife in an African Territory* (London: Oxford University Press, 1960); United Nations Development Programme/Food and Agriculture Organization of the United Nations, *Luangwa Valley Conservation and Development Project: Game Management and Habitat Manipulation* (Rome, Italy: FAO, 1973).

10. Stuart A. Marks, *Large Mammals and a Brave People: Subsistence Hunters in Zambia* (Seattle: University of Washington Press, 1976), 88–89.

11. Stuart A. Marks, "Profile and Process: Subsistence Hunters in a Zambian Community," *Africa* 49 (1979): 53–67.

12. Stuart A. Marks, Hapi Mutelele, and Kangwa Samson, *Interviews with Local Hunters, Lupande Game Management Area* (Chipata, Zambia: Luangwa Integrated Resource Development Project, 1989).

13. For insights into Northerners' earlier perceptions of their worlds, see Keith Thomas, *Man and the Natural World: A History of the Modern Sensibility* (New York: Pantheon Books, 1983); Thomas R. Dunlap, *Saving America's Wildlife* (Princeton, N.J.: Princeton University Press, 1988); and H. Ritvo, *The Animal Estate: The English and Other Creatures in the Victorian Age* (Cambridge, Mass.: Harvard University Press, 1987).

14. Stuart A. Marks, *Southern Hunting in Black and White: Nature, History and Ritual in a Carolina Community* (Princeton, N.J.: Princeton University Press, 1991).

15. R. Rorty, *Contingency, Irony, and Solidarity* (Cambridge: Cambridge University Press, 1989.)

9

Linking Cultural and Natural Conservation in National Park Service Policies and Programs

Benita J. Howell

Recent program initiatives and policy changes affecting ethnography and applied cultural anthropology have reconfigured the national park system's cultural mission and definition of cultural resources. Better management of natural as well as cultural resources and better relations between parks and neighboring communities should follow. It is useful to view these developments as the result of a decade or more of gradual organizational change, the outcome of interaction between stresses that provoke new responses and barriers that inhibit change. Both philosophical and organizational barriers have slowed progress toward the kind of integrated approach to natural and cultural resources that cultural conservationists advocate.

Nature and Culture in the National Park Service Worldview

The impetus to create national parks in the United States emerged from the wilderness preservation movement initiated by John Muir and supported by affluent easterners who visited the West, experienced its scenic wonders firsthand, and lobbied Congress to protect Yellowstone as the first "crown jewel" of the park system. In 1872 Congress established Yellowstone as a "pleasuring ground for the benefit and enjoyment of the people." Congress reiterated this dual mission of resource preservation and public access when it created the National Park Service in 1916. Over the years its preservationist ethic led the Park Service to separate nature from culture and to value historical over contemporary cultural expressions. Its orientation to a national constituency meant that it was concerned primarily with visitors rather than local people, whether residents of neighboring communities, former landowners, or indigenous native peoples with traditional and treaty claims to park resources.[1] Conventional historic preservation programs devoted to interpretation of sites and structures flourished within this framework, but it was philosophically incompatible with the broader agenda of cultural conservation, particularly encouragement or support for cultural survival that might entail recognizing local peoples' prior claims on park resources. Progress toward integrated natural and cultural resource management has been gradual and deliberate because it has required dedicated professionals in the National Park Service to rethink their organization's most fundamental values.

As the national park system grew to include historic shrines and battlefields as well as scenic attractions, the important philosophical distinction between nature and culture was expressed in unit designations and resource management. At present most units of the national park system are designated either as natural or cultural parks and administered accordingly. Yellowstone and Yosemite, for example, are natural parks, while Mesa Verde is a cultural park. Many units, however, have significant natural *and* cultural components, particularly in the eastern United States, where local populations have been removed within living memory. The Great Smoky Mountain National Park and the Blue Ridge Parkway were established in the 1930s to conserve natural and scenic resources, yet tangible elements of Appalachian cultural history—places, buildings, and artifacts—have long been preserved, documented, and interpreted in these parks. Parks with complex resource bases, particularly the national recreation areas created since the mid-1960s, also strain this system of unit designations. Dichotomous unit designations do reflect management practice, however, in that historic preservation programs and natural resource management activities are planned and administered separately.

Cultural conservationists looking beyond historic preservation would argue that humans, like all other species, are part of the complex web of life that forms an ecosystem; moreover, important aspects of ecosystems (e.g., knowledge of resources and customs through which people interact with their environment) are cultural phenomena and lie within the purview of cultural conservation. Concerns for human impact within ecosystems potentially draw cultural specialists into closer association with natural scientists and should foster collaborative research and management efforts within the national park system. Yet the practice of defining a park's cultural resources narrowly in terms of historic preservation and interpretation means that these opportunities for linkage usually are missed, however obvious and desirable a synthesis of natural and cultural resource management may appear to ethnoecologists working outside the system.

Separation of natural and cultural resource management at the park lev-

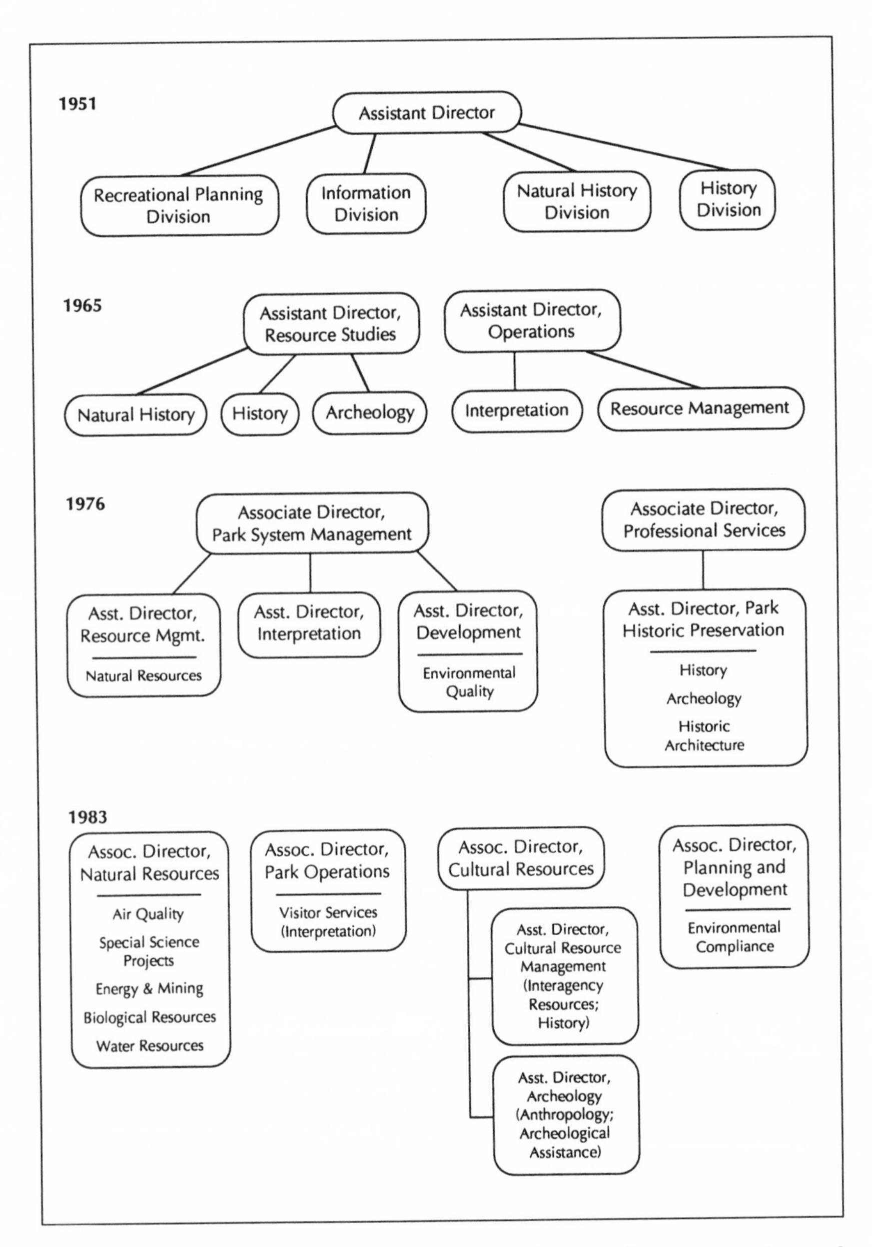

Figure 9.1. National Park System: Organization of Research, Interpretation, and Resource Management. (Adapted from Russ Olsen, *Administrative History: Organizational Structures of the National Park Service, 1917 to 1985* [Washington, D.C.: National Park Service, n.d.])

el also reflects the administrative structure of the regional and Washington, D.C., offices of the National Park Service (see figure 9.1). As historic preservation activities became more numerous and diverse in response to the National Historic Preservation Act of 1966, the organizational distance between cultural resources and natural resources increased.[2] A 1965 organizational chart of the Washington, D.C., office showed archaeology, history, and natural history as three coordinate divisions under a single assistant director of resource studies. By 1969 there was a separate Office of Archaeology and Historic Preservation reporting to the Director's Office, while the Office of Natural Science Studies reported to an associate director for management and programming. Ten years later natural resources, natural history, and social science (visitor studies) reported to an associate director for science and technology, while cultural resources reported to the associate director for management and operations. Similar arrangements prevailed until a 1985 reorganization placed different associate directors in charge of each major function: natural resources, park operations (including visitor services/interpretation), cultural resources, and planning and development. At the same time natural and cultural resource management responsibilities were being separated structurally, however, certain new legislative mandates called for more integrated planning and management and thus provoked ad hoc changes that set precedents for reformulating policy.

Innovative Responses to New Legislative Mandates

Two different forms of legislation can create special opportunities for expanded treatment of cultural resources in national parks. The first is legislation that affects the standing of particular groups to claim rights or special consideration not available to all Americans. One example is the American Indian Religious Freedom Act of 1978 (AIRFA), which grants protection of sacred sites and ritual activities to all Native Americans. More restricted in its application is the Alaska National Interest Lands Conservation Act of 1980 (ANILCA), the settlement that placed in the park system huge tracts of land claimed by native Alaskan tribes. This legislation obliges the Park Service to permit indigenous peoples to continue traditional use of their subsistence resources, even though regulations prohibiting hunting, fishing, and collecting by visitors and other Alaskans, and by anyone for commercial purposes, remain in effect.

The second form of legislation responsible for new approaches to resource management is enabling legislation that informs the National Park Service what Congress intends in adding each new unit to the system. While enabling legislation typically outlines goals in general terms and leaves management details to the Park Service, specific provisions of enabling legislation can be grounds for contesting management policy. For example, the Missouri Trappers Association successfully sued the National Park Service to enjoin an attempted ban on trapping along the Ozark National Scenic Riverways because the ban conflicted with specific provisions in the enabling legislation that permitted fishing and hunting, provisions the Park Service originally had interpreted as including trapping.[3]

Enabling legislation may imply a need for cultural research that would not typically figure in planning for a new park unit. The folklife survey conducted for Big South Fork National River and Recreation Area, for example, was funded because the enabling legislation explicitly called for interpretation of archaeological, historic, and cultural as well as natural resources.[4] Innovations stimulated by a specific enabling act are not immediately applicable to other units in the park system or to other groups whose relationship to park resources may appear similar; but these cases do become useful exemplars in the continuing dialogue that changes managers' attitudes toward local people, their cultures, and the cultural resources in parks.

Old patterns of national park system management based on preservationist assumptions have been challenged since the 1970s by the addition of multiple-use recreation areas like Ozark Scenic Riverways and Big South Fork, but innovative park units established in heavily populated areas have had even greater impact by stimulating entirely new approaches to resource management planning. The Pinelands National Reserve in New Jersey, a park without boundaries in the usual sense, involves the National Park Service in comprehensive regional planning through formal management agreements with local, state, and other federal agencies. This structure for cooperative planning goes far beyond typical efforts to cooperate with park neighbors who live on the other side of a clear park boundary. In the case of the Pinelands Reserve, for example, it seems critically important that future fire control policies be based on a thorough understanding of how local people have dealt with fire in the past, assessed the fire index, and made constructive use of controlled burning both to reduce the risk of massive conflagration and to enhance their resource base. The documentation of cultural land use patterns presented in Mary Hufford's *One Space, Many Places* includes an overview of this critical information, which has much more than interpretive significance.[5]

ANILCA has been instrumental in establishing the importance of ethnographic research as a planning and resource management tool. To conserve subsistence resources for sustained use, wildlife management plans developed for the Alaskan parks must be based on a detailed understanding of traditional subsistence patterns and any other demographic or sociocultural features that might affect the resource base over time. Substantial ethnohistoric and ethnographic research is thus required for management planning. Resource ethnographies undertaken for the Lake Clark National Park and Preserve and the Glacier Bay National Park and Preserve gathered information on a broad range of sociocultural phenomena that are linked to resource use, such as land tenure and land use, settlement types, population dynamics, and family and community life.[6] Because Alaska alone now contains more national park acreage than the rest of the system combined, resource ethnography has assumed considerable importance for the Park Service overall;[7] moreover, in Florida, Hawaii, and Minnesota, recent enabling legislation instructs the Park Service to grant other Native American groups similar access to traditional subsistence resources.[8]

Permitted use of park resources has also required managers to adopt new procedures and to shift their thinking from preservation to conservation. Because this innovation forces them to deal with potential "multiple-use" conflicts of interest, it has made management planning more complex. Difficult management issues have, however, stimulated active collaboration between parks and tribal peoples to develop workable and culturally sensitive plans for resource management. For instance, at Canyon de Chelly National Monument, where Navaho have grazing rights because the monument is on tribal lands, regulation to prevent overgrazing has been sensitively handled as one issue in an extended cooperative planning effort involving the Navaho Nation, Bureau of Indian Affairs, and National Park Service.[9]

AIRFA may have far-reaching impact on natural resource management because it requires federal consultation with tribes to identify and protect places (and their resources, such as medicinal plants) that are linked to religious traditions and ethnic identity.[10] As with special arrangements that permit use of subsistence resources, this legislation also entails ethnohistoric and ethnographic research. Moreover, because federal protection extends to places outside as well as inside of park boundaries, AIRFA can stimulate greater appreciation for Native American cultural traditions and closer interaction between park managers and neighboring tribes, even where use rights inside the park are not at issue.

Policy Shifts in the National Park System

General management policies for the national park system were revised in 1988 for the first time in ten years. The revision process created an opportunity for new perspectives and procedures generated in response to AIRFA and ANILCA to be codified as general policy guidelines. In developing measures to protect Native American rights, the Applied Cultural Anthropology Program in the Washington, D.C., office laid the groundwork for general acceptance of the notion that natural resources used for religious purposes or subsistence are ethnographic resources and integral to cultural resource management.[11] Managers' needs for ethnographic research and inventories are explicitly discussed in the new policy statement:

> Certain contemporary Native American and other communities are permitted by law, regulation, or policy to pursue customary religious, subsistence, and other cultural uses of park resources with which they are traditionally associated. Such continuing use is often essential to the survival of family, community, or regional cultural systems, including patterns of belief and economic and religious life. . . . the National Park Service will conduct appropriate cultural anthropological research in cooperation with park-associated groups. The purposes of this research will be to meet management needs for information about such groups; to develop inventories of traditional ethnographic resources associated with them; to determine the effects of their traditional ceremonial and consumptive uses of park resources; to evaluate the factors guiding their traditional systems for managing natural resources and creating cultural properties; to define their traditional and contemporary relationships to these resources; and to assess the effects of NPS [National Park Service] activities on these groups. Research findings will be used to support planning, resource management decisions, and activities; to develop interpretive programs accurately reflecting native American and other cultures; and to facilitate consultation with and meet management responsibilities to park-associated communities.[12]

Since ethnographic resources gained this official recognition, a second cultural anthropologist has joined the staff of the anthropology division in Washington, D.C., and positions have also been created for cultural anthropologists in several regional offices. These staff anthropologists will plan and manage the additional research and consultation with local groups required by AIRFA and other special agreements. One hopes that as ethnographic research becomes more commonplace in parks and as managers experience the benefits of closer collaboration with Native American neighbors, this program, initiated in response to issues of Native American rights, will be expanded to include groups representing other ethnic and regional cultures.

The NPCA Commission on Research and Resource Management

Policy change is driven in part by challenges, like ANILCA and AIRFA, which demand people working inside an organization to make innovative responses, but external pressure also guides the policy of pubic agencies. Drafts of regulations and policy statements are available for public comment; by taking advantage of the opportunity to review and comment on draft documents, cultural specialists helped develop the final version of the 1988 policy statement on ethnographic resources and research. Advisory boards and review panels are another means by which outsiders can influence agency policy.

In 1988–89 I participated as the cultural anthropologist on an interdisciplinary commission assembled by a private organization, the National Parks and Conservation Association (NPCA), at the request of National Park Service Director William Mott. The NPCA had just completed a comprehensive review of all aspects of the park system.[13] This commission would follow up by focusing on the especially critical problem of research and resource management policy for the parks, supported by a grant to the NPCA from the Andrew W. Mellon Foundation. Disciplinary affiliations of the seventeen academics and professionals on the commission reflected the diversity of natural, cultural, and social issues that park research and resource management must address. Five commission members—a historian, an art historian, a geographer/landscape architect, an archaeologist, and a cultural anthropologist—were cultural resource specialists.

Although our commission was organized by an independent agency, it functioned more as a sounding board for concerns already felt inside the Park Service than as an independent overseer. The NPCA, which publishes *Parks* magazine, is a large, nonprofit organization of members who enjoy parks and support Park Service programs through lobbying. The NPCA organized this commission to provide public visibility, outside confirmation of needs the Park Service already felt, and a basis for lobbying Congress to fund research and resource management adequately. Director Mott's office thus nominated commission members to the NPCA on the recommendation of professionals in the Park Service. The director's office also appointed a liaison group of Park Service employees—administrators and researchers from Washington, D.C., regional offices, parks, and research units—who became key consultants in the fact-finding that preceded writing the commission report.

Over the course of a year the commission met several times as a body and in topical subcommittees, with and without members of the liaison group; we read a voluminous amount of background literature and position papers prepared by the liaison staff and other Park Service professionals; and we made site visits that permitted interaction with personnel from Washington, regional administrators and scientists, park superintendents, staff researchers based in parks or research units, park resource specialists, and contract researchers. The entire commission met again early in 1989 to rework drafts of the report that had been prepared with assistance from the NPCA staff.

The final report grouped recommendations under four broad headings: (1) ecosystem management, (2) implementation of the research program needed to support ecosystem management, (3) improvement of professional standards and rewards for researchers and resource managers in the park system, and (4) improvement of public education functions.[14] The remainder of this essay considers the issues surrounding ecosystem management and the potential for linking natural and cultural conservation in an ecosystems framework.

Ecosystems as a Philosophical Issue: Old Values Die Hard

Global issues have heightened public concern about the environment, while recent media coverage on the plight of rain forests and their inhabitants has communicated the idea that indigenous peoples possess sophisticated knowledge of environmental resources, such as economically important plants. Given current public interest and the education mission of the National Park Service, local peoples' knowledge and use of natural resources is an apt theme for park interpretive programs. There is thus a close connection between the NPCA Commission's advocacy of an ecosystems perspective in management and specific directions it recommends for public education programs.

More compelling than interpretation, however, is the manager's primary responsibility—stewardship of park resources. Resource ethnographies provide more than just interesting information to convey to an environmentally aware public. Cultural specialists engaged in ecosystems research can argue persuasively that park managers need better knowledge of past and present *cultural* patterns to manage *natural* resources effectively. Images of pristine wilderness, however, still color the Park Service worldview and have impeded recognition of this linkage between culture and nature. Somehow in drawing the contrast between sublime nature and urban, industrial America, the champions of national parks lost sight of the fact that Native Americans and other groups have been shaping seemingly "natural" ecosystems for millennia.

The legacy of this thinking was a "natural" ecosystems concept at odds with the understanding of cultural or human ecology developed since the 1930s in archaeology, cultural anthropology, and geography. Park managers have been socialized to accept a value system that characterizes natural ecosystems devoid of human contamination as good and human intrusions on those ecosystems as bad. Nature is the museum; humans are curators, docents, or patrons, but they are not part of the exhibits. In critiquing this conception of "natural" ecosystems, the NPCA Commission supported and, one hopes, ultimately furthered the cause of integrated natural and cultural resource management.

Ecosystem management was on the NPCA Commission's agenda from the beginning, because this group was viewed as a successor to an earlier advisory board on wildlife management led by A. Starker Leopold, a professor of zoology at Berkeley. Foremost among National Park Service requests was a call for the commission to reconsider the 1963 Leopold Report's prescription "that the biotic associations within each park be maintained, or where necessary recreated, as nearly as possible in the condition that prevailed when the area was first visited by the white man. A national park should represent a vignette of primitive America."[15] The title of the commission report, *National Parks: From Vignettes to a Global View,* reflects that charge to reconsider Leopold's goal of restoring ecosystems by eliminating exotic species, erasing human impacts, and reversing the effects of human interference with natural processes.

Since the Leopold Report appeared, a massive facilities-building program launched in the early 1960s and subsequent developments have vastly increased visitation and the impact of visitors, their vehicles, and their wastes on park resources. Development has accelerated in areas adjacent to park boundaries as well, producing a range of new threats to park resources and regional challenges for policy (e.g., fire control). Despite increased threats of various intrusions into park ecosystems, the difficulty with Leopold's conceptions of park ecosystems is more fundamental: scientists recognize the dynamic, interactive nature of ecosystems and in fact use the ecosystems concept to model change as much as stability, yet establishing "primitive America" as a temporal benchmark disallows the very changes that are inherent in a functioning ecosystem. The goal of preserving stability in ecosystems that have experienced tremendous changes following the removal of human inhabitants and the cessation of their use of resources quite predictably creates intractable problems for managers.

The 1988 park system management policy reflects some of the confusion in the national park system concerning implementation of Leopold's intent for "natural zones": "Interference with natural processes . . . will be allowed only (1) when directed by Congress, (2) in some emergencies when human life and property are at stake, or (3) to restore native ecosystem functioning that has been disrupted by past or ongoing human activities." Implicit here is a "wilderness" ecosystem devoid of humans in the past and, ideally, in the present. The next statement, however, suggests that certain past human activities were desirable (e.g., grazing livestock on balds or burning underbrush to maintain parklike game and livestock habitat): "Ecological processes altered in the past by human activities may need to be abetted to maintain the closest approximation to the natural ecosystem where a truly natural system is no longer attainable. Prescribed burning is an example."[16] Balds created by timber cutting and grazing may enhance scenic values in natural parks, and in cultural parks, such as battlefields, the goal is to maintain or re-create a *cultural* landscape.

From the standpoint of the NPCA Commission's resource management subcommittee, which included the cultural geographer (our chair), the archaeologist, and me, the artificial separation of nature and culture in the underlying philosophy and management policy was an obvious cause of the difficulties ecosystems management had presented in the past. Based on similar academic training and interests, we shared a common understanding of ecosystems as spheres of interaction between humans and other species, systems shaped mutually and interactively by natural and cultural forces. We were interested in both natural and cultural resource management issues, and in particular we saw the need to deal with human-environment interactions not well covered by the park system's current conceptual and organizational scheme but critical to solving new management challenges, such as continuing subsistence use rights in Alaska.

Even in the "crown jewel" natural parks, however, the missing human element needed to be reintroduced into managers' conceptual models of the ecosystem. Yellowstone is an apt example because of its high visibility in the wake of the 1988 fires and because Alston Chase, author and former chairman of the board of the Yellowstone Association, has made a detailed analysis of Yellowstone management policies that speaks to these issues.[17] The appeal of preserving "wilderness untrammeled by man" unquestionably was instrumental in creating Yellowstone, but continued adherence to the myth of wilderness has created difficulties in management. Chase describes how the burgeoning bison and elk populations in Yellowstone became a perennial management problem. Both management interventions to achieve herd reduction and the periodic population crashes that are nature's solution to the problem are public relations nightmares. Chase points out that fluctuations in bison and elk populations do not indicate a "natural" ecosystem gone awry for lack of carnivorous predators. In fact, the current bison and elk population problem in Yellowstone is the result of human intervention, both direct and indirect. First, managers did all they could to increase the numbers of these species as a visitor attraction in the early years, when railroad interests and tourism dominated the construction of facilities and management decisions at Yellowstone. Subsequent development of the surrounding area in recent decades increasingly has cut off the animals' safe access to grasslands at somewhat lower altitude outside of Yellowstone, grasslands once available to Yellowstone herds as winter range. The result has been ever-greater crowding and range deterioration within the park boundaries. Chase makes the point that in "playing god" with these species, park managers were slow to recognize the true geographic extent of the contemporary ecosystem—park and surrounding rangeland—and the historic and continuing role of humans in the ecosystem, particularly the role of Native Americans as hunters and manipulators of wildlife habitat through controlled burning.

As the nature writer Paul Schullery pointed out to the NPCA Commission in an address at our first meeting, it is all too easy to criticize as naive and impractical Leopold's suggestion that parks should provide glimpses of the scenes experienced by the first white visitors;[18] but Schullery's defense of Leopold misses the crucial point. The issue is not simply that Leopold's prescription attempts to fix ecosystems in time; rather, in choosing "first visits of the white man" as the measure of "primitive" (i.e., wild and natural), Leopold obscured and ignored critical questions concerning Native American cultural manipulation of park landscapes and resources. The Leopold Report's prescription for ecosystems management is problematic for human managers-manipulators precisely because it fails to account for humans as long-term actors in "natural" park ecosystems.

After grappling with these issues for the better part of a year and achieving common understandings with the Park Service natural scientists who served as liaisons to our subcommittee, we were gratified to hear Alston Chase, in a speech to the George Wright Society in November of 1989,[19] forcefully articulate our concerns:

> By driving a wedge between man and nature, this philosophy (i.e., the dualism underlying the Leopold Report) places an impossible burden on park managers. They are charged with keeping parks—which have been affected by human activity for thousands of years and which continue to be altered by it—in "pristine" condition. And they are expected to do this by natural means, whenever possible.
>
> At the same time this dualistic approach to management encourages a fortress mentality in park administrators. Expected to protect the resource from the people, rangers are required to erect barriers, not only between visitor and the resource, but also between the park itself and the surrounding communities. This stance in turn often puts the park on a hostile footing with its neighbors, exacerbating the so-called "boundary problem."[20]

Chase's definition of the problem resonated with our thinking. His call for holism (comprehensive, integrated ecosystems research and management) and localism (attention to the interactions between historic and contemporary local cultures and park resources) foreshadowed themes in the commission's draft report, which was about to be presented to the George Wright Society members for comment.

NPCA Commission Recommendations and Future Directions

The executive summary of the NPCA Commission's report called for "developing and using the concept of ecosystem management, emphasizing the relationship among the natural and cultural resources of the system, and recognizing that an ecosystem encompasses past and present human activities."[21] To justify its recommendation for basic research on natural-cultural interactions in ecosystems and increased ethnographic research to enhance cooperation with culturally diverse neighbor populations, the commission made these arguments:

> To integrate cultural and natural resources in a broad ecosystem framework for management and interpretation, the scope of cultural resources must be expanded from a narrow focus on historic preservation to a broader focus on cultural conservation. The latter aims to protect living cultural traditions, and cultural knowledge that represents the diverse American heritage. To respond to concerns articulated in the American Indian Religious Freedom Act of 1978, the 1980 amendments to the Historic Preservation Act, and special provisions for Native American use of resources in the Alaskan parks, the Park Service needs a much-expanded capacity for ethnographic research and additional attention to facilitating harmonious relationships among park managers and diverse neighboring populations.
>
> While the National Park Service has focused its limited capacity for ethnographic research on Native American issues of pressing concern, ethnographic research is needed wherever different cultural groups have long-standing associations with park resources. Neighboring communities also have concerns that must be addressed in park planning as they transcend park boundaries.[22]

To make this transformation in park research and resource management possible, the NPCA Commission's report proposed that the park system allocate 10 percent of its operating budget to research and 35 percent of that amount to research that is autonomous from line management. The commission endorsed the cooperative park study units, which are based at academic institutions rather than in specific parks, as well as a significant commitment to contract research. These recommendations, which would reduce park superintendents' control over research in their parks, were among the most controversial when the report was presented to Park

Service personnel. If acted on, however, these strategies might help overcome resistance to new research directions that do not directly support immediate management concerns. Certainly the cooperative park study units and independent contract research potentially offer means for transcending the functional separation of cultural from natural resources that occurs in Washington, the regional offices, and individual parks.

Restructuring the national park system to unite natural and cultural resources in one directorate might seem an attractive linkage mechanism, but in fact Russ Olsen's study of Park Service administrative structures shows that they changed, on average, every twenty-two months between 1917 and 1985 as new directors took charge and as new programs (e.g., archaeology and historic preservation) were established.[23] New information needs and new approaches to planning and ecosystems management promise to have greater impact than formal restructuring does in changing Park Service goals and means. The pervasive nature-culture opposition in the Park Service worldview will therefore likely be transformed gradually as the anthropology division in Washington and cultural anthropologists now assigned to regional offices work with park managers to resolve Native American issues, or as the concept of cultural landscape utilized so effectively in Mary Hufford's description of the Pinelands encourages systematic consideration of human interaction with the environment. An ecosystems perspective incorporating human ecology must entail expanded interdisciplinary collaboration between cultural specialists and natural scientists as principles and methods found effective in dealing with Native Americans are extended to other groups. Within this shared theoretical paradigm of ecosystems management, we can work together more effectively toward our common goal of understanding and conserving the full range of biocultural diversity represented in our national parks.

NOTES

In addition to published literature, sources include discussions with Muriel Crespi, who heads the Applied Cultural Anthropology Program in the Washington, D.C., office of the National Park Service; fellow members of the National Parks and Conservation Association's Commission on Research and Resource Management; numerous Park Service professionals who met with the commission or provided information papers at our request; and researchers from various cultural disciplines who have worked in parks. I greatly appreciate the stimulation and encouragement these colleagues have given me. The conclusions expressed here are my own, however, and do not represent the viewpoints of the Park Service, its personnel, or the NPCA Commission as a whole.

1. Origins of the National Park Service are discussed in numerous works

on the conservation movement in the United States. Especially useful agency studies are William C. Everhart, *The National Park Service* (Boulder, Colo.: Westview Press, 1983); and Ronald A. Foresta, *America's National Parks and Their Keepers* (Washington, D.C.: Resources for the Future, 1984).

2. Russ Olsen, *Administrative History: Organizational Structures of the National Park Service, 1917–1985* ([Washington, D.C.: National Park Service], n.d.), presents thirty-eight organizational charts from which this information is drawn.

3. Erika Brady, "Debatable Land: Frontier versus Wilderness in the Ozark National Scenic Riverways," *Folklife Annual '88–'89* (Washington, D.C.: American Folklife Center, 1989), 57.

4. Benita J. Howell, *A Survey of Folklife along the Big South Fork of the Cumberland River,* Report of Investigations, no. 30 (Knoxville: Department of Anthropology, University of Tennessee, 1981). Her "Folklife in Planning," *CRM Bulletin* 10 (February 1987): 14–15, 29, describes how this ethnographic and ethnohistoric project provided information pertinent to facilities development and positive relations with park neighbors.

5. Mary Hufford, *One Space, Many Places: Folklife and Land Use in New Jersey's Pinelands National Reserve* (Washington, D.C.: American Folklife Center, Library of Congress, 1986).

6. Muriel Crespi, "The Ethnography of Alaska Resource Use," *CRM Bulletin* 10 (February 1987): 24–25.

7. C. Mack Shaver, "Traditional National Park Values and Living Cultural Parks: Seemingly Conflicting Management Demands Coexisting in Alaska's New National Parklands," in *International Perspectives on Cultural Parks* (Washington, D.C.: National Park Service, 1989), 311–16.

8. Muriel Crespi, "Cultural Anthropology and U.S. National Parks," *Anthropology Newsletter* 30 (September 1989): 35.

9. Joan Mitchell, "Planning at Canyon de Chelly National Monument." *CRM Bulletin* 10 (February 1987): 19–21, 30.

10. Barbara L. Reimensnyder, "Cherokee Sacred Sites in the Appalachians," in *Cultural Heritage Conservation in the American South,* Southern Anthropological Society Proceedings, no. 23, ed. Benita J. Howell (Athens: University of Georgia Press, 1990), 107–17, describes a site inventory done in connection with U.S. Forest Service long-range planning for the Nantahala and Pisgah National Forests.

11. Crespi, "Cultural Anthropology and U.S. National Parks," 35.

12. U.S. Department of the Interior, National Park Service, *Management Policies, Part One: Management of the National Park System* (Washington, D.C.: National Park Service, December 1988), 5:1.

13. National Parks and Conservation Association, *Research in the Parks: An Assessment of Needs,* vol. 2 of *Investing in Park Futures: A Blueprint for Tomorrow* (Washington, D.C.: NPCA, 1988).

14. NPCA Commission on Research and Resource Management Policy in the National Park System, *National Parks: From Vignettes to a Global View* (Washington, D.C.: NPCA, 1989).

15. A. Starker Leopold, Stanley A. Cain, Clarence Cottam, Ira N. Gabrielson, and Thomas L. Kimbell. "Report on Wildlife Management in the National Parks" (The Leopold Report), *National Parks Magazine,* April 1963, Insert 4–63, ii.

16. U.S. Department of the Interior, National Park Service, *Management Policies, Part One,* 4:2.

17. Alston Chase, *Playing God in Yellowstone: The Destruction of America's First National Park* (Boston: Atlantic Monthly Press, 1986).

18. Paul Schullery, "Feral Fish and Kayak Tracks: Thoughts on the Writing of a New Leopold Report," *George Wright Forum* 6, no. 1 (1989): 44.

19. The George Wright Society, an organization founded in 1980 by two former chief scientists of the National Park Service, is "dedicated to the protection, preservation, and management of cultural and natural parks and reserves through research and education." Although membership is not restricted to Park Service personnel, the society provides a scholarly forum for Park Service professionals.

20. Alston Chase, "The Role of the National Park Service in American Education," *George Wright Forum* 6, no. 1 (1989): 26.

21. NPCA Commission, *National Parks,* 4.

22. Ibid., 8.

23. Olsen, *Administrative History,* 8.

10

"The River's Like Our Back Yard": Tourism and Cultural Identity in the Ozark National Scenic Riverways

Erika Brady

In 1986 I was asked to testify in a hearing before the Parks and Monuments Committee of the U.S. House of Representatives on the history of fur trapping in the portion of the Missouri Ozarks that now constitutes the Ozark National Scenic Riverways, a unit administered by the National Park Service since 1964. A reinterpretation of the language of the legislation establishing the Riverways had resulted in a ban on trapping that clearly contradicted the original intent of the portion of the bill in question; the hearing concerned a second bill proposed by Eighth District Representative Bill Emerson to restore trapping as a legal activity in the region, to be controlled, as it had been previously, by the Missouri Department of Conservation.[1]

The ban sparked considerable anger among residents of the region. Although trapping is by no means universally practiced, it is an area where hunting of all kinds is enthusiastically pursued. Even groups traditionally hostile to trappers, such as fox and coon hunters, joined the fray, surmising that the prospective ban might be extended eventually to include all forms of hunting. At the time of the establishment of the Riverways, a hotly disputed local issue in itself, there had been much concern in the region that hunting and trapping continue to be controlled by the Missouri Department of Conservation. Local anxiety centered on the maintenance of adequate wildlife management and the preservation of a personally rewarding and culturally validated activity. Indeed, at the time of the attempted 1986 imposition of the trapping ban, Richard Ichord, the district's congressman when the Riverways was established, wrote to Emerson, declaring, "I can assure you that I would not have supported, much less sponsored legislation that would have the effect of prohibiting trapping—a practice that is so much a part of the Ozark tradition and way of life."[2]

Although the actual origin of and motivation for the reinterpretation of the regulation concerning trapping are now obscure, local people were swift to perceive the reinterpretation as the latest of many impositions of outsiders' values on local activities to accommodate the values of urban visitors flocking to the Riverways each summer. The local bitterness concerning the ban formed no part of my testimony, but it was very much on my mind as I delivered my presentation before the committee.

It was with shock, then, that I received the committee's comments and questions. Those committee members most adamantly opposed to overturning the ban were at the same time most interested in encouraging educational programs concerning the *history* of trapping as part of the National Park Service's public offerings. The committee chairman, Bruce Vento, even inquired if I knew of any old trappers who would be interested in talking to visitors about the "old-time trapping days"—some tame local, presumably, to be decked out in a quaint, rustic costume. I thought about Buck Asbridge, a tough and peppery octogenarian from Jadwin, whose published response to the ban on his favorite winter activity had been "DAMN federal! DAMN state! DAMN them all, by God!"[3] I wished Buck had been along to deliver a succinct appraisal of Vento's patronizing suggestion.

It would be agreeable to see this episode as isolated: a momentary lapse on the part of a politician naive about cultural dynamics and far from the scene where the drama was being enacted. Unfortunately, it is by no means a rare phenomenon, even among professional brokers of culture, to relegate complex contemporary realities to a mythic past, in which context they can be conveniently manipulated to ends defined by nonnative constituencies. In the course of a project documenting the folklife of the Blue Ridge Parkway, another National Park Service unit, Alan Jabbour and Howard Wright Marshall remarked on what might be called the unconscious anachronization of another contemporary rural pastime in a parkway brochure describing a location where "old-time hunters listened to the baying of their hounds in the valley below"—a location in which a visitor with good ears might be distracted from the reverie induced by the elegiac tone of the brochure by the sound of the sport vigorously pursued to this day.[4]

Like the Blue Ridge Parkway, the Ozark Scenic Riverways was established as an institutionally protected *natural* enclave. The logical contradiction implicit in the concepts of "protected" and "natural" invokes culturally sanctioned symbolic categories so familiar that it is no more striking to the casual listener than the equally contradictory notion of nature as a locus separate from most everyday human life, "other" territory to which one is nonetheless morally and spiritually drawn to make a pilgrimage. In such sites as these, where the conspicuous human element is an intrusion regardless of its origin, it is cynical but reasonable to expect that the native human presence will be symbolically marginalized by whatever means presents itself. Relegation to the status of a quaint survival is only one process by which present inhabitants are "disappeared"; physical displacement is the most radical.

One might think that institutionally administered tourist sites specifically mandated to interpret cultural and historical realities handle these contradictions more deftly, but in fact the need to objectify the focus of tourist experience is perhaps even more imperative when that focus is "human" rather than "environmental." At Mesa Verde National Park, there is a pronounced disjunction in Park Service interpretation between the romantic *essence* of a mythic American Indian past promoted in the official rangers' instruction guide and the gritty reality of the political, economic, and historical Indian *existence* both observable and conveyed by Hopi presenters. The anthropologist Kathleen Fine suggests that this disjunction is so emphatic that it actually breaks down visitors' preconceptions concerning Native American life, freeing them to construct a fresh consciousness of the meaning of that culture.[5] Though this optimistic hypothesis is attractive, one is left with little assurance that this freshly reconstructed consciousness bears a closer resemblance to the complexities of Navajo and Pueblo essence and existence—and wishing that such an admirable reconstruction could be achieved by less roundabout means.

In sum, whether the target experience of a visitor to an administered tourist site is human in content, as at Mesa Verde, or environmental in content, as at Ozark National Scenic Riverways, the mediated interpretive process requires that categories of "inclusion" and "otherness" be proposed (if not imposed) in a manner that can be swiftly and enjoyably grasped by visitors in the course of a relatively brief vacation encounter; to adapt Barbara Kirshenblatt-Gimblett's term for the parallel process in the marketing of folk art, the target experience must be "commodified" for ready consumption.[6] In the case of an environmental site, appropriate interpretation further demands that the process be unobtrusive, that visitors experience the illusion of participating in an apparently unmediated but safe experience of "the wild."

The Ozarkers who fish, hunt, trap, and picnic along these rivers in all four seasons travel symbolic waters that are very different from those enjoyed by most outsiders, who pour in on weekends and summer holidays for their taste of wilderness. Although conflict between local and visitor interests in a Park Service unit can and does pertain to any number of issues, the attempted trapping ban and the local response present a particularly instructive crystallization of the problems inherent in administering such an institution. To most urban and suburban visitors, whose ideas con-

Figure 10.1. Early in December on Missouri's Current River, Kenneth Wells launches his canoe to check his traplines. (Photo by the author)

cerning human-animal relations are drawn from animal rights tracts and nature specials on television, the trapper represents a kind of ultimate symbolic "other": a hairy, sadistic survival from a brutal past, whose bestiality contrasts sharply with the sentimentalized image of animal-as-child drawn from the same sources. Arguably, the operative image pits the trapper as a beast barely disguised as a human against a child-victim in a fur suit—the snatching of that fur only further humanizes the victim symbolically.

The fact that a majority of local people supports the right to trap as a reasonable, not inhumane, activity only confirms outsiders' stereotype of locals as dangerous denizens of the wilderness. The history of these divergent points of view, as well as the role of the Park Service as their uneasy go-between, is worth examining, for it reveals much concerning the character of the state and region, the nature of such conflicts wherever they occur, and the negotiation of policy where local and visitor interests are at odds. In particular, it is important to look at a topic typically neglected in these controversies: the roots of local attitudes toward the disputed activity in the larger context of the region's history and culture.

Although the Missouri Ozark region confounds simple images, it is possible to observe certain cultural generalities that have been noted since the nineteenth century. Cultural geographers, such as Milton D. Rafferty, Carl O. Sauer, and E. Joan Wilson Miller, have described several distinctive traits of Ozark life.[7] It is, of course, primarily rural, drawing on a heritage rooted in the southern highlands. The social system is relatively stable, despite the severe economic stress suffered in many areas. Children grow up in extended families that have often worked the same woods, fields, and rivers for generations.

Perhaps as a result of this stability, Ozarkers display a powerful sense of place. *Ozark* is a term of pride in the region, carrying no taint of Al Capp's Dogpatch, and is used frequently in naming businesses and organizations, especially in southwest Missouri. In addition to this general regional identification, the Ozarker seemingly relishes a kind of localized "claiming by naming"; the density of formal and informal place-names for physical features and communities is formidable, and their poetic ingenuity is dazzling.[8] Virtually every quarter of a mile on the Current River and its tributary Jacks Fork, for example, is designated by a descriptive name recalling a notable feature, a favored use, or an animal or human denizen.

Not only are the place-naming practices of Ozarkers proprietary, but their identification with others as part of their communal landscape is highly exclusionary as well. An Ozark address does not constitute membership as an insider in the community or region, even when maintained over decades. The conservatism of the region is expressed well by the historian Robert Flanders's characterization of the region as a "perpetuated frontier."[9] Traditional life-styles are vigorously maintained in conscious contrast to "outsider" behavior, sometimes at the expense of technological and economic improvement.

The *frontier* in Ozark usage refers to the historic era of settlement in the eighteenth and early nineteenth centuries, from which many inhabitants trace direct descent. To the Ozarker, the term also invokes the varied repertoire of skills and crafts initially related to subsistence during the earliest period in this demanding country, including hunting, trapping, fishing, beekeeping, and root-digging. Although most Ozark families no longer depend wholly on these activities for subsistence, they are still vigorously pursued. As Helen Gibbs of Salem, Missouri, remarked, "Hereabouts, some men go for deer, some men go for turkey, some go for your fur—but seems like *everybody* goes for something."[10]

Valuable furs from the rivers and forests and minerals from the hills first brought Europeans to the Ozarks in the late seventeenth century. The

French priest Father Membre remarked of the region in 1688, "Our hunters, French and Indian, are delighted with the country."[11] The swift-running rivers traversing the hilly country not only provided habitat for mink, muskrat, beaver, bobcat, bear, deer, otter, and raccoon but also offered a means of transporting the pelts to the trading posts located along the Mississippi River to the east. The timber boom of the late nineteenth and early twentieth century shifted the means of commercial transport from the rivers and poor roads to the new railways built by industry. Although timber was transported from the region primarily by rail, locating timber manufacturing centers near rivers was practical because the streams were useful for short-haul transport of logs. The most aggressive lumbering took place in the region of the Current River and Jacks Fork, wiping out the virgin stands of shortleaf pine primarily for use as railroad ties.

Ironically, the industrial despoilers of the region were also among the first to recognize its recreational potential. As early as 1888 a fishing and hunting club was built on the Current River by a group of railroad builders. Angler members and guests recorded their catches; the decline in number over the following two decades represents both an index of the region's potential attraction to sports enthusiasts and an indictment of the disastrous contemporary effect of the industries on the source of that attraction.[12]

The gradual withdrawal of the timber companies in the first decades of the twentieth century came as an environmental blessing and brought tourism in its wake as a new and unexpected industry. Pamphlets and magazines rhapsodized about the river region in the rich diction of sports writing of the era: "Full many a wielder of the rod has whipped the riffles of the stream and been rewarded by as splendid catches of beautiful bass and jack salmon as the reasonable heart could wish for."[13] The highly publicized fishing excursion of Missouri Governor Herbert S. Hadley in 1909 represented a landmark in local history. Governor Hadley and more than forty businessmen, officials, guides, and newsmen boarded flatboats at Welch Cave, arriving downstream at Round Spring the next day. Thanks to careful orchestration by the organizers, the trip received national attention, and the Ozarks began to command interest as a haven for sports enthusiasts.[14]

The full potential of tourism was not realized, however, until the writer Leonard Hall brought the region to national attention in 1958 with the publication of *Stars Upstream: Life along an Ozark River.* This classic of the American outdoors introduced the charms of the area to a wide audience and played a critical role in bringing about the legislation that placed the Riverways under the administration of the National Park Service.[15] Hall's book remains a delight to read, despite the fact that "life along the Ozark rivers" has changed irrevocably, in part as a result of his eloquence.

Figure 10.2 Canoeists on the Current River and Jacks Fork. (Photo by the author)

Hall drastically underestimated the allure of his rivers, once discovered. He predicted that recreational use of the Current River and its tributaries would always be effectively limited by the character of the rivers, enumerating their chill and swiftness, the annoyance of biting insects, and the skill required to canoe and camp as factors that would protect the streams from overuse.

Unfortunately, despite cold water and ravenous mosquitoes, the Current River and Jacks Fork are visited by hordes so eager for wilderness experience that they are willing to share the feast with any number of others. In 1972, the first year statistics were kept, Park Service officials estimated that the 130-mile length of the Riverways carried approximately 120,000 canoeists and 14,000 powerboaters. In 1979, the first year in which those floating down the river in rented inner tubes were systematically included in user counts, they numbered more than 15,000. In 1987 estimates were up to 190,000 canoeists, 35,000 powerboaters, and 35,000 tube-floaters—the latter apparently quite happy to float downstream in the chilly water that Leonard Hall hoped would discourage casual users.[16]

The Riverways has never provided the economic boost to the region that inhabitants and local politicians had hoped. The region remains among the poorest in Missouri. In 1986 the six counties in the Riverways included the counties rated first and second in unemployment in the state. That same year the mean salary of the six counties was $6,293.[17] Those owning the regulated canoe concessions have profited, but the general impression among local individuals is that the economic effect has been disappointing. If anything, friendly contact with outsiders seems to have diminished. No longer do most visitors float decorously downstream under the guidance of a familiar Ozarker. Canoes or tubes are rented from the concessions, and interaction between visitors and inhabitants is often limited to the exchange of a few bills at that time. Local people claim that the typical "floater" arrives with a ten-dollar bill and a pair of cut-off jeans—and when he leaves a few days later he hasn't changed either one.

Assuming, locals might add, that he's still wearing pants. There are many reasons why visitors are drawn to the Riverways: some seek a social experience in a scenic setting, some seek a natural experience in a controlled setting. But there is no question which visitors are the source of the greatest concern to local people: uninhibited visitors whose high jinks involve nudity, sexual misconduct, and drug use, which scandalize local observers every summer.

Although narratives concerning visitor behavior are common in the region, in the course of fieldwork interviews undertaken in the fall and winter of 1986, I found that the impending ban on trapping evoked detailed and outraged stories of floater antics told with greater than usual urgency and frequency. Indeed, I routinely budgeted time at the beginning of any interview concerning trapping to accommodate the ventilation of these feelings—the topic of trapping, understood to carry such a negative stereotype among outsiders, invariably elicited a kind of preemptive volley of narratives presenting negative stereotypes of visitor behavior and morals. Outsiders' offensive and illegal activities were perceived to be condoned by Park Service policy, while locals' hitherto legal and laudable activities were condemned or curtailed.

While some city dwellers perceive the rivers as wild, untamed, and innocent arenas for their own wild, untamed, and far-from-innocent horseplay, inhabitants of the region see a familiar part of their "backyard" and a valued productive resource now fouled by visitors' language, sexual exhibitionism, drunkenness, and other offensive behavior. Many who claim proudly that they were "raised on the river" now refuse to go there at all or limit their visits to the winter months, when the "outsider" traffic is light. On their side, visitors often regard the local people as threatening intruders in their riverbank Eden, invaders from Deliverance-land given to irrational and unprovoked fits of temper. Both sides admit exceptions to the rule—the helpful and humorous local, the decent sportsmanlike canoeist. But overcrowding on the river has tended to reinforce stereotypes and polarize relations, while increased social distance between locals and visitors reinforces the illusion that the prejudices of one group are somehow invisible to members of the other. One cannot float the river in the company of local people in the summer without hearing at least one passing canoeist derisively hum the first bars of "Duelling Banjos"—and the person always seems surprised when there is a glare of recognition in response.[18]

A perfect example of divergence in attitudes may be seen in local people's response to nudity on the river. Naked swimming, regarded by some visitors as an appropriate expression of escape from the trammels of civilization, is regarded as seriously offensive by local people if it is in mixed groups or if a naked man makes no effort to hide himself when women and children unexpectedly come on the scene. Vance Randolph remarked on the habitual sexual prudery of Ozark vocabulary in mixed company in the late twenties.[19] Although verbal taboos have loosened somewhat, those concerning actions perceived as sexually provocative or aggressive remain strong.

A whole cycle of stories told throughout the area recounts the revenge, violent or prankish, wrought on the outsider foolish enough to expose himself without shame to the wife and family of an Ozark man:

> I can't think of this fella's name, but he's a great big fella, and was raised on the river, and these people came down, and they were going to take their clothes off—*did* take their clothes off right around his wife and children. And just right out in the open, didn't hide theirself or anything. So he told his wife and his two children to get in the pickup and go up the road. And he thought all the time, he said, "Now, I'm gonna have to do *something*. I don't know what I'm going to do." There were men and women both, and he didn't know what to do.
>
> So he made up his mind what he thought he might do. He got his wife and children and they got in the pickup and left. And he got up in the bush. He always wore big overalls and a pair of big ole brogan shoes. So he took his overalls off, and stripped down to his birthday suit—and this guy weighs about 250 pounds—woolly-looking fella. He left his brogan shoes on so he wouldn't hurt his feet on the rocks. And he come crashing out of the brush, and he says "I WANT TO MAKE A BABY! I WANT TO MAKE A BABY!" and he said they jumped to get in the canoes like frogs. He broke up their nude party pretty rapidly![20]

Typical in this account is the Ozarker's sardonic assumption of the negative characteristics of exoteric stereotypes of both natives and visitors. The depiction of his sexual suggestiveness and nudity (except for the comically anomalous retention of his brogans, typical "local" footgear) alludes to the native perception of visitor behavior, while his threatening actions and bestially hirsute appearance reflect a consciousness of the outsider stereotype of crazed and violent locals.

To the Ozarkers of the region, the rivers are part of a social as well as geographic landscape. Despite the privacy one may enjoy there, they are public not only in the legal sense presently applicable but also in the older sense of being "of and for members of the community." Most adults remember when ownership of the land along the rivers was in private hands and exactly who owned specific stretches in their area. Men and women know the names and local associations for every stretch of the river in their region in exactly the sense that city dwellers can recite every shop and family home on the block where they grew up. River territory for Ozarkers, therefore, remains space in which one is socially accountable. Historically the commercial highway of their region, the river remains to some extent the analogue of the "front lawn" social space of urban dwellers—private or less acceptable behavior is better performed away from the riverbanks and paths, where accidental interruptions are less likely to occur.

For those outsiders whose behavior so offends local people, on the other hand, the river delights precisely because it is territory in which they are unaccountable for their behavior, far from the control of their own social milieu. They can and do revert with impunity to adolescent, even infantile behavior; their own presence and that of the human beings on the river they regard as incidental. Nothing is required of them in the face of the immensity of nature's apparent preeminence; they have no weight in nature's balance. Their image of the Riverways as "perpetuated wilderness" implies a limitless power of the stream to absolve them of responsibility for their behavior and absorb their waste without consequence.[21]

There is no easy answer to the issues raised by conflicting images of "frontier" and "wilderness" in the Ozark National Scenic Riverways—no simple criterion defining the "rights" of any single group. The local canons of precedent, sentiment, and survival have no legal weight, yet they must be taken into account in any equitable decisions of policy. In microcosm, the problems of this region represent similar difficulties addressed with varying consequences throughout the National Park Service and, indeed, anywhere that is "discovered" by tourists eager to escape temporarily from the pressures and demands of their own worlds.[22]

Perhaps at least what can be asked is that administrators and visitors make the effort to view the process of accommodation to visitor needs in part through native eyes. Conrad L. Wirth, director of the National Park Service from 1951 to 1963, described inhabitants of what is now the Shenandoah National Park in 1933 as poor, uneducated, and inbred. When relocated by the Resettlement Administration to "reasonably comfortable" houses in the valley, many insisted on slipping back to their familiar one-room homes in the mountains.[23] Wirth's bland astonishment at their choice exemplifies an outsider's selective myopia—crystal clear to him are the authentic historical human factors that make the Blue Ridge potentially alluring to visitors, while the distress experienced by the equally authentic contemporary heirs of that history in having their homes appropriated, their intimate connection with place marginalized and invalidated, remains mysterious and surprising. In focusing on the interpretation of historical trapping in the Ozark National Scenic Riverways rather than on the immediate dilemma of contemporary trappers in the region, Congressman Vento displayed a similar myopia at the hearing in 1986. Buck Asbridge *is* an Ozark trapper; it is not a role he would don docilely to take part in any congressman's living history scenario.

Ironically, in certain respects the Park Service–local split is not as absolute as such points of contention make it appear, presenting at least the possibility of effective mediation of conflict. Unit personnel comprise locals and localized outsiders as well as "career" Park Service employees transferred from sites elsewhere and likely to be transferred again in their upward scaling of the federal ladder of advancement. The folklore of any National Park Service unit is replete with esoteric references to employee categories emphasizing contract between "local yokels" (natives), "homesteaders" (nonnatives who have chosen to sacrifice career advancement to remain on site), and "floaters" (although this is the term for canoeing or inner-tubing visitors at the Ozark National Scenic Riverways, in general Park Service employee slang it also refers to personnel perceived as on their way up and out of a unit). The trapping controversy at the Riverways reflected this internal institutional complexity in microcosm: several local and localized rangers were enjoyably supplementing their federal income with trapping revenue each winter, and they were clearly uncomfortable with their impending role as local enforcers of a ban imposed by a directive from the remote corridors of power in Washington.

Informal canvassing of employees of several National Park Service units indicates that the categories containing the largest number of transient individuals include those most likely to have an impact on community- and culture-related issues: administration, interpretation, and enforcement. The employee category most often noted as having a high degree of stability is maintenance—a group with little impact on policy. Nevertheless, unit employees at all levels who have demonstrated commitment to the region might represent an untapped potential resource for cooperative negotiation of differing tourist and local interests—especially in matters of policy determined within a unit rather than imposed from the upper reaches of the federal hierarchy.

Meanwhile, as the National Park Service copes with the environmental consequences of the Riverways' surprising attraction, the human drama continues season after season with little successful mediation. Although the trapping controversy was adjudicated in favor of the trappers, the negative stereotypes called up on either side still haunt natives and visitors drawn to the streams—the brazenly naked tourist still confronts the brutal and bestial local in mental landscapes murky with mutual contempt. Where once there existed the opportunity, however chancy, for learning and exchange between people living very different lives, the paths for most have now parted. Fewer and fewer such opportunities are offered or sought. Kenneth Wells, a trapper, told me a quiet, little story that to me sums up the apparent finality of the division. While on his way to fish at Parker Ford, he saw a woman sunbathing nude on a gravel bank near his path. Embarrassed, he hovered at a distance for a bit.

> Well, she finally saw me, and I was probably thirty yards [away] when she saw me. So she politely walked into the tent. Now her husband was setting outside the tent. She didn't get into any hurry! But I just went on down there and went fishing. And went away on down the river, and when I came back, she was dressed. And you know what she made the comment? She says, "Is this the river they trap on?" I says, "Yes ma'am." [She says] "Boy, they oughtn't to be allowed to trap." I never said a word, Erika, I just kept walking.[24]

NOTES

I am grateful to the Eastern National Park and Monument Association, whose Herbert E. Kahler Research Fellowship supported the initial stages of the investigation. Thanks also are due to U.S. Congressman Bill Emerson of Missouri's Eighth District and his staff members in Washington and Cape Girardeau as well to Arthur Sullivan, superintendent of the Ozark National Scenic Riverways, National Park Service, Van Buren, Missouri, and to staff members James Corless, Alex Outlaw, and James Simpson. Further valuable insights concerning the National Park Service were offered by Lois Winter, Joy Lyons, and Rebecca Jones of Mammoth Cave National Park. Above all my gratitude goes to Kenneth Wells and the members of the ninth district of the Missouri Trappers Association, whose cooperation made this study possible. Portions of this essay appeared previously in *Folklife Annual 88-89*.

1. Hearing on H.R. 103, to require the secretary of the Department of the Interior to permit trapping in the Ozark National Scenic Riverways area, Committee on Interior and Insular Affairs, Subcommittee on National Parks and Recreation, September 11, 1986.

Public Law 88–492, which established the Ozark National Scenic Riverways, included specific provision permitting hunting and fishing in the unit. Trapping was considered a form of hunting and continued uninterrupted in the Riverways from its inception. In 1984, however, the Department of the Interior moved to ban all activities not specifically mentioned as permissible by the enabling legislation of a park unit. The ban was to take effect in the Riverways beginning with the trapping season in the winter of 1986–87.

After considerable legislative and judicial dispute, the issue was resolved by a suit brought by the Missouri Trappers Association against the National Park Service. In 1988 the case was resolved in favor of the Trappers Association, and the Park Service was enjoined from enforcing the ban. For a fuller account, see Erika Brady, "Mankind's Thumb on Nature's Scale: Trapping and Regional Identity in the Missouri Ozarks," in *Sense of Place: American Regional Cultures,* ed. Barbara Allen and Thomas J. Schlereth (Lexington: University Press of Kentucky, 1990), 58–73.

2. Letter from Richard H. Ichord to Bill Emerson, September 9, 1986.

3. Bill Smith, "Ozark Trapper Caught in Clamp of Ban," *St. Louis Post Dispatch,* October 26, 1986, A-1.

4. Alan Jabbour and Howard Wight Marshall, "Folklife and Cultural Preservation," in *New Directions in Rural Preservation,* ed. Robert E. Stipe (Washington, D.C.: U.S. Department of the Interior), 43–50. I am indebted to Mary Hufford for suggesting the term *anachronization.*

5. Kathleen Fine, "The Politics of 'Interpretation' at Mesa Verde National Park," *Anthropological Quarterly* 61 (1988): 177–86.

6. Barbara Kirshenblatt-Gimblett, "Mistaken Dichotomies," *Journal of American Folklore* 101 (1988): 140–55. Her discussion of the process of "aestheticization" in the process of commodification and subsequent marketing of folk art objects parallels the process of "anachronization" suggested here.

7. Milton D. Rafferty, *The Ozarks: Land and Life* (Norman: University of Oklahoma Press, 1980), 4–6; Carl O. Sauer, *The Geography of the Ozark Highland in Missouri* (Chicago: University of Chicago Press, 1920), 73–170; E. Joan Wilson Miller, "The Ozark Region as Revealed by Traditional Materials," *Annals of the Association of American Geographers* 58 (1968): 71–77.

8. For extensive treatment of Ozark naming practices, see E. Joan Wilson Miller, "The Naming of the Land in the Arkansas Ozarks: A Study in Cultural Processes," *Annals of the Association of American Geographers* 59 (1969): 240–51.

9. Robert Flanders, "Introduction," in *A Connecticut Yankee in the Frontier Ozarks: The Writings of Theodore Pease Russell,* ed. James F. Keefe and Lynn Morrow (Columbia: University of Missouri Press, 1988), iv.

10. Taped interview, Salem, Mo., December 4, 1986. Stories and conversations are transcribed from tape recorded interviews made in the course of the trapping investigation. Copies of these tapes will be deposited at the Western Historical Manuscripts Division of the University of Missouri, Columbia, and the Archive of Folk Culture at the Library of Congress upon completion of the project. Access will be restricted until 1995.

11. Quoted in Louis Houck, *A History of Missouri,* vol. 2 (Chicago: R. R. Donnelley and Sons, 1980), 34.

12. Larry Dablemont, "The History of Float Fishing, Part 1," *Fishing and Hunting Journal,* June 1986, 70.

13. "Current River," *Current River Magazine,* 1904, 15. Photocopy in collection of Missouri State Historical Society, University of Missouri, Columbia.

14. Rafferty, *The Ozarks,* 200–202.

15. Leonard Hall, *Stars Upstream: Life along an Ozark River* (Columbia: University of Missouri Press, 1969 [1958]). The 1969 edition contains a foreword by George P. Hartzog, then director of the National Park Service, which attests to the importance of this book in the establishment of the Ozark National Scenic Riverways.

16. Personal communication, Alex Outlaw, Ozark National Scenic Riverways staff.

17. Arthur L. Sullivan, "A Report on Trapping within the Ozark National Scenic Riverways" (Unpublished report of the ONSR superintendent to U.S. Congressman Bruce F. Vento, chairman of the House Subcommittee on National Parks and Recreation, and U.S. Congressman Bill Emerson, Eighth Congressional District, Missouri, May 1, 1986), 21.

18. James Dickey, *Deliverance* (Boston: Houghton Mifflin, 1970). This bestselling novel provided such a striking focus for southern upland popular stereotypes that a small literature of scholarly discussion of the phenomenon now exists. See especially Eliot Wigginton, *Foxfire Magazine,* Winter 1973, 258–59; James S. Otto, "Reconsidering the Southern Hillbilly," *Appalachian Journal* 12 (1985): 324–31; and John L. Puckett, *Foxfire Reconsidered: A Twenty-Year Experiment in Progressive Education* (Urbana: University of Illinois Press, 1989), 248–50.

19. Vance Randolph, "Verbal Modesty in the Ozarks," *Dialect Notes* 5 (1929), reprinted in *Ozark, Ozark: A Hillside Reader,* ed. Miller Williams (Columbia: University of Missouri Press, 1981), 33–40.

20. Taped interview, December 5, 1986.

21. The concepts of frontier and wilderness, among the most significant in American national mythology, are seminally explored in Roderick Nash, *Wilderness and the American Mind* (New Haven, Conn.: Yale University Press, 1967).

22. Benita J. Howell, "Appalachian Tourism and Cultural Conservation," in *Cultural Heritage Conservation in the American South,* Southern Anthropological Society Proceedings, no. 23, ed. Benita J. Howell (Athens: University of Georgia Press, 1990), 125–39.

23. Conrad L. Wirth, *Parks, Politics, and the People* (Norman: University of Oklahoma Press, 1980), 50–51.

24. Taped interview, May 16, 1987.

11

"Sweetgrass Is Gold": Natural Resources, Conservation Policy, and African-American Basketry

Dale Rosengarten

> It is a curious characteristic of intelligent people that they only begin to value their cultural inheritance highly when it is in danger of disappearing for ever over the cliff-edge of time—at which point they seize the tip end of its tail and exert tremendous energy in trying to haul it back. Usually what happens is that the tail comes away in their hands, and the body is lost.
>
> —Sybil Marshall, *Everyman's Book of English Folk Tales*

In African-American communities along the South Atlantic Coast craft traditions are enjoying a revival, while the communities themselves are threatened with extinction. How can both be true? It is not surprising that folk arts attract most attention when they are in gravest peril or that the right kind of attention can foster a fragile revival. Yet there is no doubt that demographic changes are altering the natural landscape and social complexion of the lowcountry and are endangering a distinct way of life.

I first became aware of threats to the African-American tradition of sea grass basketry in the autumn of 1984, when I was hired as guest curator of McKissick Museum's Lowcountry Basket Project. My involvement with the project may itself have been a sign of crisis. (Emory Campbell, director of Penn Center on St. Helena Island, once told me that as soon as he sees an anthropologist approaching, he looks for the bulldozer behind the scholar.) But I can honestly say I began my research with few preconceptions and wound up convinced that the problems of cultural conservation call for political solutions.

Most of today's lowcountry basketmakers live in Mt. Pleasant, South Carolina, across the Cooper River from Charleston. This community of landed black families has managed to preserve the sea grass tradition through the twentieth century by transforming what was once a common plantation handicraft into salable folk art. While coiled sea grass basketry was generally disappearing, basketsewers in Mt. Pleasant found a market; introduced new forms, functions, and materials; developed the aesthetic side of their craft; and kept making baskets.

I approached the "sewers," as they call themselves, first as a buyer (I bought a basket from every basketmaker I interviewed), second as a collector of information, and third as an advocate. Culminating in an exhibition and catalog called *Row upon Row: Sea Grass Baskets of the South Carolina Lowcountry,* the project generated a lot of press coverage and public acclaim, but it also caused confusion in the basketmaking community about McKissick's intent. Notoriously independent, entrepreneurial, and mindful of past attempts to exploit their art, the Mt. Pleasant basketsewers are suspicious of strangers and competitive with each other. Was the museum planning to make money from the exhibit? What were we in it for, and what was in it for them?

* * *

Once a sleepy backwater, the old malarial coast has become a tourist mecca and a residential frontier for retired people, young families, and urban refugees. Like the Native Americans who were driven off the land three hundred years ago by expanding white settlement, Sea Islanders are facing wholesale removal under the onslaught of resort development and population influx. "Developers come in and roll over whoever is there," Emory Campbell declared in the newsletter of the Highlander Folk Center in 1984. "We have given up on trying to protect the shrimp and crab because we, the black native population of these islands, have become the new endangered species."[1]

This message becomes more urgent with each passing year. In the case of the sweetgrass basketmakers, the dangers are manifold. Since the advent of the New South, the baskets and their makers have been struggling with the paradox of Sun Belt development: while tourists and new residents boost basket sales, basket stands on Highway 17 are being crowded out by shopping malls, office complexes, subdivisions, and fast food chains. Equally alarming, the facilities built to accommodate the newcomers have progressively destroyed or cut off access to the sewers' prime raw material, sweetgrass. Each year the "men folk" in the basketmakers' families have to travel farther afield—often as far as Georgia or northern Florida—to gather the grass.

Fifty years ago Mt. Pleasant was a quiet village, surrounded by farm settlements. Today it is a burgeoning suburb, and its old country lanes are now highways clogged with traffic. The generation of basketmakers entering middle age grew up in this time of transition. They learned to sew at the knee of their mothers and grandmothers. In the evenings they were required to finish a certain number of pieces before bedtime. During the long summer days there was little else to do. Their children, however, are growing up in a different world, with louder, brighter stimulations and many opportunities competing for their time and attention. In this environment basketmaking may strike active youngsters as boring, menial, and poorly paid. "We don't want to sit down and do this kind of stuff," eighteen-year-old Melony Manigault told me in an interview in 1985. "We want to get up and go."[2]

When pressed, youngsters reveal a deep ambivalence about making baskets. On the one hand, some feel coerced and impatient when they are expected to sew. On the other, they know how important the craft is to their parents and their people, and they want to see it continue. Melony, for example, heir to generations of sewers, expects to keep making baskets "but not as steady as grandmama and mama." She understands that sewing one day a week is "not good enough if you want to sell. You got to make 'em every day." For Melony, basketmaking may become a pastime—a meaningful leisure activity—but not her full-time occupation.

Judging by the notoriety it has attracted over the past twenty years, the basket tradition appears to be thriving. Lowcountry basketry has won high honors as an art form and wide recognition as perhaps the oldest craft of African origin in America. Markets have expanded. Charleston's tourist industry has grown by leaps and bounds, although Hurricane Hugo and the economic recession both have taken a toll. New outlets have opened—the convention trade, craft fairs, galleries, museums, and a small collectors' market. Most impressive, the level of artistic freedom the basketsewers enjoy has never been greater.

The recent aesthetic renaissance is fueled partly by the reintroduction of bulrush as a basketmaking material and partly by the sewers' response to the growing appreciation for baskets-as-art. The traditional shapes are still staples of the trade, including fruit, flower, and bread baskets; covered cord or cake baskets; hampers; picnic baskets; and trays. But the imprint of the collectors' market, which puts a premium on regular stitching, elaborate surface decoration, and expressive forms, is visible in the work of all the basketmakers. The new audience has encouraged sewers to be innovative, to follow their own "good minds" in the creation of "new style" baskets. Most basketmakers feature in their repertory a "signature" or "designer" piece, a specialty for which they or their families are known. "An African craft that began with functional intentions," asserts the George Washington University folklorist John Michael Vlach, "has become an art medium with primarily aesthetic motivation."[3]

As baskets are valued less as utilitarian objects and more as collectable art, we find them in new contexts—not only on sidewalks and roadside

Figure 11.1 Basketmaker in Charleston, South Carolina, late 1930s. (Photo by Bayard Wootten; courtesy of the North Carolina Collection, University of North Carolina Library, Chapel Hill)

Figure 11.2 Annabell Ellis and Florence Frazier, Kiawah Island, South Carolina, 1985. (Photo by the author; courtesy of McKissick Museum, University of South Carolina)

stands but also in studios, galleries, and museums. In fact, the original stands are being chased off the road. Nearly every new shopping mall or subdivision on Highway 17 displaces a basket stand, sometimes more than one. This encroachment is part of the process that has redefined whole islands as suburbs or resorts, some gradually, some in one fell swoop—islands like Hilton Head, Johns, Seabrook, Kiawah, Wadmalaw, Edisto, Fripp, Dataw, Daufuskie, and on down into Georgia. It is no exaggeration to say the Sea Islands are being repopulated with vacationers, commuters, golfers, yachters, and owners of second homes, condominiums, or time-share apartments—people who bring an affluent life-style with them. In this period of dislocation basket stands and sweetgrass plants serve as indicator species. Threats to their existence are evidence of environmental change and predict the direction of things to come.

The displacement of basket stands represents a loss of the very autonomy that, more than anything else, has enabled basketmaking to survive in Mt. Pleasant. The community's strategic location on the main road into Charleston made it possible for sewers to become independent entrepreneurs, to control both the production and the marketing of their baskets. Without direct access to a steady flow of customers, sewers on remote Sea

Islands by and large have stopped producing baskets. Even on St. Helena, where the Penn School made conscious, concerted efforts over nearly half a century to preserve native Island basketry, the only people making baskets today are a couple of Mt. Pleasant women who married Island men.

A folk art may die because it loses its functions or its markets or because the community that produces it disperses or is assimilated into the mainstream culture. Mt. Pleasant basketmakers so far have avoided these pitfalls. Contact with their market, however, has brought not only income and recognition but also dealings with insensitive tourists, curiosity-seekers, voracious journalists, and would-be middlemen. Added to centuries of exploitation that are the birthright of every black American, these encounters have made basketmakers wary of white people knocking on their door to ask questions.

When I began work on the Lowcountry Basket Project, my major concern was simply, would the basketmakers talk to me? Being a "come-here" from the North, I discovered, did not hurt my chances. At least I was *here,* not just passing through. Some sewers put up with my questions for the sake of a sale, yet many of the old-timers would not talk to me at all. In a region where "plantation manners" still hold sway, I was disappointed but not surprised. Among women of my own generation, my strongest drawing card was the documentation I was uncovering, including photographs and printed materials concerning people they knew or had heard of, which intrigued everyone.

For two years I combed archives and museums; talked to basket collectors, folklorists, and fieldworkers; and taped interviews with some forty basketmakers. At the end of each interview I would ask, how can the McKissick Museum help you and your community keep your tradition going strong? Every Mt. Pleasant sewer gave the same answer: "The supply of sweetgrass is shrinking fast. We need help finding more."

McKissick responded to this plea with a daring venture in cultural conservation. Already many basketmakers, and most of the buying public, were willing to credit museum curators and other outside agitators with driving up basket prices, which have doubled in the last five years. Certainly we have succeeded in throwing a spotlight on the tradition of lowcountry basketry. Could we now help find a way to conserve the natural resources and marketing practices on which the basketmakers depend?

* * *

Muhlenbergia filipes, as sweetgrass is known to botanists, is a long-stemmed plant that grows in tufts behind the second dune line or along the margins of marsh and woods. A renewable resource, it has been the main foundation material of Mt. Pleasant baskets since early in the twentieth century. All spring and summer, gatherers "pull" the blades of grass, which slip out of their roots like knives from sheaths, stimulating new growth. A salt-tolerant plant adapted to a narrow ecosystem, *Muhlenbergia* increasingly must share its habitat with developers hungry for beachfront lots.

The sweetgrass problem goes back at least twenty years, when basketmakers first reported having trouble getting to the plant. Recognizing that sea grass basketry faced an uncertain future, anthropologists, folklorists, and the media, armed with notepads, cameras, and recording equipment, began descending on Mt. Pleasant. In 1971 South Carolina ETV produced a film entitled *Gullah Baskets,* documenting the African origins of the art and describing the sweetgrass shortage as a major threat to the basket's survival.[4]

Over the next decade lowcountry basketry and the community of sewers became the subject of serious anthropological study. Gregory Day, Kate Young, Gerald Davis, Mary Twining, Gloria Teleki, Doris Derby, and John Vlach visited Mt. Pleasant, studied the tradition, and wrote up their findings in scholarly articles and dissertations.[5] Day and Young petitioned and won permission for the basketmakers to pull sweetgrass in Charleston County parks,[6] but this was not enough.

Faced with a crisis, the Mt. Pleasant sewers made a virtue of necessity. Without fuss or fanfare, they reached back into their tradition and rediscovered bulrush, using it in conjunction with *Muhlenbergia* to "stretch" the sweetgrass supply. Bulrush turned out to be an unexpected boon. Thicker and stiffer than sweetgrass, rush allows basketmakers to work on a grand scale, to make large fanners, market baskets, and hampers reminiscent of old-style work baskets. "I really love the large one now even more than I like the small one," commented the sewer Marie Manigault, because big baskets "show up prettier."[7] Rush can be used to reinforce handles, feet, rims, and other points of stress where a basket might break. It is hollow, hence light in weight. It turns a rich, tawny brown when dried in the sun. Above all, it is abundant.

But rush does not eliminate the need for the finer, more flexible sweetgrass. Not everyone is willing or able to use the tough, sharp "rushel," or "needlegrass," as *Juncus roemerianus* is commonly called. Binding rows of bulrush requires strength and agility and is hard on the hands. Rush is difficult to tie in a knot. It is too coarse to use in small baskets or for delicate decorative details. In the coin of the realm, as the basketmaker Henrietta Snype is fond of saying, "Bulrush is silver, sweetgrass is gold."

° ° °

The idea for a conference to address the sweetgrass problem germinated at a folklore seminar in October 1986, shortly after the "Row upon Row" exhibit opened. Conferring with community and government leaders, Gary

Stanton, then state folklorist at McKissick, defined the project in grant applications to the National Endowment for the Arts and the Ruth Mott Fund, which both generously awarded support. McKissick hired me to serve as conference director and Henrietta Snype as community liaison. The Avery Research Center for African-American History and Culture at the College of Charleston cosponsored the event and provided us with office space as well as technical and moral support.

Our first step was to recruit a community steering committee. We scheduled an evening meeting at the Greater Goodwill A.M.E. Church in Mt. Pleasant. Gary produced a flyer and Henrietta and I went from stand to stand, basketmaker to basketmaker, urging everyone to attend. Our most effective lure was the promise to distribute reprints of a popular basket brochure issued by the South Carolina Arts Commission in 1977. Announcements read in churches and on WPAL radio helped spread the word.

The campaign worked, and some seventy basketmakers showed up at the appointed time. I presented a slide show, Gary described McKissick's new Folk Arts Program, and the Arts Commission's Frank McNutt reviewed the kinds of support his agency could offer to traditional craftspeople. Then all hell broke loose, and we realized we had grabbed a lion by the tail.

The ensuing discussion revealed a backlog of community grievances and worries. Anxiety about the future of highway basket stands ranked a close second to fears about the supply of sweetgrass. Hot debate broke out over whether to sanction basketmakers who taught classes outside the community. Old apprehensions surfaced: What taxes and licenses might be required if basketmakers went *too* public? Wouldn't middlemen try to take a piece of the pie? Didn't help from government agencies always come with strings attached?

Although closely knit by family and church connections, Mt. Pleasant basketmakers had never organized as a group. Yet they were willing to table the most divisive issues and to focus constructively on how to solve common problems. Then, putting aside their historical distrust of outsiders, the basketmakers agreed to accept our assistance and take a leadership role in the Sweetgrass Conference. When we asked for volunteers to serve on a steering committee, about twenty people came forward.

This dedicated group of basketmakers began meeting monthly, then every other week, to draft an agenda, propose speakers, prepare press releases, solicit designs for a poster and flyer, and meet with members of the Charleston County legislative delegation, the mayor of Mt. Pleasant, and a host of local conservation groups. The planning process thus yielded new strategies and coalitions even before the conference commenced.

The day before the Sweetgrass Conference, on the afternoon of March

25, 1988, about thirty people set out from Charleston to Seabrook Island, a scenic barrier island twenty-three miles to the southwest, now a private residential and resort community. We were a diverse bunch—basketmakers and botanists, folklorists and environmentalists, photographers and journalists—on a mission to find sweetgrass. As we drove past substantial modern houses, a ripple of excitement passed through the basketmakers in the party. They had spotted lush tufts of *Muhlenbergia* growing on road medians and in landscaped yards, next to the more predictable pampas grass, palmetto, and yucca.

The excitement caught us all. We parked near a clubhouse and a cluster of new condominiums. Several members of the Seabrook Natural History Group joined us. We crossed a boardwalk onto the beach and walked east toward the neighboring island of Kiawah. In troughs behind the first line of dunes lay acres and acres of sweetgrass growing in the shade of myrtles.

When the conference convened at the Charleston Museum the next morning, speakers from the Sweetgrass Steering Committee opened each panel and set a tone of deep commitment. They talked about what basketmaking means to them and what it should mean to those outside the tradition. Sea grass basketry, explained Marguerite Middleton, "is an art form which demands and deserves the respect of the community and our state, for it is an integral part of our Afro-American heritage as well as our city's economy. . . . There is too much valuable history surrounding sweetgrass baskets to allow this art form to die."[8]

A distinguished roster of folklorists, scientists, land managers, public officials, and community leaders shared information and proposed ideas. The most pressing tasks, as defined at the conference, were to conduct a coastal survey of sweetgrass to identify existing sites and, wherever possible, to arrange for controlled harvesting; to propagate the plant experimentally, with a view toward large-scale cultivation; and to establish a "green corridor" along Highway 17 North to protect the basket stands.

"History must record this as a first," concluded Middleton, "for never before have we had a meeting of this magnitude where weavers, lawmakers, and others in key decision-making positions have met to discuss issues which affect basketweaving." In his closing remarks, Congressman Arthur Ravenel, Jr., stated succinctly a philosophy of development compatible with traditional arts. "Growth that preserves these valuable traditions," Ravenel proclaimed, "is fundamentally better than growth that does not."[9] The audience breathed a hearty amen.

* * *

Where the initiatives outlined at the conference will lead remains to be seen. Most promising is the creation of a new community organization.

Within days after the conference, the steering committee reconstituted itself as the Mt. Pleasant Sweetgrass Basketmakers' Association and immediately began to negotiate for basketmakers to gather grass on two privately owned islands near Charleston and on Little St. Simons Island, Georgia, 150 miles to the south. Association members have designed a letterhead; written, published, and distributed a handsome brochure on lowcountry basketry; produced newsletters; and attended zoning hearings of the town of Mt. Pleasant. To cope with the devastation wrought by Hurricane Hugo, the association served a crucial if unanticipated role as organizer and conduit for relief funds.

Several efforts to tackle the problem of the sweetgrass shortage have come from outside the community. The U.S. Department of Agriculture's Soil Conservation Service has undertaken a five-year propagation project, transplanting sweetgrass to experimental plots accessible to the basketmakers. Richard Porcher, a professor of biology at the Citadel, coordinated a coastal inventory of existing sweetgrass populations. South Carolina State College's 1890 Extension Program began a "needs assessment" in Mt. Pleasant to determine other ways—including marketing initiatives—to strengthen the basketmaking enterprise.

Least susceptible to solution, it seems, is the threat to the basket stands. Friendly realtors claim they are willing to make concessions. One who displaced several basket stands promised to set aside a parcel of land for the "basket ladies" and announced that his shopping mall would henceforth be named the Sweetgrass Market Place. "We think of ourselves as a good neighbor," said the broker in charge, T. Rushton Baker, "and certainly are concerned with not only the aesthetics of our development, but also the impact in that neighborhood, especially as it relates to an age-old marketing and art form."[10]

This expression of concern betrays an ignorance of the milieu necessary to sustain the "age-old" basket stands. It is hard to imagine, for example, where a basketmaker would find the requisite shade and space for a stand on the thirty-acre site of the Sweetgrass Market Place, which was bulldozed, graded, and posted with billboards announcing sales and leasing information before Hurricane Hugo stopped the venture.

What was proposed here was not cultural conservation but co-optation; basketmaking would be patronized and its symbols appropriated to sell other goods. The Mt. Pleasant basketmakers are not easily fooled, however, certainly not by a blatant public relations ploy. Genuine conservation depends first of all on understanding what you want to conserve. Second, it requires coordinating diverse groups and individuals, whose interests are not always in accord—in this case, the curators' interest in promoting folk arts, the ecologists' interest in biological diversity, the politicians' interest in serving constituents and securing votes, the city's interest in boosting the regional economy, the developers' interest in getting a return on their investment, and the basketmakers' interest in preserving their heritage and making a living.

In the end the vagaries of market forces will determine the success of this last objective. Sentiment aside, a basketmaker's ability to sell baskets is a function of the state of the economy and the elasticity of the tourist dollar. Campaigns to protect the highway stands and to gain access to sources of sweetgrass are, however, vital to secure the foundations on which the tradition rests.[11]

Young people will still be drawn by mainstream culture away from basketmaking, despite the new glamour attached to African-American folk arts. One thing we can count on is the adults' determination to pass on the torch, to fulfill their responsibility to the next generation and to past generations. "That responsibility," according to Marguerite Middleton, "has been none other than that of preserving the tradition of sweetgrass baskets. As history has proved, our people weaved in spite of the times. So it must be with our generation, for—it's OUR time now!"[12]

NOTES

1. Quoted in "Cultural Activity in the Sea Islands," *Highlander Reports* (newsletter of the Highlander Folk Center, New Market, Tenn.), November 1984.

2. Interview with Melony Manigault, Mt. Pleasant, S.C., June 12, 1985. All tapes, transcripts, and fieldnotes are at the McKissick Museum, University of South Carolina, Columbia, S.C.

3. John Michael Vlach, *The Afro-American Tradition in Decorative Arts* (Cleveland, Ohio: Cleveland Museum of Art, 1978), 19.

4. Elizabeth McRae Scroggins, "Gullah Baskets," *ETV Guide* (Columbia, S.C.), April 1, 1971.

5. See Gregory K. Day and V. Kay Young [Kate Porter Young], *Preliminary Field Report* (Washington D.C.: Smithsonian Institution, 1971); Gregory K. Day, *South Carolina Lowcountry Coil Baskets* (Columbia, S.C.: Charleston Communication Center, South Carolina Arts Commission, 1977), and "Afro-Carolinian Art: Towards the History of a Southern Expressive Tradition," *Contemporary Art/Southeast* 1, no. 5 (1978), 10–21; Kay Young Day [Kate Porter Young], "My Family Is Me: Women's Kin Networks and Social Power in a Black Sea Island Community" (Ph.D. diss., Rutgers University, 1983); Gerald L. Davis, "Afro-American Coil Basketry in Charleston County, South Carolina," in *American Folklife,* ed. Don Yoder (Austin: University of Texas Press, 1976), 151–84; Mary A. Twining, "An Examination of African Retentions in the Folk Culture of the South Carolina and Georgia Sea Islands" (Ph.D. diss., Indiana University, 1977), and "Harvesting and Heritage: A Comparison of Afro-American and African Basketry," *Southern Folklore Quarterly*

42, nos. 2–3 (1978), 159–74; Gloria Roth Teleki, *Baskets of Rural America* (New York: E. P. Dutton, 1975), and *Collecting Traditional American Basketry* (New York: E. P. Dutton, 1979); Doris Adelaide Derby, "Black Women Basket Makers: A Study of Domestic Economy in Charleston County, South Carolina" (Ph.D. diss., University of Illinois, 1980); John Michael Vlach, *The Afro-American Tradition in Decorative Arts,* and "Arrival and Survival: The Maintenance of an Afro-American Tradition of Folk Art and Craft," in *Perspectives on American Folk Art,* ed. Ian M. G. Quimby and Scott T. Swank (New York: W. W. Norton, 1980), 177–217.

6. Minutes of Meeting, South Carolina Parks, Recreation and Tourism Commission, Charles Towne Landing, Charleston, S.C., July 28, 1972.

7. Interview with Marie Manigault, Mt. Pleasant, S.C., February 8, 1985.

8. *Proceedings of the Sweetgrass Basket Conference, March 26, 1988* (Columbia, S.C.: South Carolina Folk Arts Program, McKissick Museum, University of South Carolina, n.d.), 72.

9. Ibid., 75.

10. Quoted in David Quick, "Developer Gives Basketmakers Space in Mall," *News and Courier* (Charleston, S.C.), January 19, 1989.

11. In April 1993 a Bi-Lo shopping mall, calling itself Sweetgrass Corner and displacing four or five basket stands, opened on Highway 17 North. In June the Basketmakers' Association, with help from a Clemson University horticultural professor and permission from Historic Charleston Foundation, transplanted two thousand sweetgrass plants to an acre on the McLeod plantation on James Island, southwest of Charleston.

12. *Proceedings of the Sweetgrass Basket Conference,* 72.

Part 3

Encouraging Folklife

12

Conjuring Culture: Ideology and Magic in the Festival of American Folklife

Robert Cantwell

The term *cultural conservation,* now a regular part of the discourse and the rhetoric of public sector folklore programs and of correlative projects in related fields, such as historical preservation, reveals, upon close inspection, a number of interesting and curious dimensions that at this point in the development of the concept perhaps call for renewed discussion. Among these is the paradox implicit in the coupling of the concept of culture with a term whose historico-political affiliation is to natural, not cultural, resources—not, to be precise, to nature *itself,* or, by analogy, to culture *itself,* but to their resources—that which may be exploited for use by the agents of production. Cultural resources are, as the phrase implies, in some sense natural—autochthonic, self-sustaining, and self-regulating—free in some paradoxical sense from conscious intervention, though human consciousness is presumably the carrier of them. In their explication of the term *cultural conservation,* Marjorie Hunt and Peter Seitel have recourse to its "sister concepts": environmental conservation, ecosystem, and the protection of endangered species.[1] Hence cultural resources, already defined by analogy to natural resources, exist in contradistinction to, or at least in some skewed relation to, the prevailing socioeconomic order and are explicitly identified in the federal document *Cultural Conservation: The Protection of Cultural Heritage in the United States* (1983) as folk cultures.[2] The point is that there are certain cultural resources that, like natural resources, can be made culturally available to their "natural" carriers and to the larger society through conservation; they can be made available, that is, for exploitation.

The rhetorical efficacy of the implied, though paradoxical, analogy emerges clearly in the federal report:

> The impossibility of completely preserving the contours, texture, and features of any specific culture, frozen in time, is generally recognized. It includes styles, institutions, attitudes, memories, and values—all of which change. Proposing governmental efforts to stem the inevitable change in society would be pointless. Further, in a free society, even expecting government to slow the process would be wrong. The natural flow of cultural developments belongs to the people as a consequence of their freedom to choose. It is possible, however, to temper change so that it proceeds in accordance with the will of the people, and in response to the pressures of faddish trends or insensitive public or private projects. Conservation denotes efforts which steward and nurture living resources and ensure natural cultural growth.[3]

Here the assimilation of "nature" to "culture" is evident in such phrases as the "natural flow of cultural development" and "natural cultural growth," which suggest a potentially odious aspect of a policy concept that requires its implementers, on the one hand, to distinguish between "natural" and "unnatural" cultural growth and, on the other, to determine, in a nonlegislative context, "the will of the people." "Faddish trends" and "insensitive public or private projects," simply as phrases, imply that as a concept cultural conservation has inscribed in it a particular moral, historical, socioeconomic, and cultural outlook, namely, that one set of forces in the national and international life, mainly technological and commercial, is working a powerfully destructive effect upon another, weaker set of forces, mainly local and traditional, to which the name "culture" seems most fittingly to attach. The idea of cultural conservation, then, suggests that it has become the duty of public policy to do what culture would otherwise do quite naturally and inevitably for itself, which is to transmit and reproduce itself. Cultural conservation denotes a competition within official culture for control of the cultural environment.

Direct grants to indigenous cultural groups, apprenticeship programs, cooperatives, consultation, in-kind assistance, legal protection of natural environments and historical structures, and the like are among the practical instruments of cultural conservation. But the discourse of cultural conservation normally includes the representation of culture as well; this embraces all the forms of documentation and presentation, scholarly and popular, that introduce ideas, images, and information about folklife and folk culture into the public sphere.

An exceptionally thorough case for the inclusion of cultural representation—in this case, the Smithsonian's annual Festival of American Folklife on the National Mall—in the discourse of cultural conservation is made in Richard Kurin's essay "Why We Do the Festival" (1989). The festival, Kurin writes, encourages "the preservation and transmission of traditional cultural repertoires"; these represent "not only continuity with the past, but the ability to enact the future with a variety of proven approaches and sensibilities." In this capacity, he continues, the festival becomes explicitly political, "an advocate for human cultural rights, for cultural equity, for cultural diversity in the context of the Smithsonian—a national institution founded with democratic, enlightment ideals."[4]

Kurin notes that in the late nineteenth and early twentieth centuries forces of industrialization, colonialism, commerce, communication, and the like had begun to lay waste the traditional cultures of what we now call broadly the Third World; the passing of these ways of life represented "a dimunition in the human cultural repertoire." "A pattern that may have taken thousands or hundreds of years to form," he writes, "is lost: there is no one to teach it, to transmit its vision of the world, the knowledge and wisdom reposed within, the skills of the generations of people who labored in its bounds. This loss extends beyond the present, for we never know how valuable would have been the contribution of that culture to a larger human future."[5]

To accomplish its ultimate goal, a "world of manifold civilizations animated by the vision of cultural equity," the Festival of American Folklife works in several ways. It "gives voice" to folk, tribal, ethnic, regional, and occupational traditional culture, all "non-elite and non-commercial" forms "not otherwise likely to be heard in a national setting"; in so doing, it legitimizes "alternative forms of aesthetics and culture," conveying, through the implicit endorsement of the National Museum, with its "standards of authenticity, cultural significance, and excellence . . . their value to artists, to home communities, to general audiences and to specialists," and thereby provides "a needed counterweight to other forms of delegitimization."[6]

The festival, then, is among other things a kind of morale-builder; it strengthens the self-esteem of folk artists otherwise neglected or even despised by mass culture and may enrich their own understanding and appreciation of the culture of which they are the bearers. The festival, moreover, provides a kind of training ground for the representation of culture. Festival participants, Kurin writes, often "develop their own means of self-presentation and interpretation as they interact with festival staff, experts, and the public";[7] some become cultural spokespersons themselves. The power of the festival to stimulate cultural activity extends beyond the participants to scholars, public folklorists, museum curators, and politicians. The legacy of its influences, through its researchers, presenters, authors, and consultants, as well as its participants and visitors, includes the American Folklife Preservation Act of 1976, the American Folklife Center, the

Folk Arts Program at the National Endowment for the Arts, and a variety of folklife programs and festivals in states and in foreign countries.[8]

Most important—and this is the aspect of the festival to which its producers most consistently point as a sign of its power—the festival has generated *its own* community of "scholars, workers, community people, volunteers and artists," with their own traditional names, narratives, foodways, dress, rituals, and ceremonies:

> The Festival is actually built and technically served by theater people, musicians, teachers, architects, government bureaucrats and other amateurs, some of whom take time off every year to work on the Festival. The temporary Festival staff and the hundreds of local area volunteers include a diversity of old and young, female and male from a variety of cultural and ethnic groups. People support the Festival and work on it as a labor of love and pride. This commitment to helping the nation represent itself is illustrated by volunteers returning year after year for five, ten, even fifteen years.[9]

The festival, Kurin concludes, "holds open the possibility of emergent, non-predictable cultural creation."[10] It embodies, in short, the very process over which it offers to exercise its influence; it has become an instrument capable of influencing cultural processes through cultural processes. Now this is a very different relation than that implied by, say, a direct grant, the preservation of an old building, a judicial ruling that diverts a road-building project away from an ethnic neighborhood, or a tax law that inhibits commercial development in a specific community. Were we in the purely natural realm, we would call the relation scientific or technical—science, after all, having developed certain specific technical instruments for influencing nature by the manipulation of its own laws. In the cultural realm, however, where no such technology exists, unless art itself can be called a cultural technology, the right name for the cultural power of the festival is what science was called in the prescientific sixteenth century: magic.

It should be interesting, then, to take a look at the fashion in which festival business is conducted in the ideological and rhetorical context of cultural conservation. I would like to report one instructive instance of the influence of the discourse of cultural conservation upon the language, the thought, and the practice of an office of public folklorists in the process of reviewing, in their final stages, plans for the production of a major public folk festival.

Let me briefly summarize, then, a small part of the proceedings of a review meeting that I attended in 1985 at the Office of Folklife Programs in my capacity as official historian of the Festival of American Folklife.

Lest there be any misunderstanding, let me say at the outset that my necessarily schematic and fragmentary picture of the meeting cannot do justice to the professionalism and dedication of the folklorists involved in it. They conducted their discussion at an exceedingly high moral and intellectual level, informed by the most current developments in folklore and anthropological theory; their understanding of the problems of representation, exhibition, demonstration, and the like reflected in its sophistication and subtlety the accumulated experience of nearly twenty years of festival production; and their decisions reflected a sensitivity to participants and visitors that was both politic and humane.

But most significant—and this is my point—the discussion, like folklife program discourse generally, was characterized by an underlying sense of intimate instrumental connection between the operations of the festival and the destiny of the cultures represented there, as if the festival were a kind of cultural engine; this sense of connection went well beyond that which normally inheres between parts and wholes, signs and signifieds, and instead tacitly ascribed to the festival an affective, dynamic, and predictive force, which seemed, on the one hand, to bestow on the planners an extraordinary power of influence in the realm of culture and, on the other, to burden them with the extraordinary and at times exquisite responsibilities that the exercise of such a power implies.

The name assigned, by agreement, to that responsibility was "cultural conservation"—explicitly analogized to environmental conservation and analyzed anthropologically, principally in terms of the intimate interdependency of traditional cultures and available natural resources. The instrument by which this cultural conservation is carried out, the festival, became in this highly ideological and articulate context itself a discourse, whose intellectual organization, internal consistency, and rhetorical tone demanded thorough interpretation and reinterpretation, careful scrutiny, and tireless vigilance—this in spite of what the planners would otherwise acknowledge to be the broadly spontaneous, unpredictable, and polymorphous character of the festival as festival. But, while the power of cultural conservation had found and would find further articulation both in the office and in the institution's public discussion, in the planning meeting itself it remained occult—a type, I would suggest, of alchemical or hermetic magic, based like all magic on the occultation of an instrumentality. I say this, incidentally, not to discredit the planning discussion but simply to point to an imaginative, as opposed to a scientific or political, dimension in it—for it is, I believe, in the purely symbolic and magical realm that festival discourse best succeeds in producing on the Mall what is ideally a symbolic form of behavior, not *ultimately* an instrument of a particular cultural policy.

Occultation in magic may be mere concealment, and instrumentalities merely mechanical; but the subtlest forms of magic are those based on similitude, resemblance, affinity, where even, or especially, the magician may be deceived by connections embodied in a figure or image that will not, or cannot, be exposed by analysis but can be pursued only by elaboration of the figure itself. The most complex magic, of course, involves both mechanical and figural operations, combining, confounding, and confusing them. That is what happens, it seems to me, in the curious and sometimes—to an outsider—amusing inflation of language that while remaining within the festival framework, almost imperceptibly transforms festival discourse into a larger cultural discourse undergirded by specific festival arrangements and relationships.

As a way of explaining what I mean, I would like to return to the 1985 meeting. The meeting opened with a charge by the chair, director of the Office of Folklife Programs, that the ongoing discourse on cultural conservation, the standard under which the festival was to be conducted, should be compared with the "Silent Spring" issue of the 1950s, inspired by Rachel Carson's book of that title—it should raise the general consciousness of traditional culture and of the impact of technology, commerce, mass communications, and so on upon it. "When they build a road or a bridge," the director suggested, "they'll have to do a study of its potential impact upon culture in addition to an environmental impact statement."

The theme of the meeting thereby in effect struck, a staff folklorist presented her plan for the leatherworker Duff Severe's saddle shop. Duff had sent photos of the shop that would be blown up to form the background of the exhibit. Benches would be placed to provide a site for conversation among the cowboys participating in the festival. The aim, which both folklorist and director attempted to articulate in a lengthy discussion of authenticity, space, and presentation, was twofold: to create an "intimate" encounter with the craftsperson, beyond the "two-dimensional" encounter of more typically theatrical museum displays; and to reproduce what the folklorist called "life"—she wanted the shop to become in effect what it was in its "natural" setting.

A similar aim was expressed for the cornrowers' exhibit, which, it was hoped, would become a kind of informal "hangout" on the Mall. To achieve this end, the cornrowers would be placed in a small, "embracing" semicircle at a height of about one foot—although discussion reduced this to six inches—and one of the hairdressers, a Tanzanian, would bring some of her own clients.

As the sites of what all hoped would be lively social activity, both the saddle and the hairdresser's shop offered solutions to the knotty problems of crafts presentation not so readily overcome in either the Makah woodcarvers' exhibit or that of the Puerto Rican maskmakers. The folklorist opined, to general assent, that craftsmanship *is* performance but that the long and painstaking process of woodcarving would require, at the Makah exhibit, least twenty minutes of the visitor's attention. Precisely the opposite problem arose with the maskmakers, whose technology is a relatively simple one but whose cultural context—carnival—is immensely complex, requiring a good deal of text and talk. The folklorist proposed to raise the interest of the maskmakers' site by surrounding them with a "forest of masks" and by displaying a full costume, complete with pig bladder, to one side of their workbench.

A consistent problem with crafts presentations, observed an invited state folklorist, is that craftspeople become so involved in their work that they become reluctant or even unable to talk with visitors. Presenters consequently talk altogether too much or become involved in the process themselves, opening a vacuum that volunteers or even visitors are sometimes obliged to fill by providing verbal explanations, often quite faulty, of their own.

The issue of the social character of the exhibit site was especially acute in the case of the eight Kmhmu participants—musicians, spinners, weavers, basketmakers, toymakers, and native interpreters. They would be placed in a kind of "compound"—a word to which the Office of Folklife Program's senior ethnomusicologist took strong exception—which would include a garden, a blacksmith shop, and a small platform sheltered by a tent. Both the director and the state folklorist saw potential problems of objectification with the arrangement—for the director, the exhibit too closely resembled the "cultural zoo" phenomenon of earlier exhibitions; for the state folklorist, the lack of a common language, which would normally provide a medium of negotiation between participant and visitor, was paramount—it would in effect turn the exhibit into a "living diorama." As a solution, the group agreed to redesign the platform so that the visitor, as the director put it, would be "surrounded by Kmhmu" rather than above them or separated from them by a barrier.

Whoever has struggled with the issues of cultural exhibition will recognize in this conversation a familiar paradox: exhibition, in a festival or a museum setting, demands representation, but the palpable substance and intrinsic forms of representation shape both that which is represented and the awareness to which it is represented—even though the aim of representation is ultimately to dissolve itself and its frame, bringing the visitor and the participant into a kind of mutual imaginative absorption that normally is the province of acknowledged formal fictions in which the very consciousness of fictionality underwrites such absorption. Devices of representation, such as stages, platforms, and amplification systems, and mediators, such as presenters and texts, permit the festival planners to define to the visitor the reality they hope to represent—but they also stand in the way of the thoroughgoing self-transcendence that the ideal representation would achieve.

The paradoxes of representation percolated to the surface of the discussion later in the meeting when cultural representation itself became part of what the festival would be representing. A staff assistant introduced her plans for the Louisiana component of the festival. Mardi Gras, she explained, is "about stereotypes"—its exaggerations constitute in effect a "reverse ethnicity" that converts all ethnic signs into stereotypes and hence "denatures" them. A photograph of a Mardi Gras float on its way up from New Orleans on a flatbed truck was passed around, and the state folklorist noted offhandedly that a "Mayan snake" on the float represented the transformation of one culture's religious symbols into another's comic exaggerations—a sort of "cultural appropriation."

It also appeared from the photographs that the float was decorated with Mayan glyphs—a fact especially significant since, as the director earlier explained, the Guatemalan component of the festival, on the other side of the Mall, would be calling attention through photographs and other texts to the systematic extermination of Highland Mayas by the Guatemalan army. This it seems was a particularly urgent instance of the necessity of cultural conservation with a keenly political edge, since the participation of Guatemalan refugees placed them under some threat of reprisal. Should we permit, then, on one part of the Mall, the director asked, an exhibit that would seem to subvert the purposes of an exhibit on the other side? The danger of a folk festival, he warned, is that it may do what the commercial media do: demean and "commoditize" a people's symbol. What the festival was attempting to do was to "keep symbols and their meanings together." The Mardi Gras, he continued, is a "discourse in ethnicity . . . its symbols are manipulated in a racist way."

A long, heated discussion ensued. The staff assistant insisted that had she and her coworkers understood that the float would make fun of Indian culture they would not have accepted it; but she was not convinced that it *did* make fun of Indian culture. The idea, she argued, was to portray a family making Mardi Gras floats in the traditional way. Several others pointed out that virtually all Mardi Gras imaging stereotypes the culturally other—the black Mardi Gras "Indians," for example, who would be participating in the festival in spite of the fact that the Louisiana component would include four Native American tribes to supplement the several tribes represented in the cultural conservation component. An especially graphic case was the Mardi Gras "Zulu," middle-class blacks whose traditional costume is the grass skirt and bone nasal-ornament of the cartoon primitive; but they had not been invited to the festival.

The director nevertheless feared possible embarrassment to the festival should some savvy reporter catch the ironic relationship between the Guatemalan presence, under the rubric of cultural conservation, and the Mayan symbols on the Mardi Gras float, and he rejected the float. Some effort had to be made, less than a week before the opening of the festival, to alter the design of the float or to substitute a new one altogether.

Interestingly and ironically, the director's fears were confirmed when, at festival time, a new float arrived with a gigantic image on its prow, in blue and pink, of the Blessed Virgin, her arms raised in a gesture of blessing; she had been hastily reconstructed from the original image, that of the Brazilian goddess Iménja.[11] Near the float, in the floatmakers' tent, stood, on its collar, the monstrous head of an Abraham Lincoln, glaring maniacally through starting eyes over a grotesque monkey face, larger than a rain barrel, that lay on the grass beside it, scandalously reminiscent of one of our cruelest ethnic stereotypes. From the opposite wall of the tent, a tribunal of demons and gargoyles observed this cultural dreamwork impassively, with just the slightest suggestion of indignation.

All icons and symbols fell, it seems, within the floatmakers' purview; their art consisted of the recognition of type and their ability to render it in palpable form. The papier-mâché images in the tent and on the float, like the Mardi Gras Indians and Zulu, were of course caricatures—not signs of signs but signifiers of signs: effigies. Grotesque and monstrous, as the tradition dictates—for the basis of the tradition is to profane what is sacred—they absorbed the entire pantheon of figures that furnished the cultural imagination with a flimsy, ephemeral, and spurious embodiment, whose implicit promise is that when they are finally torched at festival's end, the symbols they signify—and merely signify—and the customary weight of those symbols that has become such a burden upon the heart will have been lifted, and the original icons, sacred and secular, will be refreshed, ready to preside again for another year over the life of the soul.

The exhibits in the Cultural Conservation section in some respects fulfilled the planners' hopes for them and in other respects did not. The cornrowing exhibit became a genuine living place—though not, perhaps, precisely what it is in its Southeast Washington neighborhoods—where people, children especially, lingered, looked on, asked questions, and engaged in conversation with the hairdressers, while girls and young women, black and white, submitted their hair to braiding. The concentrated activity at the cornrowing exhibit, rooted in the tender, sensuous intimacy of the process itself and the community of girls and women formed around it, made it an appealing place to loiter and rest and provided considerable opportunity for the participants to express their opinions and personalities.

Duff Severe's shop proved not so popular, but it did provide the cowboys with a place to linger and talk; in that sense it became a place *for them,* men who had become friendly with one another partly through participation in the Smithsonian and in other festivals. It is likely that the success of the shop in that respect had a chilling effect for visitors, who may have felt they were intruding. The Puerto Rican maskmakers' booth and the Makah woodcarvers' were simply too spare; in each case the worker's absorption in his work seemed to discourage inquiry, except for the occasional crafts enthusiast willing to watch over long periods and to ask technically pertinent questions—but that is perhaps as it should be.

There is a kind of flexion in the encounter of the festival's typically middle-class visitor with participants situated across sex, class, or racial lines that would otherwise be sites of tension, rancor, or jealousy; here the cultural encounter inspires a mutually gratifying spirit of charity and goodwill. But there is such a thing as a too habitual or commonplace otherness. The cowboys, working men with considerable sophistication about the festival enterprise, were often eager to share their lives and lore with festival visitors but sometimes found themselves isolated because, in fact, the visible differences between them and many visitors were almost negligible, though of course certainly not meaningless. Only the western costume, however, which in the festival setting is almost a cliché, made the cowboys appear, at first blush, as characters, cranks, or mere interlopers.

The Kmhmu area, however, became what the state folklorist feared it would—a living diorama. Communications between participants and visitors were difficult, and, in fact, except for the old toymaker, the participants tended to ignore visitors as, it seemed, a matter of propriety, actuated by a kind of embarrassment or modesty. To approach the Kmhmu as closely as the festival setting permitted was profoundly disquieting. They are, after all, a mountain tribe of Southeast Asia, culturally enigmatic and physically exotic, catastrophically dislocated by a bizarre war. Only children, unburdened by stereotypes and undaunted by language barriers they could not anticipate, communicated with them; even certain federal dignitaries, whose interest in the Kmhmu was largely responsible for their presence, were visibly uncomfortable at the special flower ceremony prepared for them. On the discussion and music stages, some of the mystery of the Kmhmu was dispelled in music, dance, and conversation through an interpreter and with the aid of a young Kmhmu man with some English; but the feeling here was largely one of relief that through the narrow opening in the silence between the two cultures the visitor could communicate some sort of welcome, and participants could find their own humanness certified in the visitor's awkward but sincere recognition of it.

For me the questions that arise from this review meeting and from its actual outcome in the festival are these: what were the aims of the festival planners, and by what agency did they hope to achieve them? What values governed the progress of the discussion and justified its conclusions, and to what extent, if any, do those values intersect with the values of cultural conservation in which the discussion, and the entire festival, was framed? Assuming these aims to have been even partially achieved, is it to be imagined that success in the festival will encourage a revival of Makah woodcarving, as it is claimed that anthropological work among the Makah has done, or a revival of Puerto Rican Carnival maskmaking? Is it to be imagined that the festival, however successful, will contribute anything to the continuing vitality of African cornrowing or western leatherworking, except in very local and specific ways? Still more: will censorship of the Mayan glyphs on a Mardi Gras float in any way curb the unfortunate tendency of Mardi Gras players to caricature, satirize, ridicule, cartoon, and in general appropriate the cultural sign in the uncouth semiotic plenitude characteristic of festivity? Will displays of brilliant Mayan weaving and marimba music in any way enlighten our government's long-benighted Central American policy sufficiently to protect the lives of Mayan Indians still victimized by official repression?

The answer to all of these questions may be yes—often, no doubt, in the direct instrumental ways usually outlined in cultural conservation documents but far more significantly through the magical influences that move mysteriously, over time, from obscure and ephemeral works of art, visionary philosophies, and certainly folklore and folklife into the central zones of culture and history. If this is not the case, then the planning meeting, as well as the festival itself, was an idle, myopic, self-indulgent exercise.

The prevailing problem of magic in the Renaissance, as Frances Yates explains, was to grasp reality as a whole—something that could be done only through the contemplation of ideas and images, stuff of the spirit, which to Neoplatonists were nearer to absolute reality than to the shadows and chimeras of the outer world.[12] No radical ordering of the psyche could be achieved by introspection alone, however; it required a mechanics of imaging, such as memory theaters and Lullist systems of wheels and circles inscribed with signs and symbols through whose manipulations the mind could grasp and organize itself, and the reality beyond it, in concrete and visible terms. The aim of these manipulations was to animate the statues, images, characters, signs, or numbers that were the magicians' stock-in-trade with the virtues and powers of life. To do this meant to fashion these images, symbols and characters, and their relationships according to the divine principles of harmony, fitness, and proportion—attributes capable of summoning astral forces into the sublunary world. It was a kind of aesthetic science, whose aim was to gain mastery of the universe through beauty.

To me these essentially philosophical impulses, far more than the social, psychological, and political precipitates of the folk-cultural exhibition, however admittedly real and important these are, underlie the process of conceiving the Festival of American Folklife. There is no doubt that the design of an exhibit, the height of a platform, the placement of texts and images, the situation of the participants, and so on all have significant and immediate intellectual and aesthetic impact on observers; but the process of fine-tuning these factors in intimate consultations in the various sanctums of festival production is itself deeply intuitive, imaginative, and mystical, and it aims at ultimate effects that are separated from the planning process itself by a gap that neither theory nor practice can bridge. Those effects are, in fact, to call down not astral but cultural forces into the festival and to animate the participants and visitors with them—to create, in effect, what the staff folklorist calls "life," or what Richard Kurin calls "emergent, non-predictable cultural creation."

The counterfeit shrine that practice sacralizes, the imitated trance that in performance becomes harrowingly genuine, the craftsworker who momentarily forgets himself and stoops to wash his hands in a creek that isn't there, the Saints' Day procession in which participants and visitors from other parts of the Catholic world spontaneously participate—these "enviable moments in which displayed enactment and real activity merge," as Richard Bauman puts it,[13] are, again, what Smithsonian folklorists consistently point to as indications of the success of their enterprise.

The transformation of the festival, for its creators, into a cultural calculus, a purely symbolic space, a microcultural instrument for influencing the macroculture occurs because the festival plan in its various abstract and schematic manifestations indicates and empties the socioeconomic, geographic, cultural, and other boundaries that folklorists and anthropologists routinely cross in order to define their area of study and to conduct their fieldwork in it. No longer diffused on the margins of the social center, the folk-cultural universe, bounded by the National Mall and differentiated into several realms, each distinguished by a specific culture or cultural theme, is collapsed into a center, whose margin is the social-scientific gaze.

There is nothing particularly magical in this—until we realize that the festival scheme, a product of thought and as mobile as thought, works, or seems to work, like a draughtsman's mechanical arm to reproduce itself in the behavior and the experiences of participants and visitors. It is not quite as if in the midst of the game a Monopoly board were suddenly to represent the real Boardwalk and Reading Railroad and play money to become negotiable currency; but if we used the game for modeling a Festival of American Capitalism on the Mall, to which we had invited real bankers, brokers, speculators, and investors, we could not play it without supposing that by some occult instrumentality it might eventually make its impact on Wall Street. What has developed in the Festival of American Folklife, particularly in the context of cultural conservation, is the unstated assumption that the festival has in effect become the cultural marketplace itself.

Were that the case, obviously, we would play the game differently. We might open a visitor's access to a hairdresser's shop by lowering the platform on which she works or restrict a visitor's access to a harnessmaker's shop by providing seating for him and his friends, even though such tactics might run in some ways contrary to what we claim to be doing at the festival; we might even decide to turn back a thirty-foot Mardi Gras float; and we would do it not because we are thinking only about the festival but because we are in fact thinking beyond it, to what we want culture to be.

If festival planning and discussion becomes to any extent purely symbolic and combinatory, as I am claiming it does, it is worth thinking about what the manipulations of such an instrument may mean morally for the festival participants themselves. Preparing the ground for or summoning into existence specific forms of behavior is not tantamount to reproducing culture. The Festival of American Folklife, from one point of view, is a form of internment, however contractual, which in order to achieve "emergent, non-predictable cultural creation" regularly practices several forms of deception, including what is called "induced natural context," through which, by a kind of transport, simulated experiences become real ones, and the "inner audience," through which members of one cultural group feel themselves swept on a tide of enthusiasm into copartnership with another, their hearts swollen with the intimation of a brave new world that has such people in it.

But a folklife festival is by definition discontinuous—a time and space set apart; cultural reality, on the other hand, is a continuity that writes the narrative of consciousness onto the people, places, and things that come, in culture, to constitute it. Culture is an environment of reminders. In a culture the stuff of experience is over time so finely sifted and resifted that it passes without impediment through the membrane that divides the outward and inward worlds and in effect obliterates the distinction between them. To reproduce this condition in participants or visitors on the Mall through transport in effect reduces them to semiconscious or unconscious beings who do not know where they are, restoring the pernicious unbalance between folklorist and folk, between awareness and unawareness, the sophisticated and ingenuous, the self-conscious and unself-conscious, which is purely an illusion of the social boundary and which for a generation or so we have been trying to think and work beyond. Conscious beings know where they are; culture, indeed, *is* where they are.

Yet I am uncomfortable with the perspective on the festival I have just offered and recognize its incompatibility with what we actually experience there—which is, and should be, magical. I suspect I am not alone if I confess that I attend the festival at least partly in search of the transport I also expect from, say, music or, in the case of a crafts demonstration, the absorption in process all of us sometimes experience while at work. Further, I look forward to transient and perhaps superficial, but in any case actual, exchanges with people I could otherwise never come to know, and tally such associations into the sum total of my social experience, consider myself enriched and enlarged by them, and incorporate them among the elements of my conscious identity. Moreover I consider the consummation of my experience and that of the participants to be connected somehow to these expectations—that the participant has something to gain by winning my appreciation of his or her art and that I have something to gain by appreciating it, in more than a merely "educational" sense. The outcome of this mutual negotiation is what the ideology of cultural conservation is largely designed to account for.

But the terms of that negotiation are a unique form of representation, whose formal cause is not, as we casually suppose, folk culture or cultures but social encounter itself; the Festival of American Folklife has over the years elaborated a complex set of framing devices that mark and replace daunting and often insurmountable barriers of class, race, language, and the like, reducing them to a set of ephemeral physical structures, symbolic in their slightness and ephemerality but in their physicality capable of shaping socially and psychologically the nature of the encounter framed by means of them. These structures are the bridge between the mundane and the magical worlds, and within them virtually *any* form of cultural performance can be framed and our encounter with it to some extent manipulated—even, say, the performances of Washington trial lawyers.

It is magic when the frightful and tangled forces that divide human beings suddenly vanish, effaced by the sheer power and excellence, the authenticity, of performance, on the one hand, and by the willingness of the visitor, on the other, to recognize power and excellence as such, even if he or she is unacquainted with the specific cultural values that inform it. To suppose that the festival-maker can "induce" or in any other way summon up this moment is to fall into the most persistent intellectual infirmity of science and magic, the illusion that what we conjure we can control. The festival-maker can prepare for this moment; but only the participant and visitor together can create it. That participants during two weeks on the Mall should make their workplace or some related site familiar by means of culturally informed practices and habits adapted to new circumstances, or that they should become briefly absorbed in their performances, whether technical, artistic, or religious, is so typically and universally human it is surprising that we should be so surprised by it; but each acquires a magical character because under the festival's influence a suppression or dissolution of the festival frame seems to have occurred in the participant's mind. That is naive, though; the same could be said of reading fiction or listening to music, when to an observer not concomitantly engaged we will seem to have departed the real world when in fact we are consciously and deliberately enjoying the special immunity granted by art.

In fact it is the participant's own resourcefulness and imagination, not the festival-maker's ingenuity, that has produced the magic; the magic is a sign not of the folklorist's sovereignty, or of the festival's influence, but of the participant's independence of these factors. This is not culture induced or culture reproduced or culture renewed or even culture conserved but culture invented: the original response of particular people, informed by a culture of their own, to new conditions in which they learn to shape, at a particular historical moment, a reality in conformity with their own beliefs and values. It is *festive* culture, not only in a local and accidental sense but comprehensively and totally.

For the visitor the matter is a bit more complicated. The festival's framework for representation both indicates and reestablishes a social boundary; but it also conscientiously occludes most of the social, economic, and other factors that account for the boundary to begin with, particularly such potentially alienating differences as those of class, education, taste, and so on. To understand this, it is only necessary to consider for a moment what the festival would be were the participants to be fully represented in their own home circumstances, complete with such signifiers of disadvantage as a diurnal diet of fast food and daytime television, or worse. Participant and visitor meet instead on a single footing, the folk-cultural performance, which, when it is successful, becomes a metonym for an entire way of life, an essence made to stand in for an existence. Visitors cannot but understand and interpret the performance in terms of their own cultural endowment; visitors generally respect the cultural authority of the institution whose endorsement participants implicitly have won and are willing, certainly on the issue of their own advantages of class and education, to appreciate, however imperfectly, cultural difference.

Even these complex preconditions, however, will not guarantee that the festival magic will work on the visitor. That belongs, again, to participants, whose technical skill, passion, judgment, and sheer personal presence must be impressive enough to eclipse even their own cultural medium and become signs of the culture-making power itself. That is a profound magic indeed, when the cultural garment, blown in the breeze that rises out of the ground of human generativity, reveals, with a thrilling intimation, the natural form of the life that animates it.

No one is more susceptible to the power of magic than the magicians themselves, the Smithsonian folklorists, who in the final stages of festival production have arrayed before them in ductile and symbolic form, a form that as the review meeting I think indicates is even at that late stage capable of manipulation, the vast, variegated folk-cultural universe they have constructed. It is magic to wield the world about as the folk festival does and to assemble in one place a fantastic variety of folk-cultural performers, craftspeople, spokespeople, and presenters; and no doubt the Renaissance magician would have found it so, particularly if he had been as unconscious as the festival visitor typically is of the jet flights, the phone calls, the road travel, the computer and photocopy operations, not to mention the years of planning, the bureaucratic hassles, and the enormous expenditure of private and public funds required to produce the Festival on the Mall. It is not only that the world's variety is summoned up from distant and foreign parts, as other fairs and exhibitions have done, but that the Folklife Program's own fieldworker-Ariels can have been sent out to retrieve from those parts what the office explicitly names as the esoteric performance forms that however inherently excellent typically fall beneath the notice of commerce, mass communications, and official ministries of culture. What Prospero could do only once, the Office of Folklife Programs, it seems, does every summer.

With the world thus apparently delivered repeatedly into their hands, the folklorists confront—as is clear from the tone and intensity of their deliberations—what ordinary mortals are happily mostly free of, the necessity of discovering a principle upon which that world might be framed. Cultural conservation, among other ideologies, political and social-scientific, competes for this role and injects itself with other viewpoints persistently into the discussion. In the end, however, the folklorists, like the astronomers, mathematicians, sorcerers, and other wizards who know the right spells, incantations, and formulas, incline unerringly toward those divine attributes, harmony, fitness, and proportion, which for folklorist, participant, and visitor alike are still it seems the forces that wed reality to consciousness. What may actually constitute harmony, fitness, and proportion in this context we can find in the planning meeting only obscure and minute suggestions; but it is possible at least that beyond the explicit politics and the implicit theory, as well as the moral urgency and idealism, of the planning meeting lies a perennial longing for the regular fellowship and the quotidian rhythms of traditional community as we conceive it, for a fuller sovereignty than we in a consumer society can enjoy over the material forms of life, and a dream, rooted perhaps in a sense of personal exclusion arising from our own society's specific alignments of class and culture, of what Alan Lomax has called "cultural equity"—a dream that, when it fails to acknowledge the whole depth and intractability of cultural difference, can realize itself only as cultural spectacle, tragically perpetuating in the isolate spectator the very evil it seeks to overcome.

If a platform moves six inches up or down or changes shape, a photo accepted or rejected, public access opened or closed, if the semiotics of one area of the Mall are brought into alignment with those of another, if indeed we think we are elsewhere and the whole world is different from what it is, it may be for the same reason that the sun moved to the center of our solar system magically, before it was politically, mathematically, or empirically necessary that it do so—because it belonged there. We are justified in hoping that a sun moved first in imagination, and for imagination's own reasons, may in the end move in fact and warm us with a warmth that is as much a consequence of the chemistry of human desire as a reaction of hydrogen and helium.

NOTES

I thank Mary Hufford for her encouragment and assistance in the preparation of this essay. A slightly different version first appeared in the *Journal of American Folklore* 104 (Spring 1991): 412. Used by permission of the American Folklore Society.

1. Marjorie Hunt and Peter Seitel, "Cultural Conservation," in *1985 Festival of American Folklife,* ed. Thomas Vennum, Jr. (Washington, D.C.: Smithsonian Institution, 1985), 38–39.
2. Ormond Loomis, coordinator, *Cultural Conservation: The Protection of Cultural Heritage in the United States,* Publications of the American Folklife Center, no. 10 (Washington, D.C.: American Folklife Center, Library of Congress, 1983).
3. Ibid., 29.
4. Richard Kurin, "Why We Do the Festival," *Program Book of the Smithsonian Festival of American Folklife,* ed. Thomas Vennum, Jr. (Washington, D.C.: American Folklife Center, Library of Congress, 1989), 10.
5. Ibid., 11–12.
6. Ibid., 15.
7. Ibid., 17.
8. Ibid., 18–19.
9. Ibid., 19.
10. Ibid., 20.
11. I would like to thank Nick Spitzer for this identification.
12. Frances A. Yates, *The Art of Memory* (Chicago: University of Chicago Press, 1966).
13. Richard Bauman, Patricia Sawin, and Inta Gale Carpenter, *Relections on the Folklife Festival: An Ethnography of Participant Experience* (Bloomington: Folklore Institute of Indiana University, 1992), 31.

13

Cultural Conservation and the Family Farm Movement: Integrating Visions and Actions

J. Sanford Rikoon, William D. Heffernan, and Judith Bortner Heffernan

This essay links aspects of the social and political action programs advocated by midwestern farm groups loosely joined together as the family farm movement with the cultural policy agenda of cultural conservationists. Specifically, we explore links between the two agendas and suggest efforts to meld the goals of cultural conservation activity with the objectives of family farm groups.

Individual and group concepts of the family farm have psychological, cultural, social, and political implications. For the general nonfarm public, the term typically connotes very alluring and very attractive images. Public opinion surveys conducted during the 1980s on the ongoing farm crisis in the Midwest, for example, reported a vast majority of nonrural respondents viewed farmers as more honest, more hard-working, and closer to their families than urban workers are. The nonfarming sector also typically cited family farm life as more moral than city life and felt family farms were important to America.[1] Although recent agrichemical and environmental alarms may be motivating some widening breaches in the public's generally favorable attitudes, opinion surveys continue to reveal widespread positive evaluation of farmers and support for programs to "save the family farm."[2] Such instruments rarely probe causalities or provide detailed explanations of results, but their scholarly heuristic weaknesses are perhaps overshadowed by their documentation of enduring affirmative perceptions of farmers and family farms.

Public sentiment is not alone in aligning itself with an agrarian fundamentalism that holds up farming as a most honorable and virtuous way of life.[3] Over more than two centuries of intellectual thought and government programs (and sometimes the two working hand in hand), there are many examples of legislative policy and programs formulated on the basis of positive concepts of a particular structure of agriculture. A class-conscious agrarianism on behalf of independent family farmers informs the core of this ideology.

Students of American culture, for example, are familiar with the writings of Thomas Jefferson on the virtues of an idealized yeoman farmer class and with the ideology of nineteenth-century eastern Romanticists, who envisioned the Midwest as an agrarian utopia of autonomous landholders. Scholars from Frederick Jackson Turner to Henry Nash Smith to contemporary historians note how federal land policies, particularly the guidelines of the Homestead Act of 1862 as well as many lessor-known laws on preemptive settlement, attempted to translate central tenets of these agrarian ideologies into practice by encouraging the development of an agricultural structure of independent family homesteads with limited amounts of land. Nineteenth-century federal and state laws discouraged, and even outlawed at times, the ownership of exceptionally large farms or estates by absentee landlords. These programs were of course not wholly altruistic, nor were they always successful or founded on completely democratic moral social purposes. Nineteenth-century programs may well be accounted for by the availability of unsettled land in the West, desires to expand borders and markets, the need to find employment for immigrants and unemployed urban dwellers, and, certainly in the case of the 1862 Homestead Act, Republican efforts to promote aggressive free soil principles against the demands of proslavery Southerners. None of these factors, we would suggest, precluded pursuit of an overriding ideal of keeping resource and food production bases in the hands of family farmers.

A survey of twentieth-century farm-related programs reveals a vested support for farmsteads of independent owner-operators persevering well beyond the settlement of the frontier. This argument is evident in the debates and legislation of the Capper-Volstead Act of 1922, providing for the creation of farm cooperatives on the basis of the Rochdale principles (the cooperative tenets associated with one of the first cooperatives, founded in the town of Rochdale, near Manchester, England, in 1844, which included one member–one vote, education, and the like). It informs, at least in part, the guidelines of farm unit access to federal water projects or the cap on payments to participants in current U.S. Department of Agriculture price and income support programs. Again, there are exceptions and other explanations for these examples. One could, for example, view commodity payments as a form of tacit approval for low market prices, a situation that often forces smaller operators either to get bigger or to get out of agriculture.

The contemporary family farm movement believes the United States is at a crossroad in the debate over the worthiness and viability of the socio-cultural goals that have long guided public perception and vested legislative support. What many groups believe is at question today in Washington, D.C., and around the country is not merely the definition of a family farm or its cultural values and behaviors but also whether the unit itself will exist into the next century. Midwestern rural residents are asking whether an integrated program will be developed to empower farm families to continue in an occupational niche developed over many generations with the direct support of the American citizenry.

The family farm movement agenda targets the maintenance of a structural pluralism in agricultural production. The North American Farm Alliance, for example, calls its multigroup coalition "one of the last bastions of widespread individual entrepreneurship and a democratic alternative." Family farm activists often view their cause as a movement for continued democratization in agriculture, that is, for the preservation of independent, full-time, family-owned-and-operated farms. They point to two major threats to this continuity: an economic menace in the form of corporate mergers and vertical integration in agricultural production, and a social disenfranchisement on the part of a government that appears, at best, disinterested in what rural sociologists often designate as the "disappearing middle" or mid-sized family farm.[4]

The farm movement's major concern today is general socio-occupational survival, not the retention or conservation of specific cultural forms. Group activities are based on economic rationales and political goals rather than processes of cultural identification or conservation. The movement stresses such concrete economic and political goals as market quotas, debt adjustments, program benefits targeting small and medium-sized farmers, long-term export agreements, supply management, and commodity stabilization. The particular action programs of individual farm groups are rarely identical, but their basic preservation interests (and instincts) are remarkably similar.

In essence, the movement does not fly a celebratory banner of farming as a way of life as much as it raises a red flag of occupational endangerment due to corporate and governmental policy. Political resources target such legislation as the Save the Family Farm Act or Farm Policy Reform Act rather than proposed bills affecting cultural resource management. Indeed, family farm leaders rarely refer, and then only vaguely, to the preservation of specific cultural orientations as a reason for supporting family farms. In 1989, for example, delegates to the National Farmers Union (NFU) meeting in Little Rock, Arkansas, approved programs that fill a hundred-page booklet.[5] The term *culture* does not appear at all, much less references to concepts or activities of the type normally associated with cultural conservation. The NFU maintains the family farm is worth saving because "family farmers are the most efficient producers of food and fiber. This has been proved time and time again. The family farm provides the greatest protection for consumers. The small business structure of the family farm is the nation's strongest bulwark against communism and fascism. It is essential to the democratic way of life."[6]

The NFU statement is typical of other family farm group arguments in its complexity and style. The economic emphases partly represent an in-kind reaction to (and perhaps acceptance of) contemporary government and corporate rhetoric stressing farming as a business, not a way of life. The family farm movement's responses to the recent farm crisis avoid discussion of cultural identification, at least in public arenas. With the abandonment of arguments based on cultural values, groups have turned to production, economic, and social patterns as the bases of self-identity. The resulting dialogue directly counters charges of business inefficiency with examples of economic competence. At the same time, the lack of cultural foregrounding allows the retention of public support for stereotypical images that, however syrupy, are strongly positive and favorable to the movement's efforts.

Consensus self-definitions of the family farm typically focus on family ownership of the land, assumption of economic risk, overall control of the decision-making process on the farm, and responsibility for most of the farm labor. Framing identity on the basis of economic process and labor, rather than on overt cultural forms, is significant in many respects. It enacts barometers for demarking boundaries; for example, corporate farms are different because they depend on hourly hired labor and a salaried managerial class. It also defines membership on the basis of ascribed objectives and social relationships. The particular cultural stuff marking a family's life at a particular point is less important than the maintenance of group processes, values, and objectives.

The family farm movement's conception of its identity also provides occupational and social frames for the construction of symbolic meaning. The labels of "family farmer" and "family farm" are emblematic for both insiders and outsiders, serving as powerful ideational constructs around which farmers and the general public may negotiate identity and cultural attributes. In the Midwest the family farm remains an immediate and powerful symbol, invoked as a rallying point for families seeking to maintain a structural niche and occupational identity in what they perceive is a threatening world.

The cultural conservation movement agenda also includes various symbolic and ideological constructs. Most important, in contrast to the family farm movement's positive valuation of structural pluralism (or the democratization of agricultural social structure), the significant ideological objective of cultural conservation is cultural pluralism (or the democratization of cultural difference and identity).[7] If one accepts this primary difference in agendas, an important initial question to ask is whether cultural pluralism exists (or can exist) without corresponding differentiation in social structure. If the answer is that it is highly improbable that a single social structure (in agriculture or any other sphere) is likely to enhance the continuity of cultural difference, then the goals of the family farm movement and cultural conservation are *mutually* supportive, at least on levels of theory and ideology. The ability of farm families to make choices on the retention of cultural forms and lifeways requires continued existence of, and access to, social alternatives. Simply stated, if compulsion reigns—whether in the form of a single social structure or cultural model—individual freedoms are curtailed.

The rhetoric of cultural conservation recognizes the importance of structural pluralism. Activities generated thus far in terms of family farm culture, however, are very few and have yet to demonstrate much affinity for the fabric of contemporary rural farm life or the structural objectives of the family farm movement. Passages in a 1983 report published by the American Folklife Center recognize the social basis of cultural performance and, by extension, infer that the lasting impact of rural cultural conservation efforts would be well served by parallel successes of the family farm movement. The report notes, "Families and communities have the fundamental and primary place in cultural conservation. The interaction between relatives and close associates establishes the base from which all cultural attributes derive. . . . The role of family and community working together to foster cultural awareness and pride is of utmost importance in the conservation of traditional ways of life."[8]

The broader sentiments and accuracy of these sentences are perhaps open to question. The passage does, however, point to a crucial aspect of cultural continuity—the influence of social structure and interaction on people's ability to freely select among multiple and often contradictory cultural forms. The continuity and meaning of many midwestern farm traditions derives from a specific structure of agriculture, land ownership, tenure, and community. Independent family-owned farmsteads form the core of this structure. They are the crucial component in an affective interweaving of family, neighborhood, and the local community. Together these social units provide the cognitive templates for deciphering meaning as well as appropriate social contexts for performance, evaluation, and consumption. Cultural conservationist interest in processes of cultural continuity and interpretation hence must inherently include abiding concern about changes in agricultural and community social structures as well as the traditions reflective of shared experience and ideology.

Elsewhere the American Folklife Center report affirms that "the diversity of private efforts dedicated to ensuring the continuity of group traditions is awesome. . . . The pervasiveness of such efforts reflects both pride in community heritage and a profound desire to keep alive the context and expression of cultural identity."[9]

Cultural conservationists typically want to assist local efforts aimed at preservation and encouragement, yet outsiders often have difficulty locating rural groups pursuing mainstream cultural conservation activity. The lack of any strongly identified formalized support for family farm culture, combined with a general bureaucratic naivete of rural affairs, is especially alarming in the light of increasing institutionalization of cultural conservation action. The significance of the family farm movement to cultural specialists, however, derives precisely from its existence as an emic force striving for the maintenance of a diverse social base of cultural performance and for the stability of family farms and rural communities.

However one defines the cultural conservation or family farm movements, each group clearly possesses a particular range of expertise and a specific set of perspectives. Integrating the interests of the two groups requires a coalescence of outsider ascription and insider evaluation—a kind of convergence that is not easily accomplished. The programs promoted by outside cultural conservation specialists are characterized by the use of a set of ascribed, semi-objective cultural evaluations marked by a less thorough knowledge of actual cultural performance.[10] Existing public activities typically focus on continuity in overt expressive cultural forms, with ascribed meanings tending to parallel constructs of the ideal yeoman farmer type: conservative, solid and stable, close to the land, hard-working, honest, and so on. Outsiders seldom base these constructs on farm experience or farmer knowledge but rather form them through recasting older dominant themes and imposed stereotypes. In fact, a group of moral, law-abiding, hard-working families might be extremely useful to an American public needing to believe that there is (or was) a group happy and good in their work and their lives. But such messages say that everything is (or was) okay in rural America at the same time many rural Americans are saying that things are not at all okay today. As much as outsiders would like the family farm "preserved" as the last bastion of stability in a postindustrial or postmodern society, more accurate portraits recognize a multitude of voices, a strong strain of protest, and a cacophony of lifeways in farm areas.

The fashionable concern of outsiders to save family farms may be not only socially misguided but also economically manipulative.[11] Recently, for example, multinational corporations targeted as threats by the family farm movement have expressed support for the small farmer. These industries occasionally donate financial support to public projects celebrating rural heritages and often include pabulumized family farm images in their advertising and public relations activities. Part of the reason for promoting family farm continuity, however, may be a sort of economic exploitation meant to advantage corporate interests in large livestock-feeding and meat-processing industries. Small family farms are good for big business in these markets as long as the independent producers can provide labor-intensive inputs, for example, feeder pigs (or pigs from birth to forty pounds) and broilers (poultry for meat), more cheaply than can corporate farms dependent on hired labor and capital-intensive operations. This two-tiered agricultural structure plainly encourages the continuity of small, marginal farms as input-suppliers in contractual obligation to the corporation.

In spite of a long history of citizenry support for family farms, public agencies charged with cultural missions have devoted almost no attention to the contemporary occupational culture of farming. Indeed, projects on present-day rural culture typically include everything but farming, and projects on the occupation seem to focus on every period but the present one. As a consequence, cultural conservation efforts in rural areas tend to ignore current occupational considerations or to impose ethnographic and aesthetic criteria out of sync with present local norms.[12] The social ideology and agenda of the family farm movement is generally more developed and politically integrated than is the cultural ideology of rural cultural conservation. There are a number of reasons why this is so, including (1) a continued outside ignorance of the occupation and its present-day culture, (2) the perpetuation of romantic and nostalgic stereotypes, (3) assumptions about the death of the family farm, (4) institutional guidelines that seem to discriminate against rural communities and, (5) a type of personal anxiety about a postindustrial order that requires our imagination to take refuge in some yeoman ideal of an American preindustrial past.

An appropriate starting point for redefining and integrating visions and actions is the rationale for the most ambitious project planned to link cultural conservation ideas to the contemporary family farm. Conceived by the Smithsonian Institution in 1988, "The Heartland Family Farm: An American Tradition" is a program intended to yield a wide range of end products, including a major festival exhibit, recordings, books, symposia, a movie, and educational materials. As of September 1990 the project was on hold, pending funding to carry out its plans.[13] The publicly circulated document on this project opens with the following rationale:

> Today the integrity and continuity of family farming in the United States is threatened by national and world-wide economic change,

> environmental stress, and forms of popular culture which discount rural community life ways. Most public attention on the "farm crisis," has been focused on the economic conditions under which thousands of American farmers have lost their land. Less attention has been given to the nature of the loss, what that land represents, and the ways of life it has nurtured. In an era where depersonalized workplaces are the norm, when neighbors do not know or interact with each other, where we are so removed from natural cycles, so consumer oriented, specialized and mobile, the culture of family farming provides a historically important and instructive counterpoint. The endangerment and destruction of family farming represents a loss of material skills, a reduction in the ways we organize our household and community life, a lessening of our sense of daily, seasonal and life cycles, and a disjuncture in our relationship to natural resources and other living species.[14]

There are a number of striking aspects of this statement. One which we shall not pursue here is the fact that its brand of agrarian idealism could easily have been authored by a reincarnated St. John de Crèvecoeur or Thomas Jefferson. Having devoted time to the Smithsonian project, we remain committed to its general aims and products, but we also can locate in this publicly distributed rationale certain ideas and assumptions to avoid in building constructive relationships between cultural conservationists and family farm groups.

The quote is typical of much outsider rhetoric in posturing the family farm as a rather helpless entity, whose demise is threatened, and perhaps ensured, by forces outside rural communities. While there is accuracy about the point of origin of external sources of change, the statement portrays farmers as largely passive and static, with no control over their own lives. Ultimately this pessimistic prognosis may be proven correct, but it is neither true to the history of midwestern agrarianism nor a foreordained outcome of the present situation. Family farms have for a long time been directly or indirectly subjected to external change. They have, moreover, a rather startling history of success in coping with change and emerging intact as a structural unit, though perhaps with a different objective appearance in terms of visible cultural traits.

More important, positing family farmers as passive actors in a postindustrial world is dangerous because it implies the group is unable to design and implement its own survival and salvation. This is a scary proposition because power brokers who regard groups as passive or as having few means of controlling their own destiny typically deny them the opportunity to effect their own fates. We have suggested that an important contribution of outside cultural specialists would be to enhance the ability of farm families themselves to resolve issues of cultural continuity and change. Cultural conservationists are important for their perspective, training in observation and technical skills, and ability to use their institutional status to bring recognition to the fabric of rural life. But farm families are in many obvious respects the true cultural specialists, not simply because they live the life and hence have a more differentiated esoteric knowledge but, more important, they are (or should be) primarily responsible for deciding on the continuity and future of their lifeways. Indeed, a potent example of the group's active attempt to influence their own destiny is the family farm movement itself.

The Smithsonian project statement, "In an era where depersonalized workplaces are the norm, when neighbors do not know or interact with each other, where we are so removed from natural cycles, so consumer oriented, specialized and mobile, the culture of family farming provides a historically important and instructive counterpoint," posits some other questionable assumptions. There is an implication here of family farmers as a homogeneous group that is—or rather has been—especially social with one another, close to nature and natural cycles, diverse in their interests, and conservative in their residence. These notions certainly reflect some of the central positive images many people have associated with family farm operations since the colonial period. As assumptions to guide public attention to the plight of family farmers, such concepts are overly simplistic and ultimately may hinder, as much as help, any dynamic plan to enhance the continued existence of family farms.

These notions are simplistic in the way that generalizations about a sizable group of people are normally suspect. Some family farms span many generations, are host to appropriate conservation practices, and are integral parts of rural communities. Other family farms are specialized producers, do not practice effective natural resource stewardship, and are socially segregated from their neighbors. In fact, these issues are precisely some of the problems with which family farmers—like most Americans—must deal as they chart their future.

To imply family farms as a group once achieved this harmonious existence is at best reflective of superficial scholarship; at worst, it can backfire on the very group it is intended to benefit. The rhetoric not only romanticizes the lifeway but also implies models of behavior a group can never wholly live up to. As it becomes increasingly apparent to the nonfarm public that not all family farmers live up to this ideal, there is a danger of reactionary sentiments directed against the group. The problem is further complicated by suggesting the lesson family farmers offer is a "historically important and instructive counterpoint." The assumption lurking here, of course, is the notion that there is (or was) some kind of golden age of family farmers who met all the requirements of our cognitive template on the good family farmer, and now even that lifeway is dying.

To conclude this essay on a more optimistic tone, we want to suggest five major ways of appropriately integrating cultural conservation work with the family farm movement. First, cultural conservation efforts should be more closely linked to the dialogue occurring in farm houses, communities, government policy forums, and other contexts in which issues impacting on family farm culture are being discussed. It is perhaps not so important now to deconstruct notions of a golden age of family farms or to disprove romantic rhetoric. Cultural specialists might more usefully examine or reexamine concepts of family, community, and occupation or look seriously at the impact of public policy on the structure of agriculture and community life and hence the patterning of local tradition. One need not be an economist or agronomist, for example, to look at the relationships between environmental or technological issues and the ability or opportunity for farm families to address change and still maintain a chosen style of life.

Such activities would seem to be a natural extension of individuals employed in public agencies and therefore already involved in aspects of public policy discourse and formation.[15] Reactive inquiry might target the social and political causes of cultural change in family farm culture. Studies of contemporary change—including the alienation, marginalization, and centralization of culture—would enhance understanding of present-day social tensions and, perhaps, contribute to new theoretical assumptions to guide public-sector work. More proactive inquiry could address the impending impacts of emerging public policies in the form of arts council programs, the approval of biotechnologies, the inheritance clauses of tax bills, the implementation of land use ordinances, or the charter of cultural institutions.

Second, cultural conservation proponents should be as concerned about the identification and maintenance of social and economic process and context as they are about the cultural stuff in these contexts. Without championing any particular economic or rural plan, we can note that additional cultural expertise ought to inform decisions on social and economic development programs carrying significant implications for farm families' ability to make decisions about their own futures. As much as natural resource accessibility is important to various material folk cultural traditions, as much as performers need spaces in which to perform, so also do the traditions of family farmers depend on maintaining the rural social nexus in which traditions are enacted.

Third, programs on cultural conservation must go beyond the documentation of cultural forms and the preservation of overt evidences of family farm life. There is much of interest in a threshing ring, quilt, or bank barn, but these things are in themselves ambiguous and temporary symbols of identity. As noted, the family farm movement avoids self-identifications made up of discrete cultural forms because it recognizes group continuity in the midst of cultural differentiation and change. Similarly, cultural specialists ought to be highly conscious of the consequence of depicting family farm culture in series of one-to-one correlations between a set of overt cultural items and group identity. Cultural expression needs to be related back to particular group attitudes, values, and objectives. We must demonstrate that this lifeway enjoys (or at least should enjoy) flexibility, change, and dynamism. The family farm is not dead. The family farm of 1800 or 1900 or 1960 may be dead, but there is still a group continuing to identify itself as family farmers and sharing common templates of cultural values, behaviors, attitudes, and idealized social relationships.

Cultural conservation efforts aimed at the family farm sector must therefore avoid emphasis on discrete and individual performance traditions dissected from the social systems in which they normally reside. Such artificiality ignores spatial context in denying interrelationships between diverse cultural forms. Perhaps most important, it confers respectability on an academic methodology based on artificial disciplinary boundaries. Given the institutional base of cultural conservation activity, it makes sense that particular aesthetic, historical, or ethnographic primacies inform outsider evaluations. These judgments, however, generally do not parallel native categories; certainly cultural specialists rarely demonstrate sufficient attention to economic, social, and political considerations.

Fourth, cultural conservationists can contribute to the dialogue on quality of life and the relationship between quality of life and particular social structures. Documentation and public presentation of rural art forms and performers help challenge the notion that the quality of rural life can be determined simply by measures of material possessions, accumulated resources, percentages of dwellings with indoor plumbing, or average number of hours spent in leisure time activity. Without making difficult value judgments, cultural projects reveal the richness and excellence of the variety of cultural expression tied to community, group, and family cohesiveness and difference. The rather negative lessons of popular culture in terms of creativity and cultural participation are not lost on the family farm movement, which views the impact of the corporatization of agriculture in much the same way that cultural conservationists evaluate the bureaucratization or homogenization of culture.

Finally, the ultimate success and impact of the family farm agenda will depend partly on whether the American public remains convinced of the necessity of conserving a pluralistic agricultural structure. Appeals for public support must be economic, political, social, and cultural. If the family farm movement itself has largely abandoned the "way of life" rationale in the political and legislative arena, it cannot rely solely on economic arguments in dialogues with the general public. Popular ideology still connects the family farm with a way of life. Frankly, many Americans would view the movement's economic arguments about low market prices as less important than consumer desires that sufficient food supplies exist, reach supermarkets, and remain relatively cheap. The cultural rationale needs to be developed more fully, understood more generally, and put back into the political arena. A recent Ralph Nader report containing recommendations to the North American Farm Alliance notes that farmers constitute "a different kind of culture, and we've got to preserve that culture."[16] This is hardly an effective cultural appeal or political agenda. The viability of the debate and the potential impact of the movement will be greatly enhanced by demonstrating in a clear, accurate, and informative manner exactly what that different kind of culture is, what it looks like, what it means, how it feels, and why it is important to conserve.

NOTES

1. For examples, see "Trouble Down on the Farm," *Time*, October 27, 1984, 43–44; and "Report of Polls Taken by CBS and *New York Times*," *North American Farmer*, February 28, 1986, 1, 5.

2. Recent examples include Fern K. Willits, Robert C. Bealer, and Vincent L. Timber, "Popular Images of 'Rurality': Data from a Pennsylvania Survey," *Rural Sociology* 55 (1990): 559–78; and J. Sanford Rikoon and William D. Heffernan, "Farmer and Non-Farmer Perceptions of Groundwater Issues: Research Results from St. Charles County, Missouri" (Research report the for Environmental Protection Agency, Region 7, 1991).

3. Three major philosophic frameworks of an agricultural fundamentalism (a term borrowed from economist Theodore Schultz) are treated in James A. Montmarquet, "Philosophic Foundations for Agrarianism," *Agriculture and Human Values* 5 (1985): 5–14.

4. Kevin F. Goss, Richard D. Rodefield, and Frederick H. Buttel, "The Political Economy of Class Structure in U.S. Agriculture: A Theoretical Outline," in *The Rural Sociology of Advanced Societies*, ed. Frederick H. Buttel and Howard Newby (Montclair, N.J.: Allanheld-Osmun, 1980), 83–132; Sonya Salamon and Karen Davis-Brown, "Middle-range Farmers Persisting through the Agricultural Crisis," *Rural Sociology* 51 (1986): 224–39; and Sonya Salamon, "The Myth of the Disappearing Middle: A Case for Family Farm Persisters" (Paper presented at the annual meeting of the Society for Economic Anthropology, San Francisco, Calif., 1987).

5. National Farmers Union, *1989 Policy of National Farmers Union: Common Values, Common Goals for Rural America* (Denver: National Farmers Union, 1989).

6. [National Farmers Union], *Questions and Answers*, NFU Publication NO-15 (Denver: National Farmers Union Employees, 1989), unpaginated.

7. The paradigmatic importance of cultural pluralism in cultural conservation activity is especially stressed in public folklore activity and occupies a growing position in historic preservation rhetoric. See, for example, Archie Green, "A Keynote: Stitching Patchwork in Public," in *The Conservation of Culture: Folklorists and the Public Sector,* ed. Burt Feintuch (Lexington: University Press of Kentucky, 1988), 23–26; *Folk Arts: Application Guidelines Fiscal Years 1989/90* (Washington, D.C.: National Endowment for the Arts, 1988), 4; and Ormond Loomis, "Links between Historic Preservation and Folk Cultural Programs," in *Conservation of Culture,* ed. Feintuch, 184–88.

8. Ormond Loomis, coordinator, *Cultural Conservation: The Protection of Cultural Heritage in the United States,* Publications of the American Folklife Center, no. 10 (Washington, D.C.: American Folklife Center, Library of Congress, 1983), 5.

9. Ibid.

10. This model is more familiarly applied to ethnic groups. See, for example, Frederick Barth, *Ethnic Groups and Boundaries: The Social Organization of Cultural Difference* (Boston: Little, Brown, 1969), 11–18. The identity process used by ethnic groups to distinguish between themselves and others is similar to that used by diverse occupational groups.

11. The best in-depth study of the myriad social, political, and economic contexts and consequences of cultural conservation (i.e., intervention) remains David Whisnant, *All that Is Native and Fine: The Politics of Culture in an American Region* (Chapel Hill: University of North Carolina Press, 1983).

12. Some recent efforts have been partially able to address these biases. For example, the State Historical Society of Wisconsin's exhibit "Culture and Agriculture" begins to address some twentieth-century issues within a regional framework, and "Women in Rural Iowa: A Photo Exhibit" breaks down some of the gender stereotypes characteristic of presentations of rural occupational life.

13. The prime funding candidate through 1989 was Philip Morris, owner of Kraft Foods and General Foods among other companies, but corporate support was never forthcoming. In November 1990 the Smithsonian received funding from the USDA to produce a scaled-down version of the festival component during the 1991 Festival of American Folklife. Schedules, participants, and related articles on the 1991 FAF event are in the Smithsonian Institution's *1991 Festival of American Folklife* (Washington, D.C., Smithsonian Institution, 1991), 32–54 and appendices. None of the other related activities (e.g., conferences, books) has materialized.

14. "The Family Farm: An American Tradition" (Unpublished report of the Office of Folklife Programs, Smithsonian Institution, Washington, D.C., 1988), 2.

15. The need for more rigorous political intercession in public-sector folk-

lore work is more generally discussed by David E. Whisnant, "Public Sector Folklore as Intervention: Lessons from the Past, Prospects for the Future," in *Conservation of Culture,* ed. Feintuch, 233–47.

16. Randall Mikkelsen, "Nader: Family Farms Should Be Saved," *North American Farmer,* December 30, 1985, 4.

14

Folklife Assessment in the Michigan Low-Level Radioactive Waste Siting Process

Laurie Kay Sommers, Yvonne R. Lockwood, Marsha MacDowell, and Richard W. Stoffle

Although folklorists conduct cultural conservation studies, they seldom engage in environmental and social assessment of highly controversial projects and their effects on traditional culture. We believe our study, *Cultural and Paleontological Effects of Siting a Low-Level Radioactive Waste Facility in Michigan, Candidate Area Analysis Phase,* is the first to use folklorists in this kind of assessment.[1] In the present essay we discuss the process of folklife data collection and evaluation and the significance of these data to public policy development and implementation.

Our work was part of a larger environmental assessment study, or "siting process," mandated by Michigan Public Act 204 in 1987. This legislation defined the social and environmental criteria used to evaluate potential low-level radioactive waste (LLRW) locations and divided them into two categories: "exclusionary" criteria automatically eliminated an area from further consideration; "favorability" criteria, those not explicitly protected by either state or federal law, would be avoided if possible. The ninth objective of the siting criteria, for example, states that Michigan must "comply with federal and state laws which protect environmentally sensitive areas and which protect cultural and heritage values."[2] The National Historic Preservation Act, mentioned in this context, provides maximum feasible protection, but the language does not specifically preclude the adverse impact of projects on National Register sites. Under Michigan Public Act 204, all cultural resources were listed under favorability criteria.

As required by Public Act 204, Michigan's LLRW siting process included the formation of the Public Advisory Committee (PAC), which provided independent technical review of the findings. PAC members assigned to cultural resources represented the Michigan Folklore Society, the Michigan Archaeological Society, the Michigan Commission on Indian Affairs, and the local communities under consideration. These individuals worked with us to define the research methodology, identify cultural resources, and evaluate potential impacts.

The Michigan Low-Level Radioactive Waste Authority (MLLRWA), the agency responsible for locating and constructing a storage facility, divided the siting process into three steps. First, a statewide analysis applied the siting criteria to existing data bases. Because statewide data bases do not include systematic information about cultural resources, the analysis did not include cultural data. This step eliminated 97 percent of the state from further consideration. Second, the MLLRWA selected the three largest remaining land areas, termed "candidate areas," for further study (see figure 14.1). This was a pre–environmental impact assessment based on several months of research and analysis. The MLLRWA subcontracted our team to identify cultural resources that might be affected by a LLRW facility, map their locations, and "scale" or prioritize potential impacts. Before we collected and analyzed all the data, the MLLRWA eliminated two of the three candidate areas on the basis of wetlands criteria. Only one candidate area remained for complete analysis, Riga Township, Lenawee County, in southeastern lower Michigan. The third evaluation step, an environmental impact assessment based on up to eighteen months of fieldwork, was to focus on smaller areas called candidate sites. This phase did not occur, however, because the Lenawee County location also was eliminated after candidate area analysis. As of May 1993 the process to select a site was stalemated. Meanwhile, producers are storing their own waste.

Creating a Research Strategy

The scholars of our interdisciplinary cultural resources team conducted separate studies of local folklife, American Indian sacred resources, archaeology, paleontology, and historic features. We integrated our data into one report to provide a more holistic perspective, methodological synergy, and greater impact on policymakers. We evaluated our own findings rather than rely on MLLRWA staff members, who were not cultural experts or familiar with the data.

As we began to draft the folklife research plan, we became aware of the lack of models. Studies of the Atchafalaya Basin, Grouse Creek, Big South Fork, and the Pinelands did not provide a workable methodological framework.[3] On the other hand, Patricia L. Parker and Thomas F. King's *Guidelines for Evaluating and Documenting Traditional Cultural Properties* (known as *Bulletin Number 38*) was a very important and useful doc-

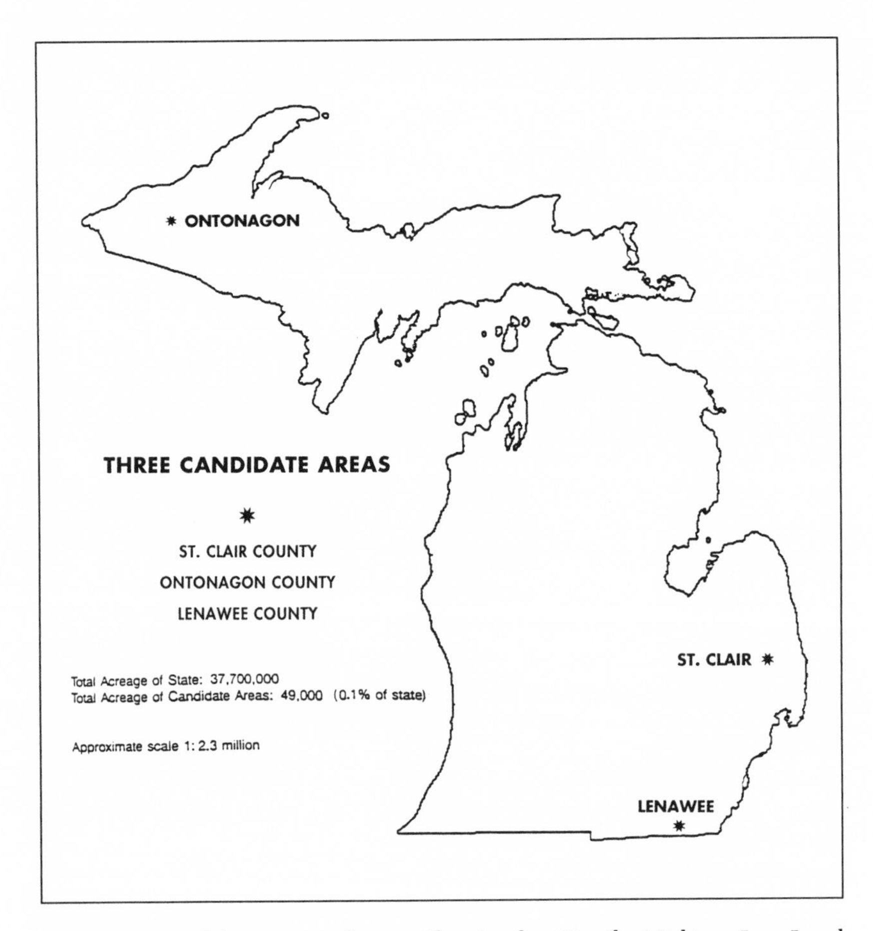

Figure 14.1 Candidate areas under consideration for siting the Michigan Low-Level Radioactive Waste Facility. (From Michigan Low-Level Radioactive Waste Authority, 1989)

ument.[4] Our research data and analysis were framed in accordance with the National Historic Preservation Act (the only legislation ultimately judged relevant to the process), which states that "the Authority must assess the effects of this project on historic properties and, if adverse, consult with the Advisory Council on Historic Preservation and/or the state historic preservation officer on means to avoid or reduce such effects."[5]

The lack of strongly worded laws for cultural conservation remains a continual problem. We have only the American Folklife Preservation Act, the National Environmental Policy Act, and the National Historic Preservation Act as general statements of federal intent. We have the National Register program and *Bulletin Number 38* as a practical tool; however, even the National Register is limited by its emphasis on tangible, physically defined properties, its exclusion of resources less than fifty years old, and its reliance on prestige rather than airtight legislation as a protective strategy.

We designed the folklife research methodology to provide preliminary identification, mapping, and evaluation of folklife resources in terms of the "significance" and impact of the project. Because of time constraints and the National Register's emphasis on mappable, tangible traditional properties, we limited our identification efforts to the following categories: (1) occupation-related traditions, (2) recreation-related traditions, and (3) community (i.e., ethnic and religious) traditions. For each of these categories we stressed the following genres: foodways, special events and festivals, vernacular architecture, and other material culture. We paid particular attention to traditional uses of environmental resources, the relationship of residents and nonresidents to community cultural resources, and evidence of community cohesiveness and stability through traditional activities and structures.

Doing Research amid Controversy

MLLRWA guidelines confined researchers to public property unless invited. Despite these restrictions and strong opposition to the project, we hoped community members would provide descriptive and evaluative information about local folk culture. This was not always the case. Some community members assisted by escorting researchers around the candidate area or by conducting a survey of family farm ownership. Other local property owners, however, denied us access as a strategy to fight the project. After a flurry of rumors that MLLRWA contractees were trespassing on private property, we kept records of all contacts.

Many residents of the three candidate areas adamantly opposed the project, and when the MLLRWA hosted open houses in these areas, opponents verbally and physically threatened the staff. In St. Clair County these threats involved guns. Frankly, we were apprehensive. Unlike most other MLLRW researchers, we depended on local people for our data. Would they cooperate? Would we be able to do adequate research in such an emotionally charged context? Would our participation in this project irreparably damage our future research in these areas?

Many local residents mistrusted the motives and abilities of project researchers. Many felt that the MLLRWA had bungled the candidate area

Figure 14.2 Cartoon by Kirk Walters in the *Toledo Blade,* posted on the refrigerator of a Riga Township resident. (Reprinted from the *Toledo Blade,* October 8, 1989, with permission)

screening process and had ignored its own selection criteria by choosing their community, an attitude expressed in a cartoon from the *Toledo Blade* (see figure 14.2). In some cases local residents taped our interviews as a precautionary measure. During initial contact we often had to pass an "inquisition," giving our credentials and our personal views about the project. Team member Laurie Kay Sommers, for example, phoned a local historian who had been described as "madder than a wet hen about this whole thing." "Laurie, what are your credentials and where are you coming from?" the historian snapped. For about five minutes Sommers explained her role. "Oh, I know what you want," the historian finally said. "You want to know if we still make German cookies around here, and we do. But let me tell you!"

Although we all encountered difficult situations, we still underestimated the intensity of local feeling until we obtained the following anonymous letter, placed in mailboxes of Riga Township residents and written in anticipation of our arrival. The James Cleary referred to in the letter was the commissioner of the MLLRWA. The first section of the letter refers to selection criteria that local people thought the MLLRWA had ignored when designating their community:

Riga Township. Home of nature's finest farmland, beautiful sunsets and peaceful family life. Riga Township, site of the next nuclear waste dump? NOT IF YOU CAN HELP IT!

It's sad but true, James Cleary is attempting to turn this peaceful community into a DMZ—by DMZ, we mean that the LLRW has turned your land into a DEMORALIZED ZONE.

In recent weeks, we have learned that EVEN THOUGH there are 500,000 people living within 13 miles of you, Mr. Cleary says it REALLY DOESN'T MATTER.

EVEN THOUGH Lenawee County is the number ONE producer of corn, beans and other crops in the entire State of Michigan, HE DOESN'T CARE.

EVEN THOUGH the area is well known for flooding and the drains to the 10 Mile Creek cannot be shut down, HE DOESN'T CARE.

So, we ask you, why would he care if some arrowheads are found on the land? Why would he care if there are ethnic groups of families? The fact of the matter is, HE DOESN'T CARE and the LLRW DOESN'T CARE.

Think about it for a minute. Can you for a moment think that this relatively minor data can make any difference? Do they actually think you believe this can make a difference? Sorry, but we're not THAT IGNORANT.

So why let them have THEIR WAY? Why would you let ANYONE connected with the LLRW on YOUR SACRED PROPERTY?

If YOU do, they will check you out. They will put YOUR NAME on a list of people who COOPERATE. If Riga IS named as a candidate site, guess whose property they will tear up first with drills and saws?

Will YOU be the ONE who aids and abets the ENEMY?

The folks coming Monday, Tuesday and Wednesday are working for the DEVIL HIMSELF.

Are you willing to live with the consequences FOREVER? Everyone will know who let the ENEMY on their land and if we lose, it could tear at the very fabric that has held this community together all along.

What can you gain by letting them have their way, really? Remember, you do NOT HAVE TO allow ANYONE on your land. When they come knocking, DON'T LET THE DEVIL IN, YOU'LL NEVER GET HIM OUT.

> It's YOUR land. Make YOUR decision. Make the RIGHT decision. The one you'll NEVER REGRET.
>
> If you are not sure what to do, think conservatively. It's better to be SAFE than SORRY!
>
> God bless you.

Clearly, this was not a "normal" folklife research situation. Local people not only distrusted us to the point of equating us with "the DEVIL" but also mistrusted the relevance of cultural resources to the siting process, a subject to which we will return later. Such experiences underscored the importance of holistic analysis that considers traditions within a larger cultural context.

Mapping Folklife Resources

After the MLLRWA eliminated two of the three candidate areas on the basis of wetlands criteria, we turned our attention to the remaining Lenawee County area. Most identified folklife resources were associated with agricultural lifeways: rural vernacular architecture, rural and ethnic foodways, worldview (including attitudes toward the land and family farm continuity), and occupational folklife associated with farming and related skills, including that of migrant workers. Virtually all other identified folklife resources existed because of, and in symbiotic relationship to, the patterns of farm-related rural settlement. The Lenawee County candidate area was a stable, cohesive rural community with a system of interrelated folklife.

The MLLRWA requested a map of our findings that would be compared with other mapped resources to determine the least disruptive location for the proposed storage facility. In many ways the mapping process was a curious return to the historic-geographic method—objectifying folklife into mappable traits. Given the proper time and approach, we have the methodological tools to map even intangible resources, but in this case the MLLRWA's goals and expectations evolved as the project unfolded. During the candidate area analysis, we planned to map only National and State Register sites and centennial farms, postponing a more comprehensive survey to the eighteen-month intensive study that would follow during site characterization. (As mentioned previously, site characterization never occurred because the Lenawee County area was eliminated.) By the end of the candidate area assessment, however, the project maps had assumed primary importance. We realized that the MLLRWA and the general public would view them as the summary of all our findings. We had insufficient data to map all the folklife resources identified though; for example, we

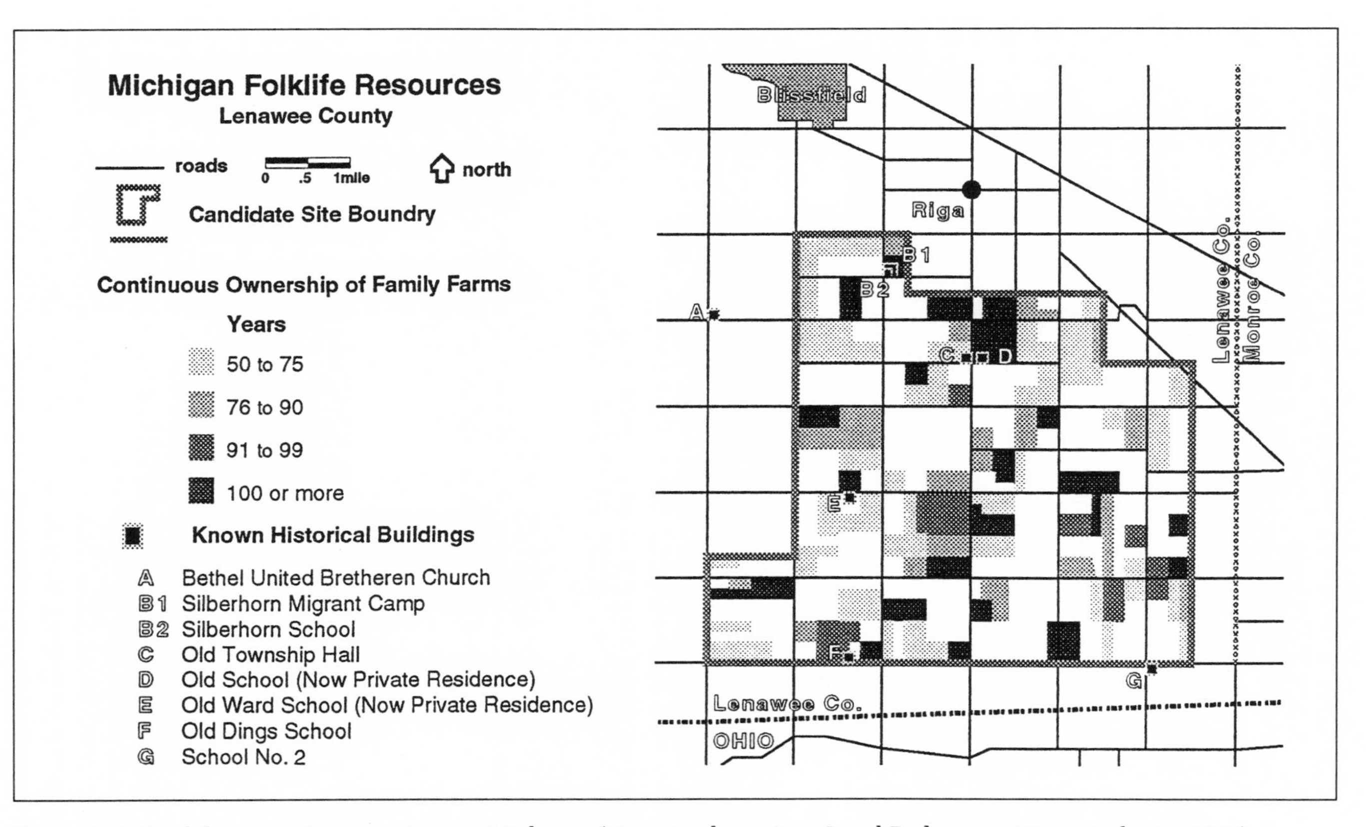

Figure 14.3 Candidate area, Lenawee County, Michigan. (From Michigan Low-Level Radioactive Waste Authority, 1989)

knew German foodways existed but did not know all of their locations. We therefore tried to map resources that would support nomination of the area as a National Register historic district.

We produced two folklife maps. Folklife Resources (see figure 14.3) depicts thirty-four centennial farms, various other farms owned by the same families for fifty to ninety-nine years, migrant farmworkers' camps, and religious and civic vernacular architecture (a township hall, church, and schools). Because of time constraints we had intended to survey farm-related vernacular architecture, by far the largest concentration of structures in the study area, during the subsequent environmental impact study of the site characterization phase. A second map, not illustrated here, showed a proposed National Register historic district that exceeds the boundaries of the candidate area. This map demonstrated that any location of a LLRW facility in or near the area would likely cause social and cultural impacts. Because the Riga Township, Lenawee County, site is economically and culturally homogeneous, we concluded that a least disruptive location did not exist within the area.

The mapping process posed an additional challenge. Could we map zones of influence, in other words, the total body of cultural resources that the proposed facility would potentially effect? Richard W. Stoffle et al. suggest a useful model of methodology in their "risk perception shadow" study.[6] They applied a combination of survey and ethnographic techniques to identify potentially affected populations and concluded that knowledge about a facility like the MLLRW facility and beliefs about risk extend in lessening degrees of intensity up to thirty-five miles from the project site. Similar methods could be used to reveal the cultural networks—such as visiting patterns; church attendance; influx of hunters, fishers, and tourists; cottage industries; and social interaction—which extend beyond the boundaries of the candidate area. Although our report identifies folklife resources located outside the candidate area and suggests that they could be adversely affected by an LLRW siting, we unfortunately lacked sufficient time to document and map zones of influence. Determining these influence zones, however, should be an essential aspect of future research.

Evaluating Folklife Resources

In addition to identifying and mapping folklife, our plan required that we evaluate our findings according to their significance and potential LLRW project impact. As mentioned previously, the MLLRWA follows Michigan Public Act 204 in defining potential impacts as either "exclusionary" (i.e., the resource cannot be adversely affected by the project; no cultural resources fell into this category), or "favorable" (i.e., resources should be evaluated and prioritized so that the most sensitive are avoided if possible). All cultural resources fell into the latter category, which we "scaled," or ranked, as either (1) "suitable for further study," in that the project may have a long-term, adverse effect on the resource that would be difficult to mitigate; (2) "desirable for further study," in that the project may have a moderately adverse effect on the resource that could be mitigated; or (3) "very desirable for further study," in that the project may have no effect or may somehow help the resource.[7]

Although the MLLRWA determined the tripartite terminology for scaling factors, we established our own definitions based on National Register language and criteria. The most sensitive category, "suitable for further study," for example, includes sites already listed on the Michigan or National Register of Historic Places and others potentially eligible according to the wording and criteria of *Bulletin Number 38:* (1) places community members deemed sacred (traditional rituals, ceremonial activities, and meeting sites); (2) rural communities whose organizations, buildings, structures, or patterns of land use reflect the stable cultural traditions valued by long-term residents; (3) an identified stable neighborhood area that is the traditional home of a particular cultural group and reflects the ongoing beliefs and practices of a cultural group; (4) those sites in which a community has traditionally carried out economic, artistic, or other cultural practices important in maintaining its historical identity; and (5) other properties of architectural or historic significance meeting the National Register criteria.[8]

Although we established scaling criteria, how could we actually rank one feature of folklife over another and make value judgments about it? According to whose value system? The researcher's? The local community's? The contracting agency's? The values expressed in existing law? In fact, we used a combination of these by fitting our professional assessments of field data, themselves influenced by the evaluative comments of local people, into the frameworks suggested in legislation and MLLRWA documents. We thought, however, that one of our primary responsibilities was to provide an evaluation that reflected the beliefs and values of the residents of the candidate areas. If all three candidate areas had remained in the running, we probably would have influenced the final MLLRWA decision, but our scaling decisions would have been much more difficult. A three-level scaling system is not sufficiently sensitive for evaluations of disparate resources. Are all National Register properties of equal value? Is a hunting camp, for example, as significant as a centennial farm?

Richard W. Stoffle et al. provide a useful technique to answer such questions in their study of the cultural significance of American Indian plants.[9] Combining survey and ethnographic techniques, Stoffle's team created an index of cultural significance based largely on Indian people's own perceptions of the value of plant resources. Ultimately, the research team ranked plants in order of importance and recommended protection for specific plants. Used during the equivalent of site characterization–level research, this technique offers a promising methodology for folklorists.

Project Implications: Lessons from the Trenches

Our work underscores the following cultural conservation implications of the MLLRW study:

1. The expression of local fear and anger as important data.

The anonymous letter underscores fears that the LLRW facility, if constructed, could destroy valued farmland, family continuity, and the very way of life that make Riga Township a desirable place to live. Protest signs dotting the Riga Township landscape also echoed these sentiments: "Farmland, Not Wasteland," "No nukes, just cukes," "Save our Riga farmland" (see figures 14.4 and 14.5). Locals repeated them orally. We would ask about folklife. They would tell us that they wanted to pass on their farms to their children; that they were afraid they would not be able to sell their crops; that they had some of the best farmland in the state; that it was crazy to build a "nuclear dump" on prime farmland.

Since the candidate areas had been selected without considering a number of criteria, including the potential impact on cultural resources, and since local people had no voice in the selection process, we became listening posts for local fear and anger. Presenting the local worldview as data made it possible to serve two clients: the MLLRWA and local residents.

2. Beliefs about the project's impact versus "science."

The anonymous letter exemplifies the folklore of radioactivity and the hysteria that can be generated by perceived nuclear threats. A wide discrepancy exists between the public's beliefs about the safety of a low-level radioactive waste site and scientific studies about the impact of such a site. This discrepancy extended to project researchers. For example, state geologists suggested that the actual LLRW facility must remain a specific distance away from wells, despite the MLLRWA's assertion that the structure would be safe and free of leaks. The contradictions did not slip by residents. They were concerned about their ability to sell crops, declining property values, their way of life, and last, but not least, their health.

3. The effects of the siting process on local people.

The anonymous letter was the result of considerable factionalism within the Riga Township vicinity. The world was divided into "cooperators"

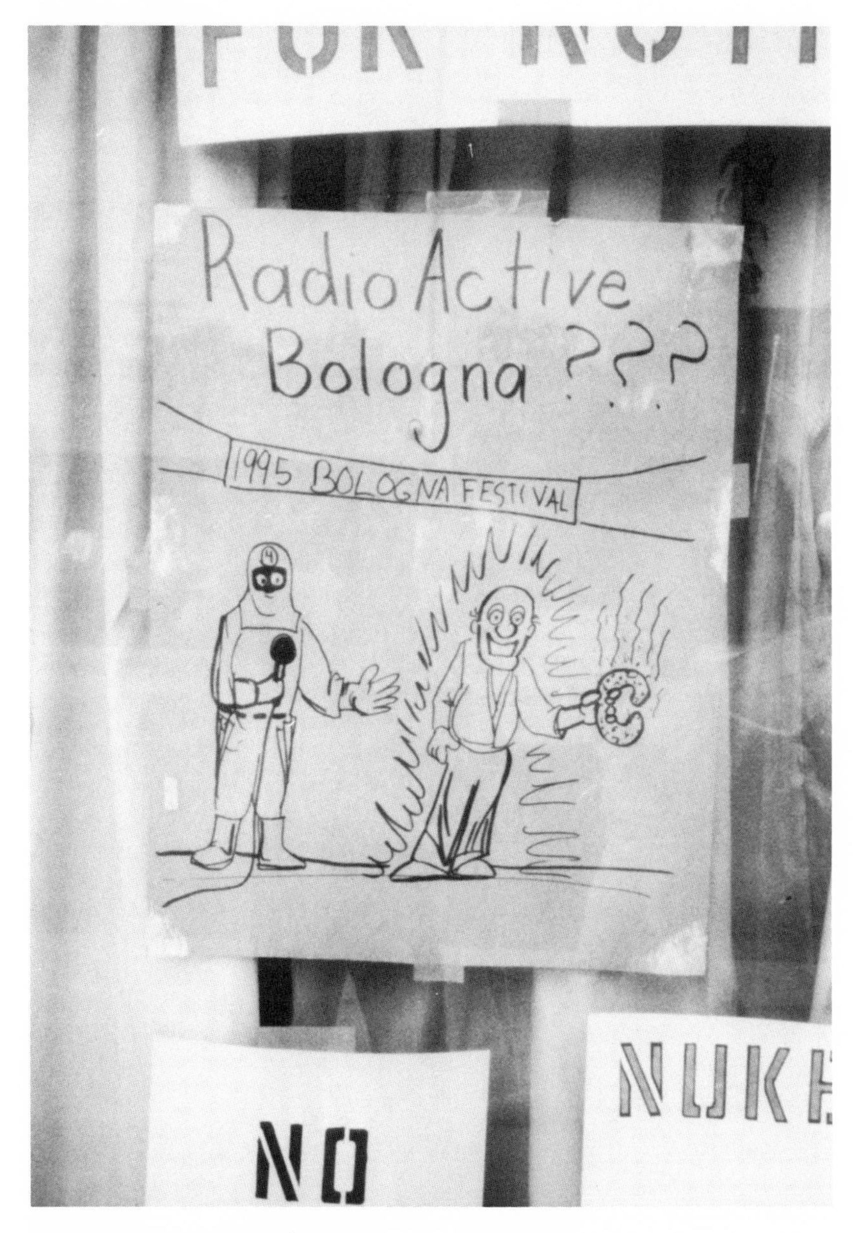

Figure 14.4 Handmade signs such as this were posted in Yale, Michigan, part of the potential candidate area in St. Clair County and home of an annual Bologna Festival honoring one of its major local businesses. (Photo by C. Kurt Dewhurst; courtesy of the Michigan State University Museum)

Figure 14.5 Nuclear protest signs register the local community reaction to the proposed candidate area in Riga Township, Lenawee County, Michigan. (Photo by Laurie K. Sommers; courtesy of the Michigan State University Museum)

in league with the "enemy" and dissenters on the side of God. The factions were complex and potentially of lasting impact.

4. The importance of a holistic strategy to present folklife resources and to argue for their conservation.

We wanted to educate policymakers about the role of tangible and intangible folklife to create a sense of community cohesion. We sought to make them aware of folklife's connections to the local economy and environment. Certainly, an isolated arrowhead or a single ethnic cookiemaker could not make an impact. An interrelated system of beliefs, objects, structures, practices, potential National Register districts, and cultural landscapes would be much more difficult to ignore.

5. Skepticism about the relevance of cultural resources to the decision-making process.

Michigan's strongest laws protect wetlands and groundwater. Many local people focused on these and other exclusionary criteria they believed would eliminate their community from consideration. Ironically, the laws do not protect folklife, but much of the protest, although not articulated as such, communicated the fear of losing those tangible and intangible folklife features that define their way of life.

Michigan has yet to site a LLRW facility, and we do not know what our future roles may be. We can, however, assess our impact to date. At the candidate area level of analysis, cultural data had no effect on the final decisions to eliminate the three proposed areas from further consideration. Only the criterion of wetlands eliminated the first two candidate areas. The MLLRWA subsequently eliminated Lenawee County using only exclusionary criteria. No favorability criteria, including cultural resources, became factors. If the MLLRWA had to weigh the pros and cons of three areas instead of just one, it undoubtedly would have used cultural and other favorability criteria to prioritize the resources of one area over another.

Despite our efforts to reflect local concerns and to underscore potential social, economic, and cultural disruption of a stable rural community, Public Act 204 mandated that all cultural resources fall under favorability criteria. A site cannot be excluded on the basis of cultural resources alone. The conclusion to the MLLRWA's *Candidate Area Decision Report* thus reads as follows:

> Protection of important cultural, archaeological, and paleontological resources is a favorability criterion. Such areas should be avoided in site development. Based on a review of the PAC (Public Advisory Committee) report and application of the scaling factors identified above, specific areas likely to contain important cultural resources can be avoided in selecting potential candidate sites within the Riga Township candidate area. . . .
>
> Folklife resources were also scaled. The results of this scaling exercise indicate that conditions within the Riga Township candidate area are generally favorable with regards to cultural resources unless another area within the State is identified that contains no important cultural resources or that such resources can be avoided during site development.[10]

If cultural conservationists are to affect the decision-making process, they must make their voices heard. In our case, no cultural specialists lobbied the state legislature for tougher protective language in Public Act 204. No cultural professionals were on the siting criteria advisory committee that created a working document from the favorability and exclusionary criteria outlined in Public Act 204. Indeed, the legislation does not even suggest that such expertise might be appropriate. Our cultural resources team would not have included folklorists were it not for the insistence of team leader Richard Stoffle.

Likewise, the MLLRWA lacked personnel with cultural expertise. Consequently, meaningful information about cultural resources seldom appears in implementation language, requests for proposals, and so forth. Take, for example, the LLRW Site Characterization Contractor Request for Proposal

(RFP).[11] This was to serve as the basis for the next phase of LLRW evaluation. Under "Scope of Work" the "field characterization" activities include detailed lists of meteorological, hydrological, and geotechnical investigations. Under the heading "Environmental Investigations" is the subheading "Human Resources" (cultural, historical, and archaeological). This implies that "culture" is equivalent to a "soil type" under "Geotechnical Investigations: Soil Classification." Presumably folklife would come under "cultural." The fact that "cultural" is one of the vaguest subheadings in the RFP is extremely troubling to those of us concerned with cultural conservation and issues of biocultural diversity. Despite the lack of specificity in the RFP, we hope our interactions with MLLRWA staff have ensured that cultural resources beyond historic and archaeological resources will be included in future siting studies.

Regardless of our future role, our work has brought cultural resource assessment to the attention of policymakers in new ways. We amassed a body of data that one PAC member compared with the Works Progress Administration data in terms of archival significance. We benefited by sharing methodology, information, and decision making with an interdisciplinary team. As a team, we also presented a unified report that deals comprehensively with a variety of cultural resources.

We also have learned the importance and the problems of identifying, mapping, quantifying, and evaluating cultural resources in terms acceptable to local people, understandable to policymakers, and scientifically valid. Unlike archaeological and paleontological artifacts and historic architecture, folklife resources are not static or always tangible. They involve beliefs and practices that projects like the LLRW can affect in complex and difficult ways. We must consider both the project site and zones of influence.

Repeatedly, we came face-to-face with existing state and federal legislation when determining our role, our impact, and our research design. In terms of folklife, the National Historic Preservation Act, the National Environmental Policy Act, and the National Register provide our only legal frameworks. Despite its limitations, *Bulletin Number 38* finally has given folklorists a voice in the National Register process, and we took full advantage of its language and implications. If we ultimately have no real impact on the exclusion of sensitive areas from LLRW consideration, it will be because we lack the mechanisms to use existing laws effectively or because we need new cultural conservation legislation.

A poignant question from a farm woman at one of the public meetings is a challenging reminder: "You mean to tell me there are laws protecting endangered species and wetlands, but none protecting me and my children from this project?" Her query was, in fact, based on inaccurate information: endangered species and cultural resources are equally unprotected under Public Act 204. However, the question should motivate all of us concerned with cultural conservation, especially folklorists, to rethink our strategies for action and advocacy. If we are truly concerned with empowering communities and encouraging and protecting biocultural diversity, we need to follow the lead of the biological scientists and lobby for their protection. The effective self-mobilization of Riga Township residents illustrates that this community was not powerless. They were, however, unable to use cultural data as a weapon to fight back because they lacked the legislative tools to do so. The recent Native American Grave Protection and Repatriation Act (PL 101-601) provides an excellent example of what can and should be done through the involvement of cultural professionals and affected community groups. We need to go further, however, by ensuring that stable, established cultural communities, defined by a network of interconnected tangible and intangible cultural characteristics, are equal in value, recognition, and protection to bald eagles and Indian burial sites. Until *endangered cultures* becomes a household expression, our work is cut out for us.

NOTES

A version of this essay was presented at the conference "Cultural Conservation: Reconfiguring the Mission," sponsored by the American Folklife Center, Library of Congress, Washington, D.C., May 19, 1990. We thank the following colleagues who worked on the Michigan Low-Level Radioactive Waste Authority Folklife Project and whose ideas and data helped shape this essay: Dennis Au, Tim Cochrane, C. Kurt Dewhurst, Ruth D. Fitzgerald, LuAnne G. Kozma, Marsha Penti, Sobha Ramanand, Ilene Schechter, Lynne Swanson, and Peter Wehr. Additional members of the entire cultural resources team included Kurt F. Anschuetz, David B. Halmo, J. Alan Holman, Florence V. Jensen, Ronald O. Kapp, John E. Olmsted, Timothy R. Pauketat, Scott G. Reid, and Henry T. Wright.

1. Richard W. Stoffle, ed. *Cultural and Paleontological Effects of Siting a Low-Level Radioactive Waste Facility in Michigan, Candidate Area Analysis Phase* (Ann Arbor: Institute for Social Research, University of Michigan, 1990).
2. *Final Siting Criteria* (Lansing: Michigan Low-Level Radioactive Waste Authority and Batelle-Lansing, May 16, 1989), 19.
3. Charles Ray Brassieur, "A Preliminary Ethnographic Survey of Atchafalaya Basin Area" (M.A. thesis, Louisiana State University, 1980); Charles Ray Brassieur, "The Modern Atchafalaya Culture: Results of the Ethnographic Survey," in "Archaeology and Ethnology on the Edges of the Atchafalaya Basin, South Central Louisiana: A Cultural Resources Survey of the Atchafalaya

Protection Levees," ed. John L. Gibson (Unpublished draft report on file with the United States Army Corps of Engineers, New Orleans District, New Orleans, La., 1980); Tom Carter and Carl Fleischhauer, *The Grouse Creek Cultural Survey: Integrating Folklife and Historic Preservation Field Research* (Washington, D.C.: American Folklife Center, Library of Congress, 1988); Benita J. Howell, *A Survey of Folklife along the Big South Fork of the Cumberland River,* Report of Investigations, no. 30 (Knoxville: Department of Anthropology, University of Tennessee, 1981); Mary Hufford, *One Space, Many Places: Folklife and Land Use in New Jersey's Pinelands National Reserve* (Washington D.C.: American Folklife Center, Library of Congress, 1986). Also of interest is William Millsap, "Folklife Research in Environmental Planning," in *Applied Social Science for Environmental Planning,* ed. William Millsap, Social Impact Assessment Series, no. 10 (Boulder, Colo.: Westview Press, 1984).

4. Patricia L. Parker and Thomas F. King, *Guidelines for Evaluating and Documenting Traditional Cultural Properties,* National Register Bulletin, no. 38 (Washington D.C.: National Park Service, Department of the Interior, 1990).

5. *Candidate Area Screening and Candidate Site Selection Methodology,* draft version (Lansing: Michigan Low-Level Radioactive Waste Authority and Batelle-Lansing, March 1990), 21.

6. Richard W. Stoffle, Michael J. Traugott, John V. Stone, Carla C. Davidson, Florence V. Jensen, and Paula Drury McIntyre, "Risk Perception Mapping: Using Ethnography to Define the Locally Affected Population for a Low-Level Radioactive Waste Storage Facility in Michigan," *American Anthropologist* 93 (1991): 611–35.

7. Stoffle, ed., *Cultural and Paleontological Effects of Siting a Low-Level Radioactive Waste Facility in Michigan, Candidate Area Analysis Phase,* 217–18.

8. Ibid., 222.

9. Richard W. Stoffle, David B. Halmo, Michael J. Evans, and John E. Olmsted, "Calculating the Cultural Significance of American Indian Plants: Paiute and Shoshone Ethnobotany at Yucca Mountain, Nevada," *American Anthropologist* 92 (1990): 416–32.

10. *Candidate Area Decision Report* (Lansing: Michigan Low-Level Radioactive Waste Authority and Batelle-Lansing, May 1990), 74–75.

11. *Michigan Low-Level Radioactive Waste Authority Site Characterization Contractor Request for Proposal* (Lansing: Michigan Department of Management and Budget, July 2, 1990).

15

Conserving Our Cities' Endangered Spaces

Steven J. Zeitlin

New York's Orchidia restaurant is gone and, with it, the Ukrainian and Italian food and the warm sense of community this restaurant brought to the Lower East Side for more than twenty-five years. On Beale Street in Memphis, Tennessee, the building that housed Battiers Drugstore and Mitchell's Hotel—where B. B. King and the chili were always hot—has been converted into office space;[1] in Baltimore, the McCormick Spice factory, a local landmark that cast its spicy aromas into the waterfront air, has become a parking lot for Harbor Place.[2] At the Reading Terminal Market in Philadelphia, a stand owner recently learned that the escalator for the new convention center above the market will descend into the center of his stall.[3] These are a few well-known examples from the thousands of significant urban spaces vanished or endangered in the swiftly changing landscape of American cities.

On Times Square, his rent raised 700 percent in expectation of the new redevelopment plan, Saul Fromkin, a born and bred New Yorker packs his tools and prepares to close up his tiny, second story, dust-filled saxophone repair shop on Forty-sixth Street and move to Florida. Sadly shifting reeds and old instruments into boxes, he is watched by the photos of the jazz greats Charlie Parker, Dexter Gordon, and all the great blowers of the jazz world, musicians whose instruments passed through the master's hands to be "over-Sauled" (overhauled) and "Fromkinized." "We were sort of like the old time doctors, we made house calls—many times I would leave my shop to run to a theater to deliver an instrument to a guy, when he had only an hour or so before the show started. That's pretty much all gone. . . . What memories—oh, if walls could talk. For all the heavies who have been in here and all the memories we should have been in the basement—I'm surprised the floor didn't collapse."[4]

In response to stories like this, City Lore: The New York Center for Urban Folk Culture initiated a project called Endangered Spaces in 1988 to document and advocate for local establishments and sites in danger of vanishing in the ebb and flow of New York's rapidly changing cultural landscape. Although historic preservationists have fought to preserve landmark buildings, we are concerned with the culture that brings those buildings to life. We began documenting and exploring ways to advocate for such places as the Essex Street Market, Brighton Beach Baths, and Schapiro's Winery—cherished places central to the vitality of particular communities in New York City.

These local establishments play a crucial role in the city's fragile human ecology, contributing to the integrity of neighborhoods and the sense of continuity between past and present that renders urban environments habitable. "Now that you can put a card in a slot and do your banking without ever meeting a teller," says Barbara Kirshenblatt-Gimblett, "now that you eat fast food without ever meeting a waitress, now more than ever we need to protect the shoemaker, the laundromat or the barbershop, places that have been there since our childhood or at least the last fifteen years and that hold together the fabric of community."[5]

As Michael P. Smith writes, "Inner-city neighborhoods and public spaces are our 'cultural wetlands.'"[6] Over the past several decades their sustenance has become one of America's most pressing issues. Urban blight and its attendant problems of crime and homelessness have affected most of the nation's large, urban areas. Local establishments represent indigenous solutions to the problems of urban living, giving people an opportunity to socialize and interact in positive ways and offering people the means to create a viable world for themselves, outside of government, corporate, or philanthropic support. "In an age of large-scale mergers," notes Kirshenblatt-Gimblett, "there is a kind of omnivorousness that swallows local efforts. It becomes crucial to protect the conditions that allow local initiatives—people doing things for themselves and for each other in places where they live, things that encourage face-to-face interaction, intimacy, and support. These become increasingly endangered the bigger cities get, the more anonymous city governments become, and the more large corporations deliver (or don't deliver) services to city dwellers."[7]

What Is an Endangered Space?

We consider *endangered spaces* to be local establishments and neighborhood institutions with a demonstrable significance in community life. We are interested only in those establishments that contribute to a community's sense of identity, that provide continuity and character to the neighborhood, and that are seen as an integral part of the community by those who use them. We consider an establishment endangered when its demise is imminent, when the neighborhood as a whole is threatened, or when the kind of establishment it represents (such as cafeterias, bathhouses) is vanishing, making its survival all the more crucial.

Many of our endangered spaces are important because they serve as the locus for a community that gathers and of memories that adhere. The community may be a group of jazz musicians, or the cadre of insomniacs and cops that gather at Philip's all-night candy shop in Coney Island for coffee and conversation, or the early morning "over eighty" crowd that met for breakfast at the now defunct Dubrow's Cafeteria. Often, they are important because they do more than provide a single service; these become a gathering point where people get to know one other, discuss issues, and share in one another's lives.

When social interactions involve more than a single interest and people become connected in a multiplicity of ways, communities are born; relationships become multilayered, moving beyond a simple use and exchange. Local establishments play a key role in the maintenance of community in New York City. A true neighborhood, according to one New York taxi driver, is where the local butcher comes to your funeral; if a butcher attends a customer's funeral, the relationship has gone beyond the purchase of meat, beyond a simple use and exchange—the two are linked together in community.

Oftentimes, local establishments and cultural sites play a role in sustaining a memory culture for those who frequented them during a particular era of their lives. Elaine Eff, formerly the Baltimore city folklorist and now the administrator for cultural conservation in the state of Maryland, takes Baltimoreans on tour to North Avenue, where the Jewish, Irish, and African-American communities resided in successive waves of migration. She talks about the "missing teeth" on the street; how people say to her, "You should have been here yesterday"; and how the missing cultural sites create a vacuum in human memory, for without them neighborhood residents have difficulty recalling what happened there.[8]

As a child in Buffalo, New York, in the 1950s, the folklorist Kate Koperski remembers shopping with her father on Saturday mornings at the Broadway market in East Buffalo. "You could squeeze in between two counters to see what was going on in back. I was very impressed by the sawdust on the floor and by the sound of the big saws going through the heavy bones when someone bought a large cut of meat. Everyone wore big white aprons and white hats behind the counters—I thought they looked very scientific."[9] Today Koperski is strategizing about ways to save the market, which, she believes, is the lifeblood of the Polish community:

> The community can get its holiday specialties—for Easter, fresh horseradish, imported Easter eggs, and butter in the shape of lamb (symbolizing Christ's resurrection); for Christmas, they get suckling

> pig, marinated herring for good luck on New Year's Eve and *opaltek,* wafers shared by Polish families as a sign of solidarity before Christmas dinner. There's about three dozen stands still at the market, and you can buy things in any quantity (the lunch counters even serve half portions). Nobody's rushing you and you can even do business in Polish. The counter ladies are part of it—they're always dressed for the season, with candy cane earrings and hearts for Valentine's day. And they still use white paper and rubber bands—plastic and butcher tape haven't caught on yet. So there's a certain rhythm to each purchase—wrap, snap, and a gruff "What else." It's incredible to me that supermarkets here in Buffalo have a phony "Olde World Section" and that people choose to shop there rather than at the market.[10]

In Baltimore the folklorist Elaine Eff and the African-American photographer Roland Freeman (who was an "Arabber" in his youth) have documented and struggled to preserve wooden stables that quarter the horses needed to pull the gaily painted fruit-laden carts through the streets. Deep blues-based cries still echo down city blocks, serenading shoppers, luring them to the carts to barter and talk. The elderly Arabbers cry,

> Well I hoop and I holler till my throat got sore
> If it wasn't for that fruit, I wouldn't holler no more.
> Got watermelon, got 'em red to the rind.
> If you want black seed watermelon
> Come to this wagon of mine.
> Watermel-o-o-o-o![11]

"We are concerned," says Barbara Kirshenblatt-Gimblett, chair of Performance Studies at New York University and president of the American Folklore Society, "about everyday people, about culture with a small *c* rather than a capital *C*."[12]

Theoretical Justification

In his classic work *Historic Preservation: Curatorial Management of the Built World,* James Marston Fitch states, "Throughout history, the cost of making anything—a city, a house, even a quilt—has been high in terms of both labor and materials. Thus every artifact was used and reused until it 'wore out' or 'fell apart'. . . . Current concepts of technological obsolescence, of objects becoming useless *economically* without reference to any *physical* utility are modern inventions, the result of the industrial revolution."[13] The same may be said about the *cultural* utility of places. Fitch suggests that the real value of a place is defined not by dollars and cents but by the quantifiable human energy that was put into it. Harry Weese, the Chicago architect, suggests that one case for preservation is the conservation of energy: "the residual value of energy built into old cities is enormous, packed into streets, utilities and buildings."[14]

Part of this, he submits, is the "time energy" that it took to create the building—but part of it too is the human energy that it took to create a life for the building, a folk culture that takes root in the place and reaps its rewards in terms of such human values as the creation of communities. Alan Lomax has suggested that folksongs are important because the creators and their communities have invested a large portion of their creative genius in them. Community establishments can be important for the same reason: the countless decisions that went into their usage—where to hang the pictures, the recipes for the food, the humor that evolved—create a working nexus for a community. Part of our job as cultural conservationists is to find ways to understand and assign value to these intangibles—because only by assigning a measurable value can we fight to protect them.

Photographic Documentation

Part of our job is documentation. We try to assure that a place is photographed and documented in case it does close. We are also concerned with documentation because it is often the first step in making a case for preserving a site. The tradition of using photographs to raise consciousness about social issues goes back as far as Jacob Riis's images of squalor on the Lower East Side in the 1890s, which did encourage a generation of reformers to address the social problems.

In addition to this strand of photographic work, there is a long photographic tradition of documenting what we are calling endangered spaces in New York and even before that in Europe.[15] By the turn of the century Eugene Atget (1857–1927) was already documenting a "vanishing" Paris. He served as one of the initial inspirations for this work by American documentarians. Jesse Tarbox Beals (1870–1942), whose images date from before World War I, photographed "cigar store indians" in New York City. Unlike the urban reformers who sought to bring about social change rather than preservation, Berenice Abbott documented old country stores and other urban forms being displaced by "modern" life. The Photo League in the 1940s and early 1950s was also interested in endangered spaces; such photographers as Sid Grossman, Arthur Leipzig, Rebecca Lepkoff, Morris Engel, Ruth Orkin, Arnold Eagle, and Sid Kerner documented street life and people in public places. In the 1960s Bruce Davidson conducted a photographic study of New York's cafeterias, most of which have closed (or been replaced by salad bars).

Intervention

As Jim Abrams has written, family businesses—and many of these cherished sites are family businesses—have a life cycle of their own. They are tied into currents in American history and economics, family history, and the aging process.[16] Today, however, this life cycle is often truncated by drastic changes in real estate values and a narrowing of interests toward mass consumption and chain stores with their coercive advertising power. At City Lore we have tried to intervene on behalf of local establishments. When a family-owned Jamaican shoe repair shop in Park Slope, Brooklyn, was hit with a rent increase from $600 to $2,300 a month and when Philip's Candy—Coney Island's only maker of old-time saltwater taffy—received an eviction notice, folklorists and other cultural specialists contacted the landlords and worked to get stories in the local papers. When the house under the Coney Island roller coaster (seen in Woody Allen's *Annie Hall*) and the old Brighton Beach Baths were scheduled for demolition, we testified at the hearings, claiming that "neighborhood life is on trial here." The Coney Island developer is now considering refurbishing the roller coaster and preserving the house, while Philip's Candy has received a reprieve partly because of our efforts.

Ethnic Social Clubs

While we were developing our advocacy efforts for endangered spaces, a tragic event in New York City caused us to shift directions.[17] In March 1990 eighty-seven New Yorkers were killed when a social club frequented by Latino and Latina, largely Honduran, immigrants was torched by an arsonist—it was the worst fire in New York City since the Triangle Shirtwaist disaster in 1911. City hall's response was to order the closing of approximately four hundred social clubs located in buildings that did not meet fire and building codes.

This was a tragedy in a city where ethnic social clubs, though ramshackle, are the bulwark of many communities. In New York as elsewhere, immigrants often organize themselves around ethnic social clubs that bring together residents of the same village in Greece, Italy, Eastern Europe, or Puerto Rico in basements and storefronts in the five boroughs of New York. These ethnic associations rise and fall and are renewed each day in New York City, as immigrant groups arrive in this country, band together for support, and try to maintain continuities with their past as they chart strategies for success in the United States.

City Lore asked to testify before a commission set up by the mayor on the city's social clubs and led by Rudolph Rinaldi, commissioner of buildings. Our testimony was important because the commission did not realize that social clubs were not a new Latino phenomenon but existed in a historical context. Social clubs and, in a larger sense, voluntary associations have helped shape the immigrant experience during each of the major waves of immigrants to the United States. During the first wave (1840s–50s) immigrants who arrived at Castle Garden established the Irish Ancient Order of Hibernians, the Lieder Kranz German choral society, and the Bohemian Benevolent Association, among many others that are still active in New York today. During the second wave (1880s–1920s) immigrants who disembarked at Ellis Island established hundreds of Italian patron saint "societies" and Jewish *landsmanshaftn* (hometown associations). During the third wave (1965 to the present) immigrants who landed at JFK International Airport established the city's newest clubs—among them the Asantemen's Association of America, West Indian carnival "mas" (as in masquerade) camps, and the Yemenite Benevolent Association.

As advocates, our perspective is simple: rather than close down the clubs because they are not up to code, the city should be assisting the clubs in bringing their facilities up to code; they should be helping to fix them up rather than shutting them down. Such a policy can be drafted if the city is willing to work with people from within the community, as well as with folklorists, anthropologists, and other culture specialists. It is possible to understand the variety of functions served by the clubs and to prioritize the role of some clubs as community centers, giving the city a way to select the clubs to be assisted—although the other clubs, including the dance clubs, also serve important functions that should not be stifled.

We are arguing that social clubs are a basic part of the human condition. If they are locked out of one space, they are likely to move to spaces that are even less safe. Many of these clubs are in low-income areas that have cramped home environments and no facilities for clubs. This is especially true in the Bronx, where hundreds of buildings have been demolished and abandoned over the past twenty years. Frequently, they serve as indigenous settlement houses, providing homegrown solutions to social issues confronting low-income and new immigrant populations. More often than not, they can serve to keep out drugs. Supporting them, Barbara Kirshenblatt-Gimblett argues, is cost effective because they provide a variety of cultural and civic services for the community that would be costly or prohibitive to replace. "What the city needs," she suggests, "is for people to take care of themselves wherever possible, and to make this impossible by taking away places where they can meet is one of the most counterproductive and costly approaches the city can take."[18]

Ethnic History

Along with City Lore's efforts to implement the Endangered Spaces Program has come an effort to expand the boundaries of historic preservation to include both vernacular architecture and ethnic history (its proponents also stress the importance of culture with a small *c*). As Dolores Hayden, working with the Power of Place, a Los Angeles–based organization, writes, "While many vernacular structures are not exceptional as architecture, their age, scale and neighborhood meaning may make them vital reminders of the ethnic past."[19] Recognizing that the meaning of particular ethnic sites often resides in locales and neighborhoods rather than in isolated building, she aptly notes the need for "territorial histories" and stresses the need for a new sensitivity to women's history and workers' histories, a history of the city from the perspective of production rather than consumption. She offers two reasons why ethnic history projects are important: "First, the awareness that every citizen's history is important can generate a new kind of pride in a multicultural city. Second, recognition of historic structures in poorer neighborhoods can support other kinds of community organizing for change."[20] Although both folklorists and the new preservationists can form a valuable alliance based on a shared vision of culture, it is important to realize the distinction between historical structures with significance in women's, ethnic, and workers' history and places with an ongoing community use, for different strategies must be devised for their conservation.

Strategies

What strategies can be used to conserve endangered spaces? The new inclusiveness and sensitivities of contemporary historians, along with the new approaches to ethnic and folk history by preservationists and folklorists, enhance the possibility that some sites important for cultural reasons might be protected by including them in the National Register of Historic Places. In their *Guidelines for Evaluating and Documenting Traditional Cultural Properties,* written for the National Park Service, Patricia L. Parker and Thomas F. King define a "traditional cultural property" as "one that is eligible for inclusion in the National Register because of its association with cultural practices or beliefs of a living community that (a) are rooted in that community's history, and (b) are important in maintaining the continuing cultural identity of the community."[21] They suggest "an urban neighborhood that is the traditional home of a particular cultural group, and that reflects its beliefs and practices" as an example of the kinds of culturally significant properties that might be included.[22] They offer Honolulu's Chinatown as a possible traditional cultural property with great significance to the city's Asian community. Their discussion of the National Register criteria suggests that a number of our endangered spaces might fit in the program, if they have made a "significant contribution to the broad patterns of our history" (see table 15.1 for specific examples).[23]

Nonetheless, there are other criteria for inclusion that may prove to be stumbling blocks—the emphasis on the places that have held cultural significance in the *past* rather than the present and the limitation to properties that have achieved significance over more than fifty years. Those concerned with endangered spaces might pursue emending or changing these criteria, as well as adding specific criteria that emphasize living communities (although not excluded, they are not emphasized). The other problems with pursuing this strategy is that once a property is on the National Register or in equivalent programs on the state or city level, changes to its facade and structure are prohibited under certain circumstances, but nothing is said about its *use.*

The legislation in historic preservation does partially address districts of historic importance. This is important to the folklorist and the social historian because a populist history is, by nature, not focused on single events, personages, and places. Dolores Hayden emphasizes the import of conducting "territorial histories," emphasizing neighborhoods.[24] The legislation on preservation, however, defines districts in terms of visual contiguity of buildings, a concept not well suited to conserving buildings important to social history or ongoing community establishments in neighborhoods.

An alternative strategy to protect endangered spaces would be to establish commercial rent control. No U.S. city has commercial rent control (though England, France, and Japan do). In New York major struggles have been mounted to pass a commercial rent control bill, to no avail. We are currently exploring the possibilities for a system of "cultural landmarking," which would define and protect certain neighborhood institutions as threatened cultural landmarks based on predetermined criteria for significance. We are arguing that the "cultural landmarking" idea would be less threatening because it would apply to a limited number of places; they could not claim that such legislation would wreak havoc with the city's overall economy. This legislation would help preserve real neighborhood institutions.

The problem, of course, is that it is hard to identify which sites would be defined as having significance in the community. This is a sticky question, but it is not insurmountable. One possibility is to ask threatened establishments or their supporters to produce a petition with a certain number of names and to establish a review board—if an establishment passed it would qualify for the same kind of rent stabilization that large residential units receive. Ultimately, we need to convince legislators that intangi-

Table 15.1. A Partial Listing of Sites Already Documented or Considered for Documentation under City Lore's Endangered Spaces Project

Recreational Areas
- Sheepshead Bay fishing piers
- Brighton Beach Baths
- Coney Island
- Gaelic Park, Bronx
- New York's public pools
- Central Park Children's Zoo

Markets
- Essex Street Market, Lower East Side
- La Marqueta, Harlem

Delis, Cafeterias, Eateries
- Katz's Delicatessen
- Automat (documented, 1989, 1990), Manhattan
- Pop's Restaurant, Woodhaven, Queens

Bookstores
- St. Marks Books, Manhattan
- Strand Bookstore, Manhattan

Candy Shops, Bakeries, Confectioners
- Philip's Candy, Coney Island
- Davies Chocolates, Queens
- The Marzipan Shop, Upper East Side
- Lemon Ice King of Corona, Queens

Work Sites
- Steinway Piano Factory, Astoria, Queens
- Brooklyn Shipping Piers
- Union Hall, Local 25, 64, Lower Manhattan

Social Clubs
- Bohemian Hall, Astoria
- Casitas: Rincon Criollo, Bronx
  Villa Puerto Rico, East Harlem

Local Landmarks
- House under the roller coaster, Coney Island
- Parachute jump, Coney Island
- Adam Purple's Garden, Lower East Side, Manhattan
- Lamppost mosaics, Grenwich Village
- Little red lighthouse under Brooklyn Bridge
- Rock monument, Farmers and Liberty, St. Albans, Queens

Barbershop
- Broadway Barber, 104th and Broadway

Religious Sites
- Our Lady of Mount Carmel Grotto, Rosebank, Staten Island
- St. Lucy's Church, Mace and Bronxwood, Bronx

bles, such as "community significance," can be quantified sufficiently to provide a basis for action.

Along with seeking landmark designations and commercial rent control, there is a third set of strategies, which are more widely applicable to the full range of endangered spaces. These are simply to bring the problem to the attention of the owner, to threaten and then go to the press, and to try to weave a protective net, not with legalities but with public approval. "Sometimes," said Baltimore's Elaine Eff, who showed the owner of the Parkway Theater on North Avenue old photographs of the building in its heyday, "just bringing the importance of a site to the owner's attention is enough to save it. With old photographs and a tour I think I was able to stall off—at least for awhile—the demolition of the Parkway Theater on North Avenue. Other times, it's just a losing battle. McCormick's Spice factory is now a parking lot. What can I say?"[25]

Government controlled properties often hold public hearings where folklorists and other preservationists can testify. Our experience is that people on the planning boards are sensitive to these issues, as are elected officials who do not want to be perceived as holding the moral lowground or as party to the demise of beloved local establishments. The press is also an effective medium, and feature stories on endangered spaces make effective copy, both in print and on the air. The local news in New York, for instance, airs a special regular segment called "Shame on you," dealing with such issues as unscrupulous landlords.

The recent work on New York's Puerto Rican casitas is a case in point. "In East Harlem and the South Bronx," writes Barbara Kirshenblatt-Gimblett,

> little country cabins pop up incongruously on vacant lots between tenements and brownstones, some abandoned and others still intact. These old-fashioned *casitas*, once common in the Puerto Rican countryside, are now scattered throughout inner city neighborhoods, where vacant lots abound and where local men can no longer afford to rent space for their social clubs. . . . Brightly painted and rich in pastoral imagery, these little cottages re-create in loving detail the veranda, wood-burning stove, latrine, chicken coop (complete with chickens), well, and gardens remembered from the Puerto Rican countryside.[26]

These fragile structures are under constant danger of demolition by city agencies—they are ramshackle constructions that do not meet city codes and are illegally built on vacant lots. In the early 1980s, working with Barbara Kirshenblatt-Gimblett and other folklorists in New York, the photographer Martha Cooper began photographing the casitas. In 1988 Betty Sue Hertz, an artist working with the Bronx Council on the Arts, initiated the exhibition project "*Casitas:* An Urban Cultural Alternative," which resulted in a magnificent exhibit installed at the Smithsonian's Experimental Gallery in Washington, D.C., in 1990 and at the Bronx Museum in 1990 and 1991. With its rich documentation, this project was written up in all the major New York City newspapers, including the *New York Times.* The publicity has enabled many of these structures to survive. Even though the exhibition and the newspaper articles are not advocacy pieces per se, they have helped create a safer climate for these community-based clubhouses; knowing the press's interest in these establishments, city agencies are increasingly reluctant to demolish them.

In working with endangered spaces, we realize, increasingly, that no single strategy is applicable to all local sites; each instance needs to be addressed on its own. In fact, research into the history of the space, its ownership, and use is necessary to build a case for conservation. Oftentimes, endangered spaces are brought to our attention by a tenant feuding with a landlord; there are numerous sides to the story, and even after research how to proceed remains unclear. Each space requires extensive field research, documentation, and thoughtful consideration before strategies can be devised and advocacy can begin.

The Best of Both Worlds

Applying principles of cultural conservation to small businesses and establishments in New York City is not an easy task. Endangerment can occur for many reasons: the loss of traditional skills, the lack of heirs for family businesses, changing tastes, aging proprietors, and, perhaps most common, escalating real estate values. Here, we draw a distinction between preservation and conservation. Sites that are crucial because of a human rather than a physical dimension can not be preserved in the sense that a building can be preserved; human factors render each cultural site exceedingly complex and often impossible to conserve; we can not serve as a life-support system to keep dying establishments alive; and keeping a neighborhood establishment open will not assure the perpetuation of the community that patronized it and brought it to life. Maintaining Coney Island's spookhouse or Madam Lily's "World in Wax" can not re-create the lifeways that characterized the neighborhood of Coney Island fifty years ago. Similarly, New York's homemade chocolate shops can not be conserved if no one wants to eat hand-dipped, calorie-laden chocolate anymore or if the owners wish to retire. Ultimately, we need to conserve the best of both worlds—to be cognizant of the present and the need for change as we try to conserve what was best about the past. This kind of work requires a philosophical outlook. New York's Essex Street Market opened in the

1930s, when Mayor Fiorello La Guardia wanted to gentrify the pushcarts that jammed Hester Street and Orchard Street by moving them indoors; half a century later, the stall-bedecked market central to the Latino community on the Lower East Side is trying to ward off a new wave of gentrification, and we are doing what we can to protect it.[27] In this line of work all of us may find ourselves fighting to conserve the places that we were fighting against a few decades earlier.

We can not, however, allow these complexities to dissuade us. To make informed choices for the future of urban neighborhoods, we must ground our decisions on what has worked to create a sense of neighborhood and community in the past. The dissolution of communities is real and costly, and cultural conservation is a preventive medicine that can keep neighborhoods and communities from falling apart. Assessing the value of community establishments may be difficult, even costly, but trying to re-create the community after their doors have closed is not possible at any price. However much some of us may profit from progress, we can not let what is most distinctive and most human about our cities be destroyed. As Alan Lomax warns, "If we continue to allow the erosion of our cultural forms, soon there will be nowhere to visit and no place to truly call home."[28]

NOTES

1. Telephone interview with Judy Peiser and Richard Raichelson, Center for Southern Folklore, November 1989.

2. Telephone interview with Elaine Eff, November 1989.

3. Telephone interview with Deborah Kodish, Philadelphia Folklore Project, November 1989.

4. Interview with Saul Fromkin, October 24, 1989.

5. Personal interview with Barbara Kirshenblatt-Gimblett, chair, Performance Studies, New York University, November 1989.

6. Michael P. Smith, "Conserving Multi-Cultural Heritage in the City; A Conference on Urban Cultural Parks and Festivals" (Unpublished grant proposal, 1991), 3.

7. Personal interview with Barbara Kirshenblatt-Gimblett, November 1989.

8. Telephone interview with Elaine Eff, November 1989.

9. Telephone interview with Kate Koperski, November 1989.

10. Ibid.

11. Walter Kelly, recorded at the Festival of American Folklife, Smithsonian Institution, Washington, D.C., October 1980.

12. Personal interview with Barbara Kirshenblatt-Gimblett, November 1989.

13. James Marston Fitch, *Historic Preservation: Curatorial Management of the Built World* (New York: McGraw-Hill, 1982), 29–30.

14. Quoted in ibid., 32.

15. I thank Bonnie Yokelson, photography curator at the Museum of the City of New York, for this discussion on the photographic history of endangered spaces in New York.

16. Jim Abrams, "Family Businesses in Philadelphia" (Unpublished manuscript, 1989).

17. This discussion of ethnic social clubs was written in collaboration with the codirector of City Lore's ethnic clubs project, Joseph Sciorra.

18. Personal interview with Barbara Kirshenblatt-Gimblett, October 1989.

19. Dolores Hayden, "Using Ethnic History to Understand Urban Landscapes," *Places* 7 (1990): 15.

20. Ibid., 17.

21. Patricia L. Parker and Thomas F. King, *Guidelines for Evaluating and Documenting Traditional Cultural Properties,* National Register Bulletin, no. 38 (Washington, D.C.: National Park Service, Department of the Interior, 1990), 1.

22. Ibid.

23. Ibid., 11–12.

24. Hayden, "Using Ethnic History," 16.

25. Telephone interview with Elaine Eff, October 1989.

26. Barbara Kirshenblatt-Gimblett, "The Future of Folklore Studies in America: The Urban Frontier," *Folklore Forum* 16 (1983): 196–97.

27. See Jill Weiner, "Requiem for Essex Street," *Village Voice,* December 4, 1990, 39–42.

28. From a personal conversation with Bess Lomax Hawes, in which she quoted her brother Alan Lomax, Washington, D.C., 1989.

16

Cultural Conservation and Economic Recovery Planning: The Pennsylvania Heritage Parks Program

Shalom Staub

The cultural conservation paradigm has emerged in recent years to redress the fragmentation among specialists in the documentation, preservation, and interpretation of cultural forms and traditions. It also has offered promising opportunities to reknit the tangible and intangible elements of cultural heritage, elements that for too long have been torn apart by academic models and bureaucratic structures. The shift that the cultural conservation paradigm signals, integrating multiple cultural forms and encouraging interdisciplinary cooperation, is particularly timely as significant portions of the United States experience economic "restructuring." Regions of the country undergoing deindustrialization have seen the related rise of cultural tourism economies, which seek to market the past (or particular images of the past) as a means of economic survival. In such cases, the new cultural conservation paradigm offers one additional potential benefit; by focusing attention on the living cultural traditions of local residents as well as artifacts from the past, cultural conservation offers a model that encourages community members to participate in shaping their community's future character.

These three key elements of cultural conservation—the emphasis on interdisciplinary collaboration, the integration of cultural resources, and the emphasis on community involvement—have found particular expression in the development of the Pennsylvania State Heritage Parks Program. This state program was introduced in 1989 to foster the planning and implementation of a system of "parks" to promote tourism and economic revitalization by conserving and interpreting the region's industrial heritage. The program emphasizes a multiphase planning process to assess and develop conservation strategies for the region's historic, cultural, recreational, and environmental resources.

Heritage parks require and initiate a shift in symbolic meaning, transforming areas of industrial decline into "cradles of American industrial heritage," with tourism potential and a revitalized community spirit that can attract new investment. Ethnographic perspectives have played a key role in the planning process and have been incorporated in the program guidelines. There is a continuing need for folklorists and other cultural specialists to take such excursions into cultural tourism seriously.[1] In examining the development and implementation of this state program, this essay focuses on the definition of *cultural conservation*, its role in public policy, and strategies to ensure that local cultural patterns and values shape tourism planning and development. My own role in the program is at the level of policy development, specifically public policy informed by fieldwork-based ethnographic perspectives and community participation.[2]

Pennsylvania's efforts in this area build on earlier heritage park models. Massachusetts was the first state to create such a program, known as the Massachusetts Urban Heritage State Park Program, and in 1979 New York State created its Urban Cultural Parks Program. Expanding the notion of a park, these early efforts challenged people to think beyond open, green space and consider urban blocks and restored mills and factories as parks. Still, in the pioneering Massachusetts model, the heritage park occupies a relatively small, circumscribed geographic boundary, akin to a historic district.[3]

The heritage parks model expanded significantly with the introduction of the heritage corridor, first implemented in Illinois in 1984 along the remains of the historic Illinois and Michigan Canal. In 1985 another heritage corridor was established in the Blackstone River Valley linking Massachusetts and Rhode Island. Each of these projects was designated a "National Heritage Corridor" by act of Congress and came into existence through joint federal, state, and local effort. The National Park Service has played a key role in developing the heritage corridor concept, adapting and refining the concept and practice as new efforts are made throughout the country.[4]

Pennsylvania is now the site of four federally assisted heritage project areas (at different stages of development): the nine-county America's Industrial Heritage Project and the Steel Industry Heritage Park in southwestern Pennsylvania, the Lackawanna Heritage Valley in northeastern Pennsylvania, and the Delaware and Lehigh Navigation Canal National Heritage Corridor in eastern Pennsylvania.

Interest in such efforts in Pennsylvania at the state and local levels goes back a number of years. In 1984 three state agencies collaborated to produce a report entitled *Pennsylvania Heritage Parks: A Concept with Applications.*[5] These three agencies, the Pennsylvania Historical and Museum Commission and the departments of Environmental Resources and Community Affairs, offered the Heritage Park Planning Project as a framework "to preserve cultural resources in a manner which provides educational, recreational and economic benefits" by promoting community revitalization and stimulating tourism.[6] The plan called for the development of a set of regional and local parks drawing on existing historical resources. It offered screening criteria for evaluating potential parks and described forty-two viable park possibilities, each based closely on existing and potential historic districts.

The initial proposal lay dormant until 1987, when the three agencies, along with the Pennsylvania Heritage Affairs Commission, revived the idea and sought to respond to federally assisted activities and growing interest in all corners of the state. The Heritage Parks Work Group, composed of staff from the Department of Community Affairs and the Heritage Affairs Commission, reevaluated the 1984 plan and reviewed the results of the ongoing efforts in Massachusetts and New York. Over the course of many months the Heritage Parks Work Group designed a program that received an initial appropriation of $550,000 in the Commonwealth's 1989–90 budget.

The Pennsylvania Heritage Parks Program does not seek to re-create the Massachusetts model of state-financed and state-operated parks or the New York model of state-mandated and state-assisted parks. Rather, the Pennsylvania program takes a "bottom-up" approach, emphasizing planning and process as much as product and local community involvement as much as the inventory of historic, cultural, educational, and recreational resources that eventually will constitute the park.

Our efforts focus on industrial heritage, appropriate enough for Pennsylvania's legacy of industrial prominence and later decline. Projects must relate to one or more of the following industries: iron and steel, coal, textile, machine and foundry, transportation, lumber, oil, and agriculture. The first five of these—iron and steel, coal, textile, machine and foundry, and transportation—exceed all others in terms of numbers of people employed, the amount of capital invested, the value of their products, and their contributions to technological, labor, and business history over a sustained period of time. For brief periods the lumber and oil industries were significant employers and producers of industrial goods in the state and nation. Agriculture has played a key role in Pennsylvania's economy from colonial times to the present; in fact, agriculture is now its leading industry.[7]

The driving force behind the Heritage Parks Program is economic development. A Pennsylvania heritage park is designed to

> complement existing economic development initiatives in a region or . . . even become a primary program for economic revitalization.

> The intent of the program is to stimulate economic activity in an area by attracting tourists for both daily and overnight visitations, resulting in direct expenditures for traditional visitor services such as food, lodging, retail sales, entertainment, etc. Other spin-off economic objectives [are] the creation of employment opportunities, development and expansion of small business activity, and the formulation of public/private investment partnerships in the region. The attraction of major businesses, manufacturing or industrial companies into the heritage park area [is] a long term goal that will add substantially to the success of the initiative.[8]

The promise of economic revitalization has allowed this state program to grow when many state programs are suffering sharp budgetary cutbacks. The State Heritage Parks Program began in 1989–90 with a $500,000 appropriation, grew to $950,000 in 1990–91, and stood at $2,000,000 in 1991–92. The increase in state support is directly linked to the need to provide matching funds to federal appropriations of $52.4 million over a two-year period (1989–91) to support the four federally assisted heritage projects.[9] The State Heritage Parks Program in turn requires projects to show matching monies from local public and private sources.

One project, the Lackawanna Heritage Valley, estimates that capital costs will total $37 million between 1991 and 1995. In turn the plan is expected to attract between 860,000 and 1,310,000 visitors annually, with annual visitor spending estimated at $12 million. The project would create construction and related employment estimated at 1,430 to 2,650 jobs, with additional service and retail jobs. Citing a multiplier effect of this investment, project consultants estimate an economic impact greater than $79 million.[10]

Although driven by a concern for economic revitalization, the development of a heritage park depends on a foundation of historical and cultural resources. The program is intended to enhance "community, regional, and state-wide awareness and pride of Pennsylvania's historical and cultural legacy through the preservation, adaptive reuse, or restoration of historic sites and properties; the conservation of other cultural resources through documentation, interpretive programs and events; and educational materials to be made available to the public." A heritage park is also intended to link and enhance the educational and recreational infrastructure of the region. These objectives are expressed in the five formal goals of the Pennsylvania Heritage Parks Program: economic development, intergovernmental cooperation, cultural conservation, recreation, and education.[11]

The lead administrative agency for the Heritage Parks Program is the Department of Community Affairs (DCA), Bureau of Recreation and Conservation, which utilizes its network of five regionally based recreation advisers to provide extensive technical assistance to local communities. The DCA heritage parks' management team,[12] continues to monitor closely the program's progress and plan for its future. A State Heritage Park Interagency Task Force (SHPITF)—composed of representatives from the departments of Commerce, Community Affairs, Education, Environmental Resources, and Transportation; the Pennsylvania Heritage Affairs Commission; the Pennsylvania Historical and Museum Commission; and the Pennsylvania Council on the Arts—reviews and makes funding recommendations on Heritage Park Program grant applications, recommends state heritage park (and planning area) designation, provides expertise and technical assistance, and coordinates heritage park efforts with other state grant and loan programs.

Obtaining designation as a Pennsylvania heritage park is a two-step process. First, a region must complete a feasibility study. Approval of the study by the SHPITF allows the region to be designated as a Pennsylvania heritage park planning area and to compete for a management action plan grant. While conducting the management action plan, a heritage park planning area can apply for early implementation project grants. When the management action plan has been completed and approved by the SHPITF, the region is designated a state heritage park by the governor. This designation allows the region to apply for special purpose study project funds, implementation project funds, and support for a state heritage park manager.

During both the feasibility and management action planning stages, the region must address the industrial theme, propose park boundaries, and inventory economic, historical, cultural, educational, and recreational resources. The program encourages applicants to utilize consultant teams with expertise in a wide range of fields, including architecture, archaeology, planning and urban design, history, and ethnography.

In the program's initial year, eight grants were awarded. Feasibility study grants were given to explore the possibilities of creating a lumber region heritage park in north central Pennsylvania, an oil region heritage park in northwestern Pennsylvania, a steel industry heritage park in the Monongahela Valley of southwestern Pennsylvania, a Schuylkill River heritage corridor in southeastern Pennsylvania, and a national road heritage corridor along sections of Route 40, the National Pike, in southwestern Pennsylvania (see figure 16.1). Management action planning grants were given to support federally assisted efforts for the Lackawanna Heritage Valley, the Delaware and Lehigh Navigation Canal National Heritage Corridor, and the Allegheny Ridge Industrial Heritage Corridor, a portion of the nine-county America's Industrial Heritage Project linking the cities of Altoona, Johnstown, and Windber.

By mid-1993 the work on these projects had progressed considerably.

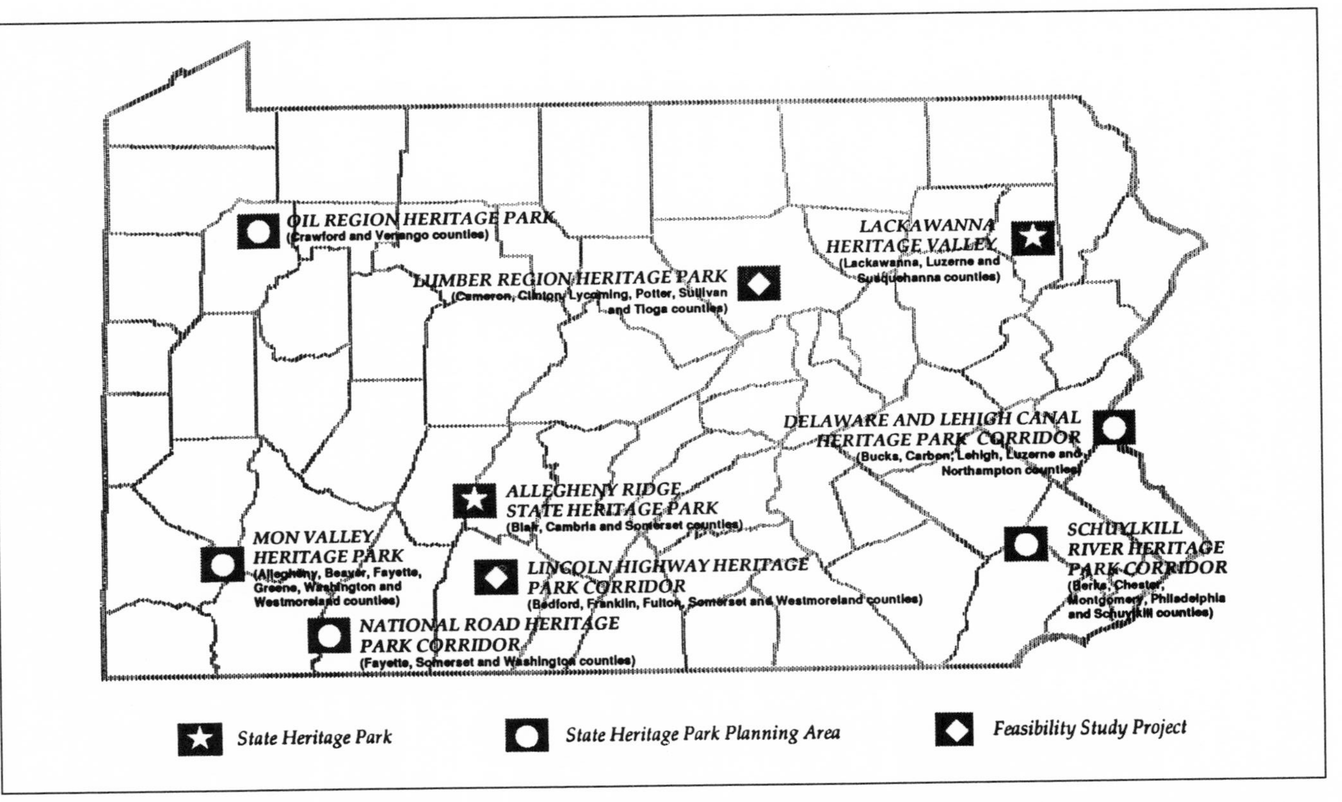

Figure 16.1 Pennsylvania Heritage Parks Program project areas, April 1992. (Courtesy of the Pennsylvania Department of Community Affairs)

The Lackawanna Heritage Valley was named the first state heritage park in April 1991. The Allegheny Ridge Industrial Heritage Corridor received state heritage park designation in April 1992, and the Delaware and Lehigh Navigation Canal National Heritage Corridor received its designation in April 1993. During December 1991 the feasibility studies for the oil region and national road were officially approved, making them official state heritage park planning areas and therefore eligible to apply for management action planning grants in February 1992. The feasibility studies for the steel industry and Schuylkill River projects were approved in January 1992, and those projects moved into the management action planning phase. The feasibility study for the lumber region project was tabled. A new project focusing on the Lincoln Highway, a portion of Route 30 in southwestern Pennsylvania, moved through its feasibility study into management action planning.

In each of these areas, the opportunity for participating in the Heritage Parks Program depends heavily on the availability and identification of "heritage" resources. Almost invariably, these "resources" are first conceptualized by applicants as the hulklike remains of industrial structures and the tangible remains of an industrial elite, what might be called the "sites and structures of the rich and famous" approach. Pennsylvania's Heritage Parks Program is set apart from similar programs nationally by its insistence that "heritage resources" encompass not only the built environment but also "the human dimension of industrial heritage: the social history of the communities and workers who built and sustained Pennsylvania's industries and their folklife, the living cultural traditions shared within occupational and ethnic groups and local communities."[13]

We have used the term *cultural conservation* to encompass these tangible and intangible elements of cultural heritage. Our focus on the people and their own understanding of their heritage is consistent with the program's overall process orientation, which demands local community involvement in shaping the goals of a particular heritage park. The program requires each project to establish a local heritage park task force to represent a broad spectrum of interest groups in the region and to guide applicants toward an open, participatory planning process, with ample opportunity for public review and comment.

Conceptually, the Pennsylvania Heritage Parks Program has built on the emerging cultural conservation paradigm, drawing on the work of the American Folklife Center and others[14] who have sought to create links between preservation efforts more broadly: historic preservation, documentation and perpetuation of folk cultural traditions, and environmental conservation. Though we adopted the mantle of cultural conservation, new terminology needed to be coined for the program manual and application guidelines to ensure that applicants would give serious consideration to both tangible and intangible elements of cultural heritage. We recognized that the field of historic preservation had developed a network of practicing professionals ready to bid on consulting contracts but that these consultants were not necessarily trained to consider "the human dimension." Furthermore, we saw a distinct lack of consultants readily available for the ethnographic component of the required studies. We recognized too that such terminology as *cultural conservation* and *folklife* is understood by professionals in the field but lacks the broad public recognition of historic preservation terminology. Ironically, these terms were developed by practicing folklorists and anthropologists to direct attention to how people actually perceive and live their "heritage," but they are either too new or, like folklore and anthropology more generally, are misunderstood or taken to refer exclusively to far-away or exotic cultures.

For these reasons, we explicitly defined the terms *cultural conservation* and *folklife* in the Heritage Parks Program manual. We used *cultural conservation* to encompass the fields of historic preservation, folklife studies, and social history. The definition of *folklife* is adapted from Public Law 94-201, the American Folklife Preservation Act, to mean "the traditional expressive culture shared within various groups . . . encompassing a wide range of creative and symbolic forms. . . ."[15]

Having defined these basic terms, we realized that further guidelines and definitions would be needed to ensure that the human dimension would be treated with the same seriousness and thoroughness that the historic sites and structures were. For example, in addition to asking for a preliminary inventory of significant historic sites, properties, and other tangible resources that contribute to the industrial heritage of the region, the feasibility study application asks for an overview of the social and cultural history of the region. Additionally, the application narrative must identify the ethnic background of the communities within the proposed heritage park region, as well as other associational groups that may relate to the industrial theme (such as unions, craftworkers' guilds, associations of retired workers).

The required scope of work for the feasibility study itself calls for further resource inventory and analysis. For the tangible resources, program participants must provide a "historic context," including "an identification of the types of sites, buildings, and other tangible resources expected to appear in the context."[16] A parallel definition of *cultural context* was needed to address the intangible elements of cultural heritage, and we added this term to the program manual and feasibility study scope of work. *Cultural context* is defined as "a body of information drawing on ethnographic and historical sources about a region's settlement patterns, social organization and folklife. A cultural context will provide information about the daily patterns of activity experienced by people of different social groups at particular periods of time, covering such elements as occupational, domestic, religious, and social life; sense of place; and attitudes towards, and interaction with the built and natural environments."[17] The scope of work in the feasibility study calls for a cultural context "including an identification of the categories of folklife resources present in the Heritage Park area and an assessment of their relationship to the Heritage Park proposal."[18]

The scope of work in the management action plan calls for "a comprehensive profile of cultural features, based upon the cultural context established during the feasibility study and expanding upon the identified categories of folklife resources. The profile of cultural features will identify significant aspects of community life relating to the industrial theme selected for the Heritage Park area, and discuss the presence and vitality of folklife resources."[19]

This definition of *cultural context* and its application in the two study stages is meant to guide applicants and program participants to the situated meanings of *history* and *heritage* for residents in the region. Through this definition, we intended to focus attention on issues of ethnicity and class in the industrial context and how these elements are variously constructed in the contemporary lives of the region's communities.

Despite the best intentions of the guidelines, the broad, interdisciplinary scope of the Heritage Parks Program and its conceptual innovations (particularly in its cultural conservation component) represented clear challenges to applicants. Though the application guidelines made it clear that a heritage park requires a lengthy planning process with public participation and must treat the living cultural traditions of a region as well as significant historic structures, one first-round applicant offered a Disneyland vision of re-created environments, with costumed locals playing historic roles for visitors. Another talked of guided walking tours along "Millionaires' Row," the historic district of elegant Victorian homes, with no mention whatsoever of working conditions for laborers during the heyday of industrial expansion.

To address the issues raised by such applications as these, applicants were invited to technical assistance workshops with representatives of all agency members of the SHPITF. In this context, I had the opportunity to provoke some discussion of the conceptual issues posed by heritage park planning, for example, the varied and ambivalent relation to the past, particularly for workers (or their descendants) whose relation to industrial "heritage" may be the recollection of harsh working conditions and exploitation. I built my presentation on a series of rhetorical questions to direct attention to the ethnographic dimension: what is the "heritage" in the proposed heritage park? Is this heritage located in the past only? What would the heritage park look like if planners stressed public participation to reflect the multiple (and at times ambivalent) visions of the past (and future) that are present in any diverse contemporary community. *Whose heritage* will be presented, and *who decides?* Who is the intended audience? What are the implications for transforming local culture into a tourist experience? What will be the impact of increased cultural tourism in the region, and particularly what will be the impact for the very cultural resources that lend the region its distinctive character? What steps can be taken to mitigate any negative impact of increased tourism?[20]

Popular attitudes about local heritage, coupled with the prominent role of leaders of business, industry, and government, contributed to early formulations of heritage parks that stressed the past over cultural continuities, a "management" view over "labor," social elites over a broader range of ethnic groups and minorities, and male perspectives over female. The technical assistance workshops helped expand and refine program participants' understanding of the issues. The Pennsylvania Heritage Affairs Commission staff has consistently stressed the need for a strong ethnographic dimension in the planning studies to enable the planners to gain access to multiple perceptions of the past and, by implication, the future of the heritage park. We established liaisons with each of the heritage park projects to provide ongoing technical assistance. We were also able to identify and make recommendations for including representatives of local ethnic and labor groups in the planning efforts.

Beyond the ongoing technical assistance, the Pennsylvania Heritage Affairs Commission has designed and conducted ethnographic survey or documentation work in all nine of the heritage park project areas.[21] All of these projects share some common elements: inventory of existing ethnographic research and collections, new survey work, selected in-depth case studies of particular cultural traditions, and the development of programmatic and policy recommendations to focus attention on the conservation of a region's characteristic traditions and the mitigation of cultural tourism's unwanted intrusions.

Ironically, the first designated state heritage park—the Lackawanna Heritage Valley—remains among the least ethnographically informed of all the current project areas. Nevertheless, a closer examination of this case shows that key elements of the cultural conservation paradigm are present and have been developed in innovative ways.

During 1989–91, project organizers in the Lackawanna River Valley in northeastern Pennsylvania created a local task force and committees (whose participants in some cases reached into the hundreds), hired consultants, held public meetings, and began regional self-study efforts to inventory resources. The Lackawanna Heritage Valley exemplifies the interaction of federal, state, and local government, private industry and business, nonprofit organizations, and the valley's residents.

Through the self-study, facilitated by the National Park Service and the consulting firms—Lane, Frenchman and Associates of Boston and Leung, Hemmler and Camayd of Scranton—it became clear that the five goals of the State Heritage Parks Program meshed well with visions of the future expressed by Lackawanna Valley residents. Residents were unequivocal in their insistence that while tourism was an acceptable strategy for economic development, the heritage park must address itself equally to needs of the local community. People expressed a desire to regain a pride of place that had been lost over the years of industrial and economic decline, and they wanted the heritage park to help preserve the valued elements of the Lackawanna Valley—the neighborhoods, the main streets, job skills, ethnic traditions, and the like. The ultimate goal is not an exclusive tourist economy; there is little interest in the valley to create the atmosphere of a living museum, with amenities directed toward out-of-town visitors. Although economic development is clearly a driving force for the planning and implementation, the focus is on preserving valued elements of "place" to contribute to increased "quality of life" and to attract new industries or major businesses.

The history of the Lackawanna Valley has been shaped by the presence of anthracite coal. Coal deposits largely dictated patterns of land use along the river corridor: industrial sites, railroad tracks and yards, neighborhoods and churches, and coal sites and culm banks at the fringes of residential areas—all clustered along the valley floor, with green hills rising sharply on either side. Survey research indicated that the physical and built environment has remained remarkably constant since the height of the valley's industrial strength in the 1920s.

The planning team organized the results of the resources inventory into three key elements: the land (the river and green hills), the people (ethnic diversity), and industry (iron, coal mining, railroading, and manufacturing). Considering these three elements led the project planning team to formulate a heritage park core scheme tying together *cultural conservation* (focusing on existing "cultural resources," such as Scranton's Steamtown National Historic Site, the Anthracite Heritage Museum, and the McDade Park Coal Mine Tour, and on ethnic community festivals in Olyphant—with rail, motor, and pedestrian linkages between such sites); *reclamation* (reclaiming the industrial wastelands that dominate the valley by using available conversion technology and innovative planning); and *greenspace* (linking existing parks, establishing "rails to trails" programs for unused railroad lines, reclaiming the river, and protecting the green ridges).[22]

Reclamation in the context of planning the Lackawanna Valley heritage park is used both literally and metaphorically. Reclaiming spoiled industrial sites and waterways represents efforts to render blighted areas both usable and livable. In public meetings, valley residents said they were equally concerned about reclaiming the valley's history, ethnic heritage, occupational traditions, and neighborhood memories. Programmatically, the planning team has proposed establishing an environmental research institute in Mayfield at the valley's north end and an ethnic folklife center in Olyphant in the middle of the valley.

Heritage park implementation continues in the Lackawanna Valley, predicated on the continuing availability of federal and state monies to leverage private funds. The Sauquoit Mill, a historic textile mill, is undergoing conversion to create 140 housing units and a neighborhood social service center. The Florence Apartments, once luxury apartments, are being restored as elderly housing. The proposal for an environmental research institute has attracted considerable attention, and funding appears likely from government and corporate sources. The creation of an ethnic folklife center with programs focusing on conserving the intangible cultural traditions of the valley is being considered, supported by recommendations based on a folklife resources survey and documentation project during 1993.

The lack of ethnographic work during the planning stages of the Lackawanna Heritage Valley is not representative of the experience of the other state heritage park project areas; nevertheless, key elements of the cultural conservation paradigm have found powerful expression. Public access to the planning process helped shape a vision of the park that responds to local concerns and seeks to balance a tourism economy with attention to rebuilding the local economic, environmental, and industrial infrastructures. Reclamation emerged as a key theme, linking concerns for the environment with the maintenance of local cultural heritage.

Now moving into the implementation phase, the Pennsylvania Heritage Parks Program offers a model of the cultural conservation paradigm in action. This program has shown that new policy and program structures can indeed overcome longstanding disciplinary and bureaucratic predisposition and inertia and, in so doing, can establish exciting new alliances and creative interaction for the encouragement of folklife.

NOTES

I wish to acknowledge the work of my colleagues at the state, federal, and local levels who are partners in developing and implementing the Pennsylvania Heritage Parks Program: Ray Angeli, Larry Williamson, Alan Chace, and Allen

Sachse of the Pennsylvania Department of Community Affairs; Randy Cooley, Southwestern Pennsylvania Heritage Preservation Commission; Debbie Darden and Deirdre Gibson of the National Park Service; Amy Skillman and Tom Jones of the Pennsylvania Heritage Affairs Commission; Doris Dyen, Steel Industry Heritage Corporation; Jim Abrams, folklife project contractor for the America's Industrial Heritage Project; LeeEllen Friedland, folklife project contractor for the Delaware and Lehigh Navigation Canal National Heritage Corridor; Alex Camayd and Harry Lindsay of the Lackawanna Valley Heritage Park Project, and many others too numerous to list here. I also wish to thank Barbara Kirshenblatt-Gimblett and David Lowenthal for their helpful comments on earlier drafts of this essay. Slightly different and considerably shorter versions of this essay appeared as "The Pennsylvania Heritage Parks Program" in *Folklife Center News* 14, no. 2 (1992): 8–10, and as "Cultural Conservation in a 'Heritage Parks' Program," *Practicing Anthropology* 14, no. 2 (1982): 27–30.

1. A session organized for the 1991 annual meeting of the American Folklore Society pointed to parallel developments outside the United States: Elke Dettmer addressed "nonconsumptive tourism" in her paper "The Newfoundland Screech-In Controversy," and Deirdre Evans-Pritchard discussed "sustainable tourism development" in her paper "Taking Tourism Seriously: Sustainable Tourism Development and Folklore Research."

2. The role of ethnographer as policy planner is distinctly different from that of the field-based project ethnographer or the academically based ethnographer as critic. The ethnographer as policy planner does not have the luxury of offering cultural critique. At the policy level, one fills the critical role of ensuring that ethnographic perspectives inform the planning process, thereby creating opportunities for cultural conservation through the program structure and guidelines. Such a role has recently been called for by Tony Bennett, "Putting Policy into Cultural Studies," in *Cultural Studies,* ed. Lawrence Grossberg, Cary Nelson, and Paula Treichler (New York: Routledge, 1992), 23–37.

3. Massachusetts's heritage parks are often coterminous with or closely follow the boundaries of existing historic districts. For example, the Western Gateway Heritage State Park in North Adams is located in North Adams's National Register freight yard district and Eagle Street and Monument Square Historic District (the historic downtown) and is linked to Witt's Ledge and Natural Bridge, two local natural resources.

New York State's program expanded beyond the confines of a downtown or urban district. The enabling legislation for the New York Urban Cultural Parks Program (Title G—Urban Cultural Parks, Article 31—General Provisions, 31.01—Definitions) offers the following definition: "'Urban cultural park' shall mean a definable urban or settled area of public and private uses ranging in size from a portion of a municipality to a regional area with a special coherence, such area being distinguished by physical and cultural resources (natural and/or man made including waterways, architecture, or artifacts reflecting a period of style or cultural heritage) which play a vital role in the life of the community and contribute through interpretive, educational and recreational use to the public. An urban cultural park may include traditional parks (pleasure grounds set apart for recreation of the public) and historic places or property on the national or state register of historic places. . . ." As an example of a New York urban cultural park, the boundaries of one park are set as "the related and cohesive geographical areas of the cities of Binghamton, Johnson City and Endicott, Broome County, associated with and revealing of immigration, migration and the region's industrial development during the nineteenth century" (Article 35.03.1.h).

4. The involvement of the National Park Service (NPS) in such heritage parks projects has sparked ongoing debate in the NPS itself between those who favor limiting the agency's role to administering the grand, outdoor parks and those who support the expansion of the agency into more contemporary, urban and industrial sites. Another element in the controversy is that the site selection of federally designated heritage parks may have to do more with the seniority and political clout of particular U.S. representatives and senators than with the inherent historical and cultural significance of a particular site. The Steamtown National Historic Site, a key attraction in the Lackawanna Valley heritage park discussed later, is one such site that has sparked allegations of pork-barrel project funding.

Nevertheless, the National Park Service has played a key role in developing heritage parks in various regions of the United States. A working definition of heritage parks used by numerous NPS field personnel stresses a planning process and beneficial societal values, consistent with the political and bureaucratic elements of identifying and obtaining congressional support for such an undertaking with federal monies: "a heritage area is a regionally identifiable and significant landscape which is the focus of a cooperative public and private decision-making effort to recognize, organize and communicate a community's natural, cultural, recreational and economic attributes in order to protect important values, stimulate the local economy and improve the quality of life." This definition appeared in J. Glenn Eugster and Deirdre Gibson, "Heritage Areas: An Approach to Integral Landscape Conservation" (Paper prepared for the Forty-third National Preservation Conference, Philadelphia, October 1989 [revised March 1990]), 2–3.

5. *Pennsylvania Heritage Parks: A Concept with Applications* (Harrisburg: Commonwealth of Pennsylvania, 1984) was released under the auspices of the Recreation Planning Program of the Commonwealth of Pennsylvania, with funding support from the federal Land and Water Conservation Fund.

6. Ibid., 1.

7. For a more complete discussion of Pennsylvania's industrial heritage, including historic preservation implications, see Bruce Bomberger and William Sisson, *Made in Pennsylvania: An Overview of the Major Industries of the Commonwealth* (Harrisburg: Pennsylvania Historical and Museum Commission, Bureau of Historic Preservation, 1989).

8. *Commonwealth of Pennsylvania Heritage Parks: A Program Manual,* 3d ed. (Harrisburg: Pennsylvania Department of Community Affairs, 1991), 2. There are significant proponents of the view that the focus on industrial heri-

tage is a misguided approach, emphasizing a nostalgic treatment of the past when what is really needed is a commitment and investment in retooling and revitalizing the industrial infrastructure.

9. The authorizing legislation for the Delaware and Lehigh Canal National Heritage Corridor requires a 100 percent match for federal money. Without the State Heritage Parks Program, this particular federal effort might not have been realized.

10. Lackawanna Valley Team, *Plan for the Lackawanna Heritage Valley* (Scranton: Lackawanna Heritage Valley Steering Committee, 1991), 16.

11. *Commonwealth of Pennsylvania Heritage Parks: A Program Manual,* 2. See ibid., 2–3, for more details on the five formal goals.

12. This is an expanded version of the earlier Heritage Parks Work Group. The management team now includes a representative of the Pennsylvania Heritage Affairs Commission; representatives from the Department of Community Affairs' Office of Policy Development and the bureaus of Recreation and Conservation, Housing and Development, Planning, Human Resources, and Local Government Services; a representative for the directors of the five DCA regional offices; and two regionally based recreation advisers who provide extensive field-based technical assistance to the network of nine heritage parks projects. The team is led by the department's deputy secretary for programs. The transformation from the smaller work group to the new management team reflects growing commitment to the program and an effort to coordinate the heritage parks work with the broader range of outreach and services provided by the department in such areas as human services, municipal planning, and local government services.

13. *Commonwealth of Pennsylvania Heritage Parks: A Program Manual,* 2. Since most of the regions participating in the Heritage Parks Program are marked by the decline of industry, high unemployment, out-migration, lack of replacement population, and an increasingly aged population, the reference to the "local communities" here refers to ethnically heterogeneous populations with deep roots in these areas, tied to the historic industries that are now the focus of these heritage projects. The exception to this pattern is limited to eastern Pennsylvania, principally in the Delaware and Lehigh Canal Corridor. Here new immigrant populations have entered the Easton-Bethlehem-Allentown urban corridor, suburbanites steadily encroach on the farmlands of Bucks County, and vacationers and retirees build homes near the former coal and canal towns along the Lehigh River. In these cases the challenge is to incorporate these new populations (and their social history and folklife), with little or no direct connections to the historic industrial experience, into the park planning process. As current residents in the park region, they have a stake, albeit different from that of long-time residents, in the ultimate outcome.

14. See, for example, Ormond H. Loomis, coordinator, *Cultural Conservation: The Protection of Cultural Heritage in the United States,* Publications of the American Folklife Center, no. 10 (Washington, D.C.: American Folklife Center, Library of Congress, 1983); and Burt Feintch, ed., *The Conservation of Culture: Folklorists and the Public Sector* (Lexington: University Press of Kentucky, 1988).

15. *Commonwealth of Pennsylvania Heritage Parks: A Program Manual,* 1.

16. *Feasibility Study Project: Application/Scope,* Pennsylvania Heritage Parks Program, PHP-FS-2 (11-89) (Harrisburg: Pennsylvania Department of Community Affairs, Bureau of Recreation and Conservation, 1989), II-1.

17. *Commonwealth of Pennsylvania Heritage Parks: A Program Manual,* 1.

18. *Feasibility Study Project,* PHP-FS-3, III-2. The reference to "categories of folklife resources," intended to lead applicants beyond lists of folk artists to the broader categories of local traditions, is based on a brief but excellent discussion of this issue in Thomas Carter and Carl Fleischhauer, *The Grouse Creek Cultural Survey: Integrating Folklife and Historic Preservation Field Research* (Washington, D.C.: Library of Congress, 1988), 6.

19. *Management Action Plan Project: Application/Scope,* Pennsylvania Heritage Parks Program, PHP-MAP (Harrisburg: Pennsylvania Department of Community Affairs, Bureau of Recreation and Conservation, 1989), III-2.

20. In her insightful commentary on the Pennsylvania Heritage Parks plenary session at the 1990 Cultural Conservation Institute, Benita J. Howell raised some of these issues with a cautionary note: the danger of constructing "too rosy a picture of the industrial past"; potential conflicting objectives of cultural conservation, environmental protection, tourism and recreation, and economic revitalization; and provision for adequate sociocultural impact assessment and public participation in planning.

21. In five of these cases, the commission has undertaken this work under contract with the National Park Service. Three of the state heritage park areas are located in the nine counties of the America's Industrial Heritage Project. Here ethnographic work proceeds within the broader scope of work of the Folklife Division of the America's Industrial Heritage Project, contracted by the Pennsylvania Heritage Affairs Commission, with funding from the National Park Service. The two other ethnographic projects under contract with the NPS supported the work of the Delaware and Lehigh Canal and the Steel Heritage projects. Ethnographic documentation has continued in the steel heritage region, guided by Doris Dyen, director of cultural conservation for the Steel Industry Heritage Corporation.

In two other areas, the commission has successfully sought funding from the National Endowment for the Arts, with matching monies from the Pennsylvania Council on the Arts. The commission contracted for ethnographic documentation work in the Lackawanna Heritage Valley in 1993, under a cooperative agreement with the Lackawanna Heritage Valley Authority and the National Park Service. For the Schuylkill River Project, commission staff designed the initial project that was funded by the Pennsylvania Council on the Arts. Further work was done by an independent folklorist as part of the management action planning phase. Ethnographic work in the oil and lumber regions along Pennsylvania's "northern tier" took place in 1992.

22. The full development of these elements can be found in Lackawanna Valley Team, *Plan for the Lackawanna Heritage Valley.*

Afterword: Raven, Mallard, and Spotted Owl—Totems for Coalition

Archie Green

Reflecting on this book's purpose to make common cause among cultural conservation professionals, I imagine a totem pole carved by the protectors of community and environment. I invoke metaphorical language to close a set of essays by colleagues on history, heritage, diversity, and vision. The American totem pole has long whispered about past and future. Lexicographers attribute the word *totem* to Ojibway speakers; travelers in the Pacific Northwest marvel at towering cedar constructs honoring ancestors and marking clan relationships. I suggest that cultural conservationists need no soaring eagle, powerful bear, clever fox, as found there. Rather, their pole might display raven, mallard (decoy), and spotted owl.

Each participant in cultural conservation comes from a different disciplinary setting and brings varied experiences. As apprentices, artisans, and old-timers, we ply trades in libraries, classrooms, and laboratories; we dwell in skyscraper suites and legislative corridors. Our many cloaks could make an American patchwork. We accept names, such as documentarian, designer, planner, curator, editor, teacher, folklorist, ethnographer, geographer, architect, historian, naturalist, conservationist, preservationist, or ecologist. No single name has emerged to reflect our similarities or soften our differences.

The raven is a useful symbol for vernacular expression, the mallard (decoy) for historic preservation, and the spotted owl for natural conservation. I have no wish to rank the three birds hierarchically, to imply that one bird's wingspread is superior to that of others. But out of familiarity with my own discipline, folklore, I place the raven at the pole's base and work upward to duck and owl.

Children in English-speaking families may hear "The Carrion Crow," a nonsense song, little suspecting its antiquity and ambiguity, or that this bird is one of nature's best recyclers. An opening stanza reads:

> There was a crow sat on an oak,
> Derry, derry, derry, day-ko.
> There was a crow sat on an oak
> Watching a tailor shape his cloak.
> Sing high-ho, the carrion crow!
> Derry, derry, derry, day-ko.

The ballad scholar Bertrand Bronson identifies this ditty as a descendant of "The Three Ravens," a text first printed in 1611 in Ravenscroft's *Melismata.* Folklorists know this text/tune family as Child 26. In early forms devoted animals—steed, hawks, hound—surround a wounded knight. In some variants the knight's lover, a fallow doe, appears: "she lift up his bloudy hed / And kist his wounds that were so red." In Scotland three talking ravens wait cynically to feast on the wounded knight. In Appalachia the ballad often loses themes of the doe's solicitude and the ravens' hunger.[1]

Here we need not explicate all the mystery in "The Three Ravens" or "The Carrion Crow." Among many chores, folklorists place texts and tunes variously in literary, musical, and community settings. Study of a song's origin and variation reveals melodic and poetic forms as complex signifiers of human experience. Further, a ballad case study ranges across boundaries of time, place, and language.

Many youngsters in American Indian families hear traditional raven stories in which the bird externalizes conflict. The raven hops from role to role—trickster, saboteur, buffoon, sage, magician—despoiling sacred places, violating codes, resisting authority, and pushing order beyond limits. The raven inhabits realms of scatology, subversion, inversion, dissidence, satire. Students who hear raven tales seek cross-cultural connections to coyote narratives, for the coyote is a fellow trickster. We ask, are raven and coyote cousins to the carrion crow who sat on an oak watching a tailor shape his cloak?

Whether we learn grandfather's story or grandmother's song, we discover that the raven also achieves dimensionality in both visual and tactile art. Rotunda visitors to the University of British Columbia's Anthropology Museum view a huge yellow cedar raven sculpted by the Haida artist Bill Reid. His bird, conjured from a four-and-a-half-ton laminated block, "speaks." For generations Haidas told of a gluttonous prankster who discovered mankind on a storm-lashed island in the Queen Charlotte Archipelago. Reid melds past and present, legend and science: "Though the [current] world view might hold that man migrated over a Bering land bridge, the Haida know that a Raven coaxed the first men from a giant clamshell on the beach at Naikoon."[2]

While the raven occupies our conservation pole's base, a duck perches above it. This second bird speaks equivocally, in that it is a carving portraying a carved object. The mallard decoy of my totem pole symbolizes the manual skill that produces material culture as opposed to the verbal creativity that gives rise to such intangibles as stories and songs. A decoy carver fashions a wooden duck designed to function in water as an economic tool (bringing food home) or on a collector's shelf as an aesthetic prize (garnering status through a recognition of craftsmanship and beauty). Like raven tales and ballads, decoys are expressive forms. Their differences lie in their appeal to different senses: folk narratives are heard, while decoys can be seen and touched.

Curiously, a pictured set of duck decoys troubled some partisans in animal rights and folklore camps. In 1985 the U.S. Postal Service issued four twenty-two-cent stamps under the rubric FOLK ART: mallard, redhead, broadbill, and canvasback decoys. Some wildlife advocates criticized these stamps for honoring the hunting of game. Meanwhile, some folklorists asserted that the presentation of quaint and inanimate objects showed their discipline as an antiquarian pursuit. I did not see the stamps as stereotypical folk art; instead, I found them attractive and welcomed postal attention to vernacular culture.

I will not enumerate all the contrasts between material and literary constructs, but I propose the duck decoy as an appropriate representation of all the artifacts to which preservationists respond: Mount Vernon, Independence Hall, Vicksburg's mansions, Galveston's Victorian "painted ladies," the sailing ship *Balclutha,* slave quarters, iron forges, textile mills, graveyard stones, urban plazas, poets' lofts, and street murals.

Professionals in the National Trust for Historic Preservation and in related public agencies agonize over decisions on the historic status of individual buildings and objects. Ultimately, a community "saves" that portion of its physical past that can be encompassed within living norms. Old decoys, like other constructs, tangible and intangible, reinforce both particular and universal myths. They have value in themselves (both aesthetic and utilitarian) and in the large ideas they symbolize. The birds in our folksongs (and a myriad other artistic depictions) help moor our sense of reality. They provide the terms under which we live out our lives.

A decade ago the snail darter, a tiny fish in Tennessee, became an instant symbol of conflict between land developers and conservationists. In recent years the spotted owl has migrated into public consciousness as a representative of old-growth forests and respect for the land. When wood-product industrialists and employees joined to confront conservationists and allies over clear-cutting and log export, publicists elevated Athena's wise bird to an emblem of present-day tension.

As passions in the redwood, cedar, and fir zones spread, the spotted owl came to roost in the newsroom, television studio, state legislative office, and U.S. Congress. A few examples from print speak volumes: "Loggers Say They're Endangered, Owl Isn't"; "The Disenchanted Forest: The Battle over the Spotted Owl"; "The Last Stand: A Logging Town Fights to Preserve Its Way of Life"; "Clearcutting Is Eco-Terrorism"; and "Farewell to the Spotted Owl?"

The spotted owl's friends and foes alike have invoked community imagery. Loggers assert their need to preserve sawmill towns, while naturalists see old-growth forests as living organisms. Forest workers and ecologists contend over who and what is endangered. Behind this divergence of opinion lies the troubled history of American lumbering. In this century's early decades many "timberbeasts" in the Northwest joined the Industrial Workers of the World. Then, rebel Wobblies—militant on the job, libertarian in ideology—saw no contradiction between action to improve living standards and commitment to "reforestation." Wobblies were brutalized for their beliefs; on Armistice Day 1919 a mob in Centralia, Washington, castrated and lynched IWW member Wesley Everest.

I invoke the ghost of Wesley Everest as an ancestor figure who would have regarded spotted owls as allies, in the same way coal miners regarded canaries underground—birds quick to succumb to deathly gas, harbingers of doom, and thus guardians of working folk. I see him in the long American tradition of dissent: Samuel Adams, John Brown, Malcolm X, Elizabeth Cady Stanton, Mother Jones, Rachel Carson. What has impelled many loggers in the generations after Everest to ignore his vision by parading with truck bumper stickers "Boil a Spotted Owl for Breakfast"? What changes in society have allowed Everest's successors to ignore the IWW legacy?

From among numerous examples of present-day disputes about the proper use of natural resources and respect for the planet, I have selected the case of the spotted owl for the way it resonates with the 1919 lynching of a Wobbly and reflects the social, economic, and political interactions in American life. By introducing the raven in ballad and tale, the mallard (decoy) in waterway and museum case, and the spotted owl in natural habitat and editorial column, I mean to suggest the complexity of the task ahead for the various partisans of living legacies.

A blue-collar outsider, leafing through this book, may see our cultural conservation professionals as looking alike—just as we may be unable to distinguish "woodbutcher" (carpenter) from "rodbuster" (ironworker) when viewing a building site. With the capacity and imagination to see separate craftworkers in linked enterprise, from excavation pit to topping-out ceremony, we might also bridge the differences among cultural conservationists. Ultimately, our working together will depend on understanding and respecting twined particularities and unities.

Beyond our particular presentations, then, we seek commonalities—to discover whether, indeed, we form a community. To my mind, the term *cultural conservation community* recalls a program from Franklin Delano Roosevelt's day, the Civilian Conservation Corps, an appropriate analogue for the mobilization of effort. The initials CCC might also stand for cause, congregation, and coalition. In the years ahead an appropriate name will emerge to characterize the joint efforts of those concerned with cultural conservation. We need a coalition, perhaps a clearinghouse/lobby/editorial chamber. We agree that efforts to preserve cultural material must include its presentation. We have not yet charted a formal organization with a constitution, bylaws, officers, and dues, but we anticipate a future alliance.

Conservationists need not dissolve particular identities to pool energies in a common cause. Our 1990 meeting in the Library of Congress's Madison Building suggested a fine political lineage for deliberations. The father of the Constitution, James Madison, understood the importance of compromise and coalition, the weakness of the nation under the Articles of Confederation, and the need for a strong union. Did he hover at the rostrum? Can we catch the spirit of political urgency that inspired his work?

Cultural conservationists cannot escape political action, whether testifying on local zoning laws or articulating outrage at the sight of oil-drenched otters in the Prince William Sound or oil-drenched cormorants in the Persian Gulf. (The otter and cormorant deserve their own totem poles.) We train to explicate artistry in all its settings, to probe metaphor's limits. We seek to preserve fiddle tune and guitar run, barn sign and scrimshaw token. But day by day news pours into parlor, den, or office about social inferno, new horrors confronting people and environments.

In recent years ethnographers and their peers in preservation and conservation have coined a potent term, *cultural genocide.* Among abundant examples, we learn that Brazilian gold miners use mercury in the Amazon's headwaters. Do any legislators in Brasilia, committed to Third World development, speak for natives who subsist on mercury-poisoned fish? Natural ecosystems are clearly dependent on parliamentary or bureaucratic decisions.

The same leaders who ordered tanks into Tiananmen Square destroyed Buddhist temples and language schools in Tibet, as other commissars who dried the Aral Sea sent armed Black Berets to Vilnius and Riga. Our nation is not immune: those who scrapped an energy-conservation policy for the United States energized death squads in Central America. The term *cultural genocide* links the death of individuals and communities to the extermination of their expressive forms.

Two newspaper items can be read, respectively, as a sermon on resisting such atrocities and a comment on the need to build coalitions. On December 7, 1989, Mary Williams Walsh reported from Fort Simpson,

Canada, "At Earth's End, Priests Try Harder."[3] More than a century ago French Jesuits had paddled down the MacKenzie River bringing Catholicism to Dene, Cree, and Inuit tribes. Hudson Bay traders, Mounties, and priests (called Blackrobes by the Indians) formed a governmental triumvirate. In recent years, as American Indians have grown disillusioned with white outsiders, young French seminarians, coincidentally, have declined to serve in Canada's "Third World."

Responding to these realities in 1986, Canadian Oblate Order fathers visited Poland to recruit new priests. The shift from France to Poland held more than geographic meaning. In the past decades Canadian Jesuits had accepted a form of liberation theology, involving themselves in secular struggles of indigenous people. Priests who had learned Slavey, a Northwest Indian regional tongue, joined in the fight against a proposed Mackenzie River pulp mill that threatened to pollute traditional fishing waters.

Canadian recruiters in Warsaw faced a political dilemma, for Polish seminarians in the 1980s identified with Solidarity's workers in rejecting their own outside exploiters. Young Polish priests viewed liberation theology as thought corrupted by Marxist dogma. The first newcomer to Fort Simpson from Poland, Father Andrezij Stendzina, knew no Slavey. Where his predecessors used canoe and dogsled, he turned to pickup truck and light plane. Despite access to modern tools, he faced overwhelming community problems: alcoholism, tuberculosis, child abuse, land claims, polluting paper mills.

French Jesuits came to arctic Canada originally to save souls. Father Andrezij Stendzina, a "conservative," learned that he would have to "sort out the traditional and the modern, the European and the indigenous, the political and the personal." I dwell at length on reporter Walsh's portrait of Stendzina to make the point that cultural conservationists under any rubric, and in all the globe's hidden recesses, face his choices.

On May 2, 1990, Steven Mufson noted a speech by Richard Darman at Harvard's John F. Kennedy School of Government: "Darman Laments the Decline of the Romantic Spirit."[4] The reporter commented on the Office of Management and Budget (OMB) director's criticism "in none too charitable a spirit" of the environmental movement. Darman (like other White House pundits) aimed at environmental neo-Luddites, ranging from Arlo Guthrie's "Alice's Restaurant" to Albert Ryder's mystical painting *Toilers of the Sea.* Darman countered their wish "to make the world safe for green vegetables" with America's "heroization of risk taking and pioneering spirit."

In traditional accounts Ned Ludd, a Leicestershire villager, broke a stockinger's knitting frame about 1779. Three decades later *Luddite* and *Luddism* emerged as terms for machine-breaking. To this day Ned has been treated harshly and called a half-wit or saboteur. Those who voice the cliché "You can't stop progress" demean the just aspects of Luddism.

Many who endured the Industrial Revolution's thrust turned to prelapsarian dreams, longing for humane societal forms. Tom Paine and Tom Jefferson felt in their bones Ned Ludd's vision.

In popular discourse the word *sabotage* stems from the notion that French workers literally threw wooden shoes into machinery. In current parlance *monkey wrenchers* drive spikes into trees. Who has not heard such charges from power brokers and image makers? Environmentalists for decades will need to deal with canards of neo-Luddism on figurative and philosophic grounds. We shall be called on to test Richard Darman's naysayers against Father Andrezij Stendzina's devotion.

Over the years conservationists have faced strings of pejoratives. (Presumably, in asking cultural conservationists to represent their work by carving emblematic ravens/ducks/spotted owls into totem poles, I become a foolish romantic.) Within the academy the term *advocate* has become a slur, implying departure from value-free norms. In popular arenas conservation advocates, from the Sierra Club to the Audubon Society, stand accused of ignoring the "real world," of violating pragmatism's message. As unabashed advocates for cultural conservation, we can chose to mire ourselves in academic controversy by responding to picayune charges or move ahead in responsible tasks.

At a quiet moment during the Library of Congress conference that preceded this book, Harris Francis, from Window Rock, Arizona, reported that four sacred mountains bounded the Navajo Nation. Referring to his tribe's cultural resources, he moved beyond prehistoric archaeological sites to places where elders continue to gather medicinal herbs and to pray. Navajos have no tradition of preserving presidential birthplaces but have long preserved sacred mountains. Francis had no wish to desecrate cathedrals during his Washington visit. He asked his audience not to violate Navajo sacred ground. Who judges such reverence to be romantic?

The tar brush of romanticism and neo-Luddism sits in its bucket ready for use. We display maturity by resisting the brush, by distinguishing rhetorical performance from physical sticks and stones. We measure growth by framing cultural-conservation discourse in the largest settings at our command. To take the high road in our strategies implies willingness to question internal language, to stand back from catch words of our respective professions (*invented tradition, pristine park, old-time music community, impact assessment, holistic reach*). In using plain speech to communicate with others inside and outside our professions, we undergird analysis, advance action, and step into coalitions. Some professionals seem surprised that their lingo remains cloudy to outsiders. Those who choose to toil for endangered species in enclaved societies have compelling need for clarity in expression.

This book's selection of essays by conservationists from various arenas notes differences and commonalities in joint endeavor. Essentially, we wish our talks and papers, allusions and representations, to recognize the gravity of shared tasks, the promise of chosen paths. Each essay contributor in *Conserving Culture* has asked particular questions derived from observation and geared to promote reflection. Should we cling to separate ribbons? By linking resources, do we vitiate tested skills? When do conservation constituents metamorphose into "special interest groups"? Does facility for elaborate rhetoric pull us away from reality? Readers may draw other puzzles and challenges from our varied case studies. Raven, mallard, and spotted owl—fixed on their totem pole and free in the sky—watch our endeavors and cheer us on the way.

NOTES

1. Bertrand Bronson, *The Traditional Tunes of the Child Ballads,* vol. 1 (Princeton, N.J.: Princeton University Press, 1959–64), 308. Bronson supplies citations for Child 26.
2. Christopher Baker, "Objects of Bright Pride," *Pacific Discovery* 43 (Summer 1990): 5–6.
3. Mary Williams Walsh, "At Earth's End, Priests Try Harder," *Los Angeles Times,* December 7, 1990, A1.
4. Steven Mufson, "Darman Laments the Decline of Romantic Spirit," *Washington Post,* May 2, 1990, A7.

Contributors

ROGER D. ABRAHAMS is the Hum Rosen Professor of Folklore and Folklife at the University of Pennsylvania. He has worked in the areas of Anglo-American folksong, Afro-American folklore and culture, children's folklore, folklore theory, and the place of the profession in American life.

JAMES F. ABRAMS is director of the Division of Ethnography and Oral History of America's Industrial Heritage Project in southwestern Pennsylvania and is completing a Ph.D. dissertation entitled "Theme Work: Constructing Personal and Public Heritage Worlds" at the University of Pennsylvania.

ERIKA BRADY is an assistant professor in Programs in Folk Studies at Western Kentucky University and edits the journal *Southern Folklore.* Her work on trappers in the Missouri Ozarks has been partially supported by a Herbert Kahler Fellowship from the Eastern National Park and Monument Association.

ROBERT CANTWELL teaches American studies at the University of North Carolina at Chapel Hill. His books include *Bluegrass Breakdown: The Making of the Old Southern Sound* and *Ethnomimesis: Folklife and the Representation of Culture.*

ERVE CHAMBERS is a professor of anthropology at the University of Maryland, College Park. He is the author of *Applied Anthropology: A Practical Guide,* the coeditor (with Setha M. Low) of *Housing, Culture and Design: A Comparative Perspective,* and the founding editor of *Practicing Anthropology.* He is currently working on a book on development and the impact of tourism in Southeast Asia.

DOUGLAS DENATALE, who has a Ph.D. from the University of Pennsylvania, is the director of the Folklife and Oral History Program at the University of South Carolina. He has had extensive experience in public sector research, programming, and administration. He was the project coordinator for the American Folklife Center, Library of Congress's Lowell Folklife Project.

ALAN S. DOWNER, JR., trained as an anthropological archaeologist at the University of Missouri–Columbia, is the historic preservation officer for the Navajo Nation, where he has been developing the first historic preservation program established by an Indian tribal government. He is coeditor (with Anthony L. Klesert) of *Preservation on the Reservation: Native Americans, Native American Lands and Archaeology* and the author of articles dealing with Native American preservation concerns.

HARRIS FRANCIS, who grew up on the Navajo Reservation in Teesto and Chinle speaking Navajo and observing traditions in daily life, holds a paralegal certification from Northern Arizona University. Since 1987 he has worked as a Navajo culture specialist, with a focus on protecting Navajo sacred places and other cultural resources.

ARCHIE GREEN is a retired professor of folklore, University of Texas. His interest in conservation partly stems from serving in the New Deal's Civilian Conservation Corps in the Siskiyou Mountains in California and as a lobbyist for the American Folklife Preservation Act. His publications include *Only a Miner* and *Wobblies, Pile Butts, and Other Heroes.*

JUDITH BORTNER HEFFERNAN is the executive director of the Heartland Network for Town and Rural Ministries, a response by the United Methodist Church to the ongoing social and economic changes in the Heartland region, and a research associate in the Department of Rural Sociology at the University of Missouri–Columbia. Her major academic research interests have focused on farm women, farm families, and rural communities.

WILLIAM D. HEFFERNAN is a professor of rural sociology at the University of Missouri–Columbia. His main research interests are in the area of the sociology of agriculture, particularly the social consequences of changes in the structure of agriculture. He is a past president of the Rural Sociological Society.

BENITA J. HOWELL is an associate professor of anthropology at the University of Tennessee–Knoxville. In 1988–89 she served on the National Parks and Conservation Association's commission to evaluate research and resource management in the national park system. She is editor of *Cultural Heritage Conservation in the American South: Preserving Our Community Heritage.*

MARY HUFFORD, who holds a Ph.D. in folklore and folklife from the University of Pennsylvania, is a folklife specialist at the American Folklife Center, Library of Congress. Her publications include *Chaseworld: Foxhunting and Storytelling in New Jersey's Pine Barrens; One Space, Many Places: Folklife and Land Use in New Jersey's Pinelands National Reserve;* and *The Grand Generation: Memory, Mastery, Legacy* (with Marjorie Hunt and Steven J. Zeitlin).

KLARA B. KELLEY received her Ph.D. in anthropology from the University of New Mexico in 1977 and has taught at the University of New Mexico and Navajo Community College. She has worked in Navajoland since 1973. Her publications include *Navajo Land Use: An Ethnoarchaeological Study* and *Navajoland: Family Settlement and Land Use* (coauthored with Peter Whiteley).

YVONNE R. LOCKWOOD, who has degrees in folklore and history from the University of Californa, Berkeley, and the University of Michigan, is a Michigan folklife specialist with the Michigan Traditional Arts Program at the Michigan State University Museum. She works with public-sector folklife and does research on ethnicity and regional cultures.

SETHA M. LOW is a professor of environmental psychology and anthropology, Graduate School and University Center of the City University of New York. She founded the Cultural Aspects of Design Network and coedited (with Irwin Altman) a volume entitled *Place Attachment.* She is currently writing a book on plazas and urban public space.

MARSHA MACDOWELL, an associate professor of art history at Michigan State University, is the curator of folk arts and the coordinator of the Michigan Traditional Arts Program at the Michigan State University Museum. She served as coadministrative coordinator of folklife research for the Michigan Low-Level Radioactive Waste Project.

STUART A. MARKS has studied events in Zambia's Luangwa Valley since the 1960s. He has worked as an ethnographer and ecologist for the government and academia and currently is an independent scholar and consultant. His works include *The Imperial Lion* and *Southern Hunting in Black and White.* He is currently writing an environmental history of the British in central Africa.

CLARENCE MONDALE is a professor of American Civilization at George Washington University. He has coedited a book-length bibliography on

American regionalism and has authored articles on the geography of aging and on the experience of migration.

J. Sanford Rikoon is a research associate professor in the Department of Rural Sociology at the University of Missouri–Columbia. He currently is conducting research on agricultural and environmental issues in the Midwest and the former Soviet Union.

Alexandra Roberts, an anthropological archaeologist, received her Ph.D. in anthropology from the University of New Mexico. She has worked in cultural resource management in private and public organizations and since 1988 has served as deputy director and anthropologist with the Navajo Nation Historic Preservation Department.

Dale Rosengarten, a graduate of Harvard University, was guest curator of the McKissick Museum's Lowcountry Basket Project, director of the Sweetgrass Conference, and coordinator of the Sweetgrass Transplantation Project. Her publications include *Row upon Row: Sea Grass Baskets of the South Carolina Lowcountry* and *Between the Tracks: Charleston's East Side during the Nineteenth Century* (coauthored with a team of researchers for the Charleston Museum).

Laurie Kay Sommers, who has a Ph.D. in folklore from Indiana University, is a folklorist with the Michigan Traditional Arts Program at the Michigan State University Museum. She has worked as a freelance consultant in both historic preservation and public-sector folklife. She conducted the Lenawee County folklife study for the Michigan Low-Level Radioactive Waste Project.

Shalom Staub, who has Ph.D. in folklore and folklife from the University of Pennsylvania, is the executive director of the Pennsylvania Heritage Affairs Commission and the executive secretary of the American Folklore Society. As a member of the Pennsylvania Heritage Parks management team, he was responsible for developing the program's cultural conservation guidelines.

Richard W. Stoffle is an associate research anthropologist at the Bureau of Applied Research for Anthropology at the University of Arizona, Tucson, where he specializes in developmental change, social impact assessment, risk perception, and ethnohistory. He served as principal investigator for the study *Cultural and Paleontological Effects of Siting a Low-Level Radioactive Waste Storage Facility in Michigan, Candidate Area Analysis Phase.*

Steven J. Zeitlin, who has a Ph.D. in folklore and folklife from the University of Pennsylavania, is the director of City Lore, the New York Center for Urban Folk Culture, which initiated the Endangered Spaces Project in New York City. He is the coauthor of *A Celebration of American Family Lore; The Grand Generation;* and *City Play* and has coproduced documentary films on American folk culture. He is currently a commentator for National Public Radio's "Crossroads."

Index